Garfield
keeps his chins up

BY: JIM DAVIS

BALLANTINE BOOKS · NEW YORK

D0523261

Sale of this book without a front cover may be unauthorized.
If this book is coverless, it may have been reported to the
publisher as "unsold or destroyed" and neither the author
nor the publisher may have received payment for it.

Copyright © 1992 United Feature Syndicate, Inc.
GARFIELD Comic Strips: © 1991, 1992 United Feature
Syndicate, Inc.

All rights reserved under International and Pan-American
Copyright Conventions. Published in the United States
by Ballantine Books, a division of Random House, Inc.,
New York, and simultaneously in Canada by Random
House of Canada Limited, Toronto.

Library of Congress Catalog Card Number: 92-90049

ISBN: 0-345-37959-4

Manufactured in the United States of America

First Edition: October 1992

10 9 8 7 6 5 4 3 2 1

YOU KNOW YOU'RE GETTING FAT WHEN...

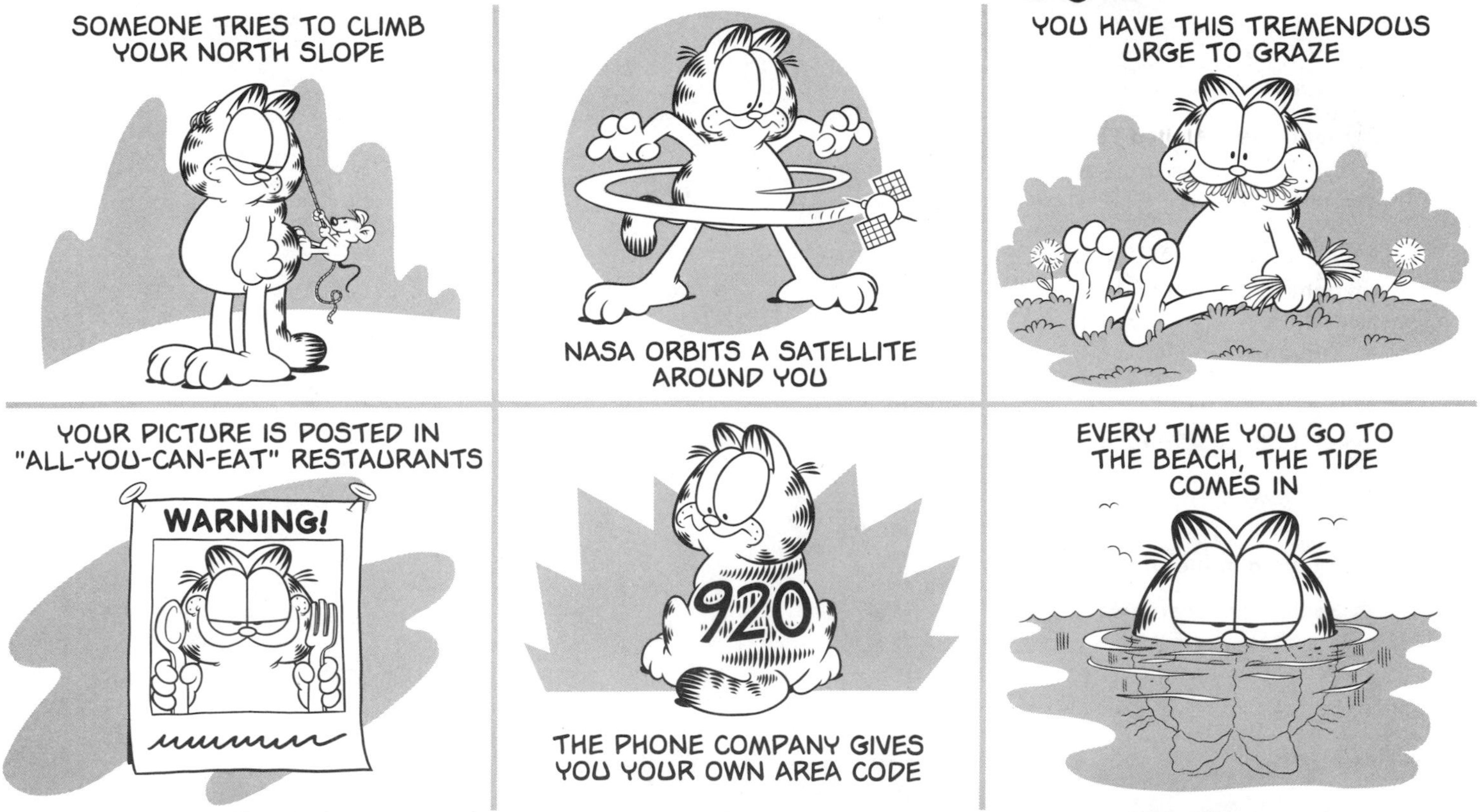
SOMEONE TRIES TO CLIMB YOUR NORTH SLOPE
NASA ORBITS A SATELLITE AROUND YOU
YOU HAVE THIS TREMENDOUS URGE TO GRAZE
YOUR PICTURE IS POSTED IN "ALL-YOU-CAN-EAT" RESTAURANTS
WARNING!
920
THE PHONE COMPANY GIVES YOU YOUR OWN AREA CODE
EVERY TIME YOU GO TO THE BEACH, THE TIDE COMES IN

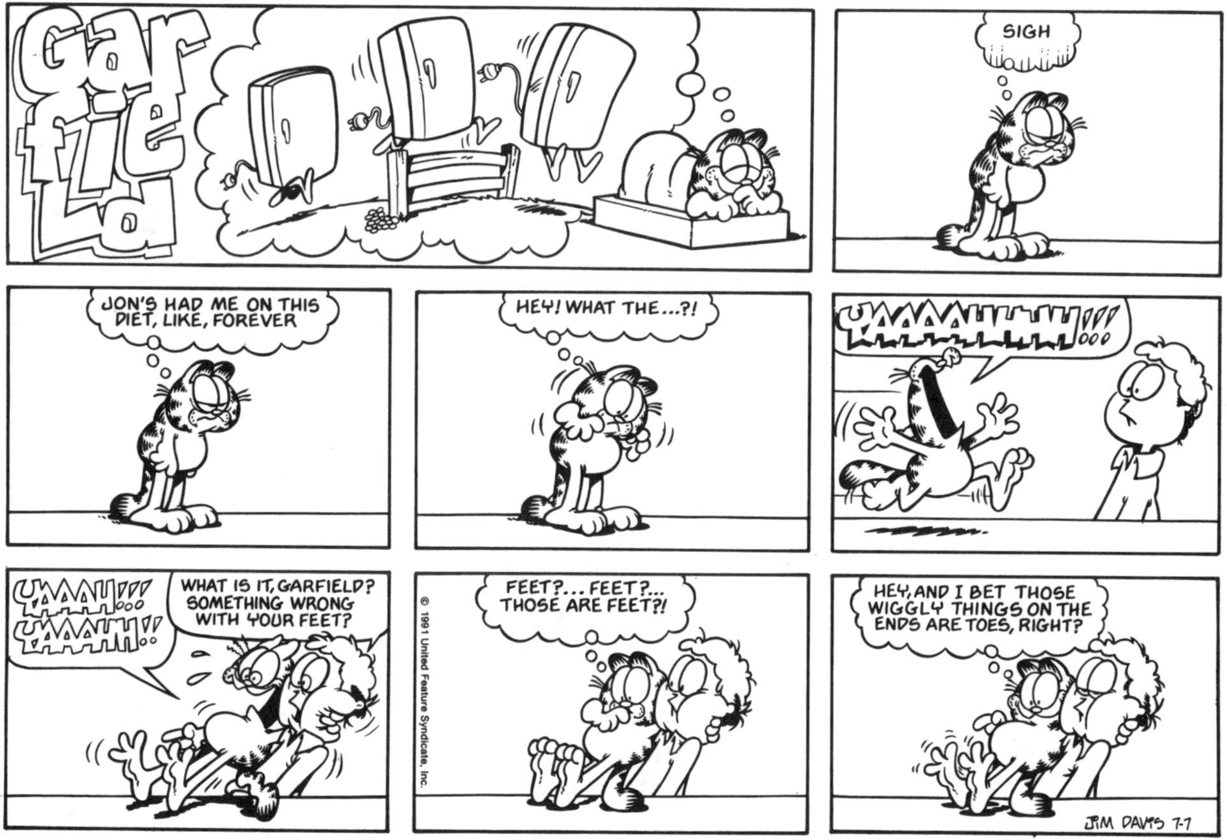
GARFIELD
SIGH
JON'S HAD ME ON THIS DIET, LIKE, FOREVER
HEY! WHAT THE...?!
YAAAAHHHH!!!
YAAAH!!! YAAAHH!!
WHAT IS IT, GARFIELD? SOMETHING WRONG WITH YOUR FEET?
FEET?... FEET?... THOSE ARE FEET?!
HEY, AND I BET THOSE WIGGLY THINGS ON THE ENDS ARE TOES, RIGHT?
JIM DAVIS 7-7

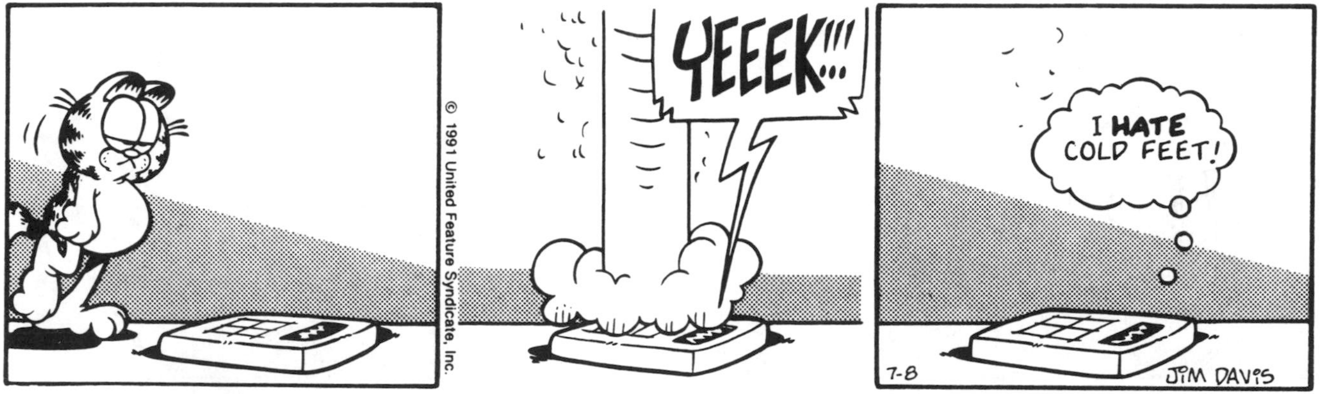
YEEEK!!!...
I HATE COLD FEET!
© 1991 United Feature Syndicate, Inc.
7-8
JIM DAVIS

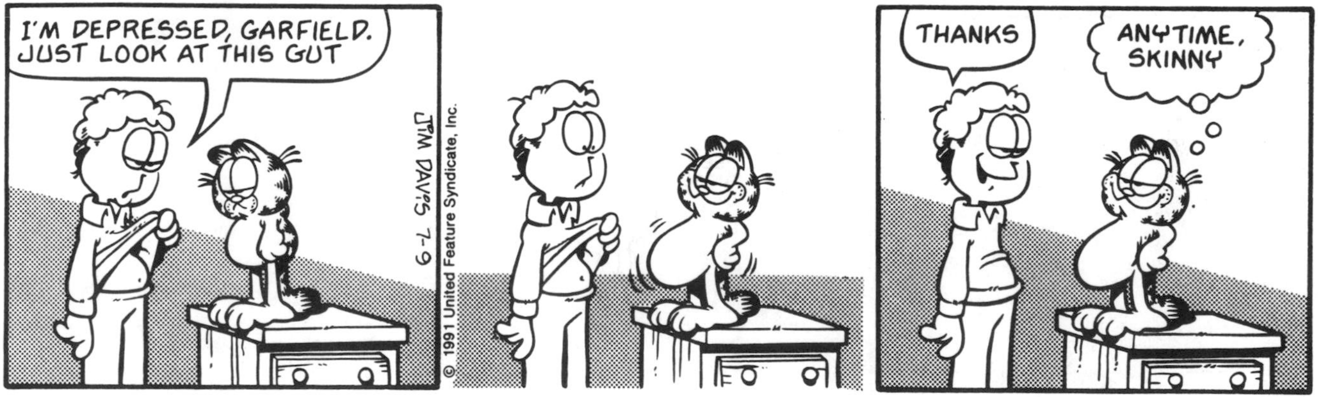
I'M DEPRESSED, GARFIELD. JUST LOOK AT THIS GUT
JIM DAVIS 7-9
© 1991 United Feature Syndicate, Inc.
THANKS
ANYTIME, SKINNY

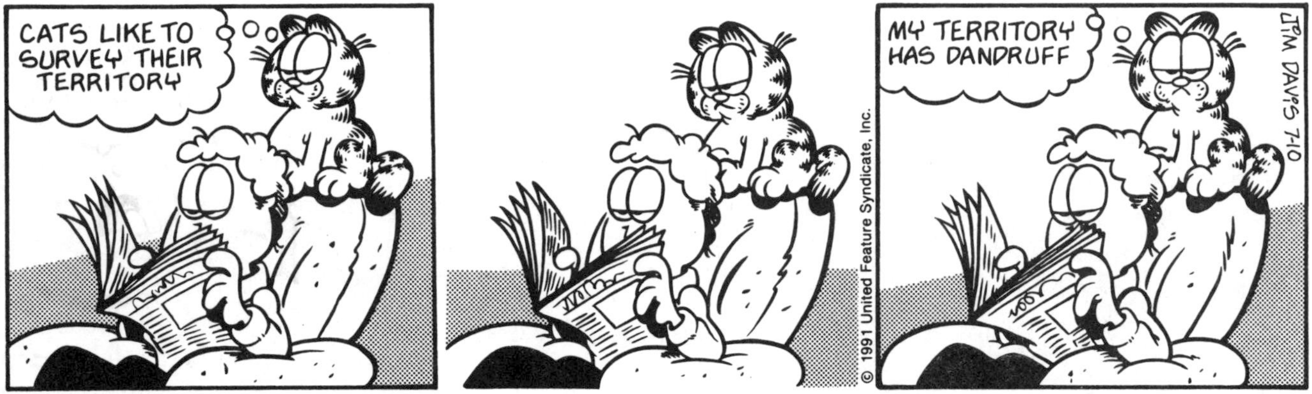

CATS LIKE TO SURVEY THEIR TERRITORY
MY TERRITORY HAS DANDRUFF
JIM DAVIS 7-10
© 1991 United Feature Syndicate, Inc.

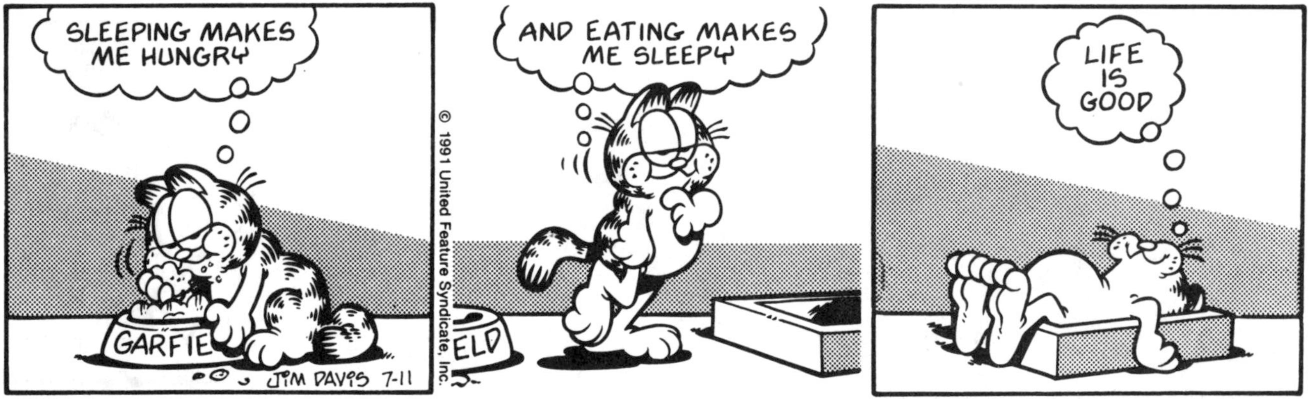

SLEEPING MAKES ME HUNGRY
GARFIE
ELD
JIM DAVIS 7-11
© 1991 United Feature Syndicate, Inc.
AND EATING MAKES ME SLEEPY
LIFE IS GOOD

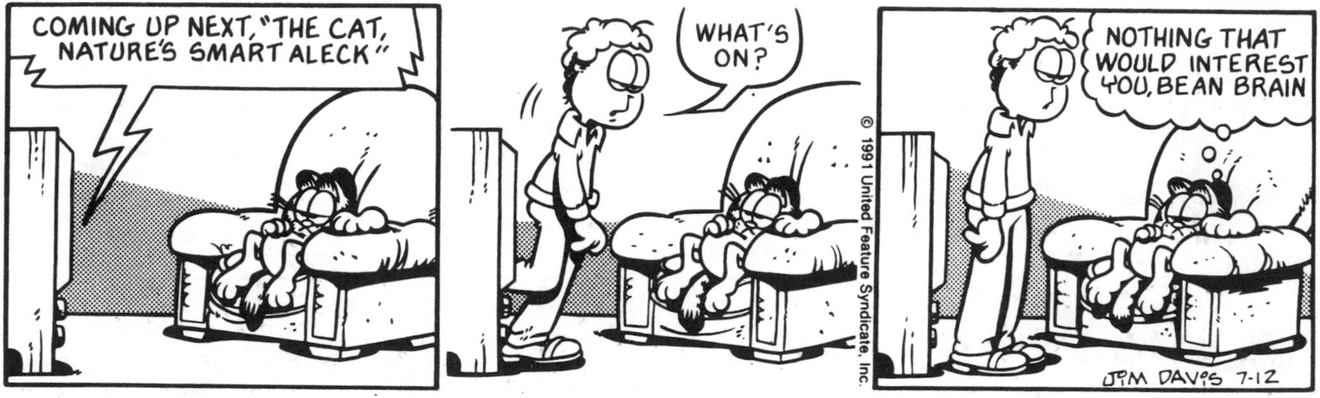
COMING UP NEXT, "THE CAT, NATURE'S SMART ALECK"
WHAT'S ON?
NOTHING THAT WOULD INTEREST YOU, BEAN BRAIN
© 1991 United Feature Syndicate, Inc.
JIM DAVIS 7-12

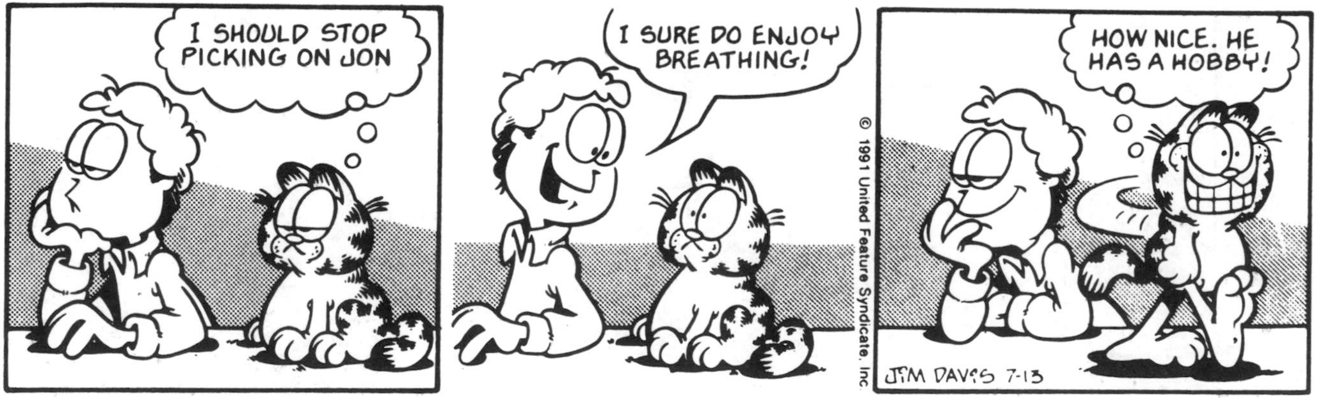
I SHOULD STOP PICKING ON JON
I SURE DO ENJOY BREATHING!
HOW NICE. HE HAS A HOBBY!
© 1991 United Feature Syndicate, Inc.
JIM DAVIS 7-13

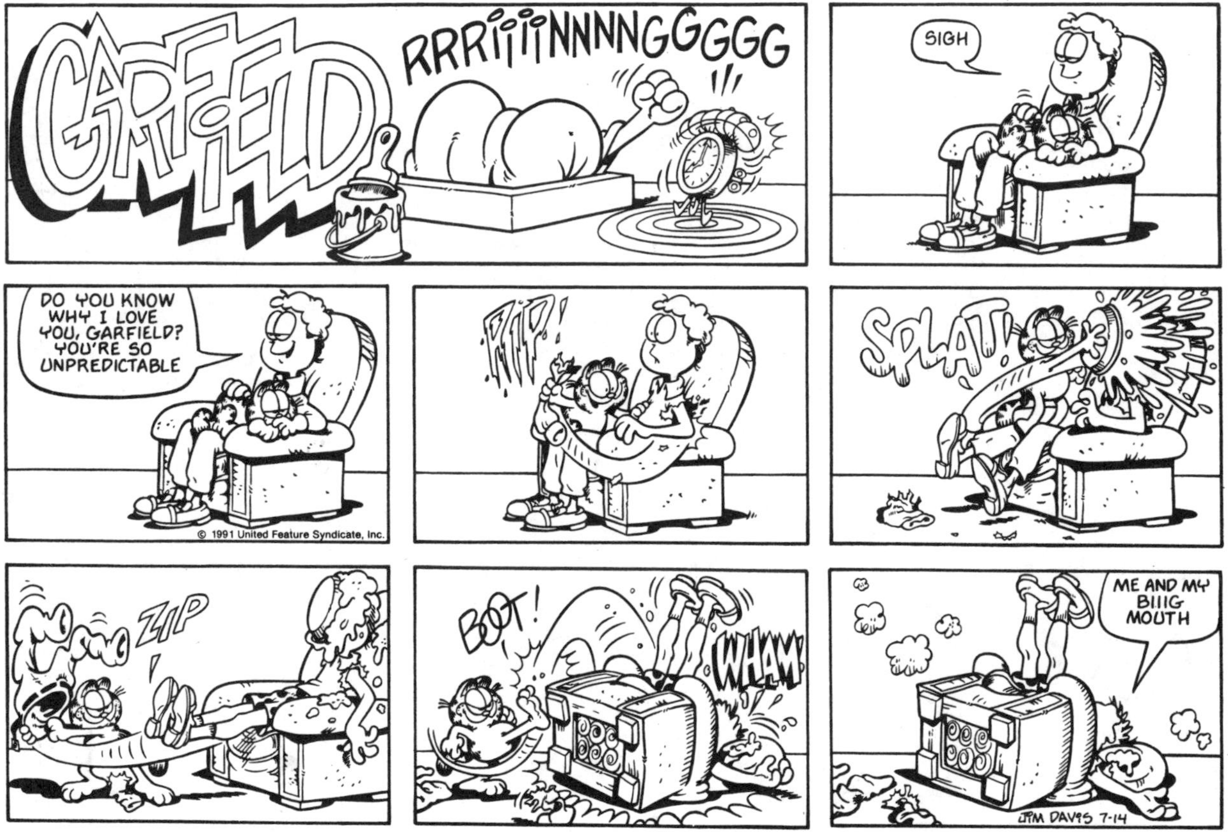
GARFIELD
RRRiiiiNNNNGGGGG
SIGH
DO YOU KNOW WHY I LOVE YOU, GARFIELD? YOU'RE SO UNPREDICTABLE
© 1991 United Feature Syndicate, Inc.
RIP!
SPLAT!
ZIP
BOOT!
WHAM!
ME AND MY BIIIG MOUTH
JIM DAVIS 7-14

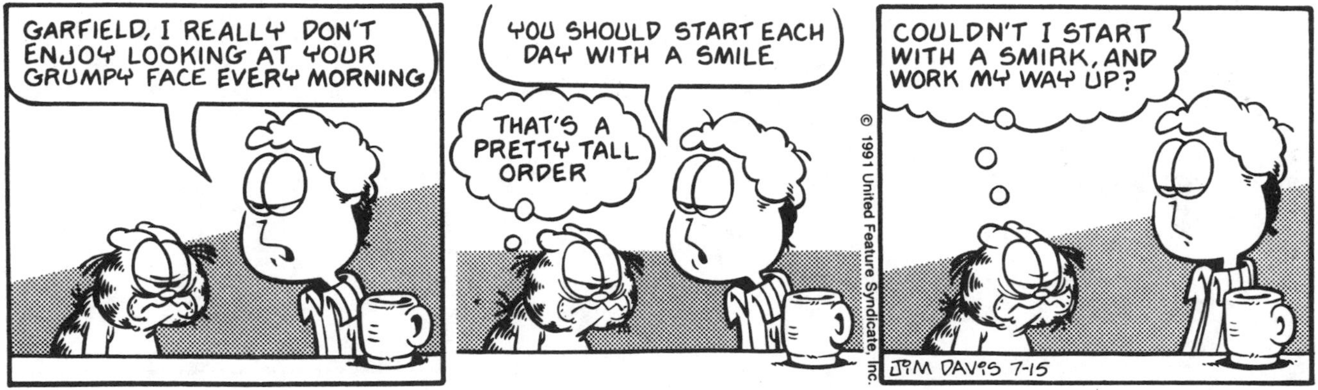
GARFIELD, I REALLY DON'T ENJOY LOOKING AT YOUR GRUMPY FACE EVERY MORNING
YOU SHOULD START EACH DAY WITH A SMILE
THAT'S A PRETTY TALL ORDER
COULDN'T I START WITH A SMIRK, AND WORK MY WAY UP?
© 1991 United Feature Syndicate, Inc.
JIM DAVIS 7-15

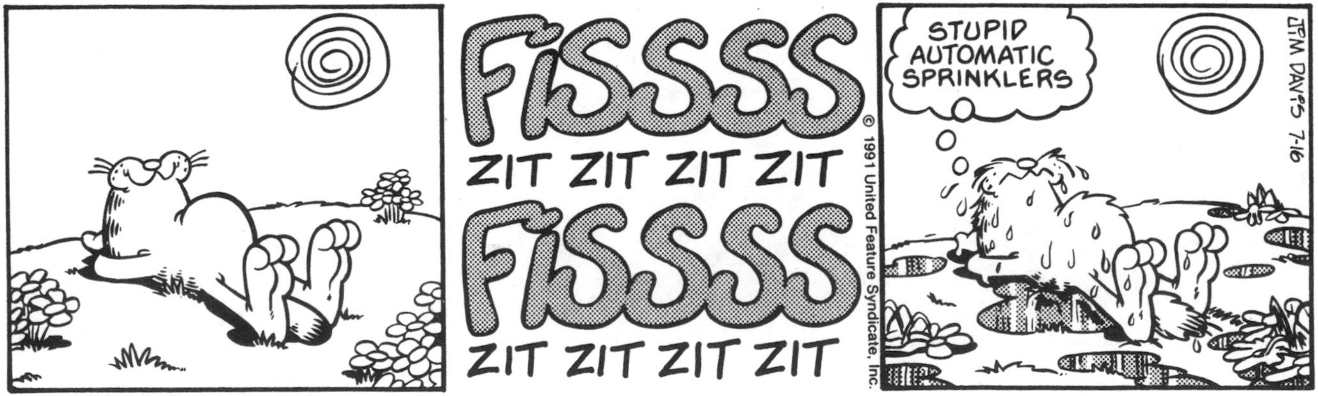
FISSSSS
ZIT ZIT ZIT ZIT
FISSSSS
ZIT ZIT ZIT ZIT
© 1991 United Feature Syndicate, Inc.
STUPID AUTOMATIC SPRINKLERS
JIM DAVIS 7-16

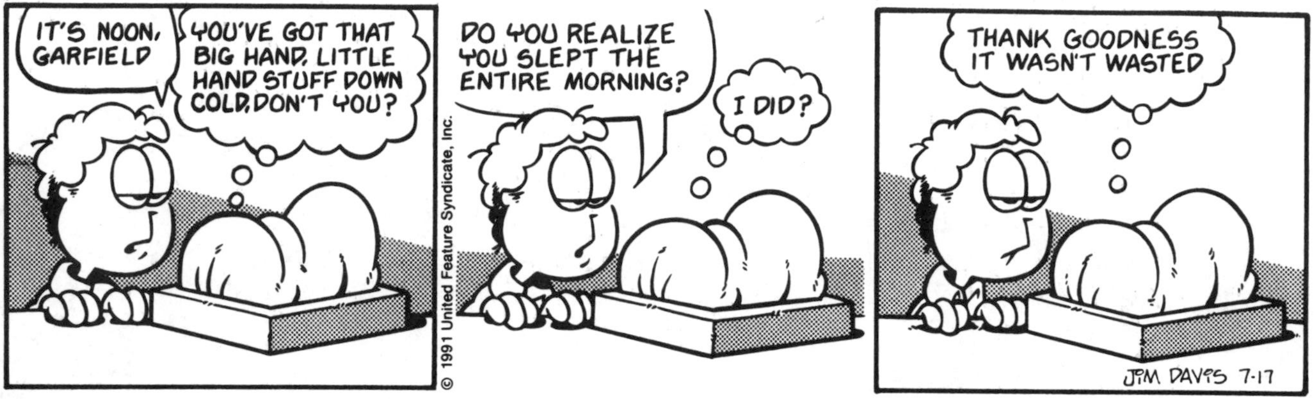
IT'S NOON, GARFIELD
YOU'VE GOT THAT BIG HAND, LITTLE HAND STUFF DOWN COLD, DON'T YOU?
© 1991 United Feature Syndicate, Inc.
DO YOU REALIZE YOU SLEPT THE ENTIRE MORNING?
I DID?
THANK GOODNESS IT WASN'T WASTED
JIM DAVIS 7-17

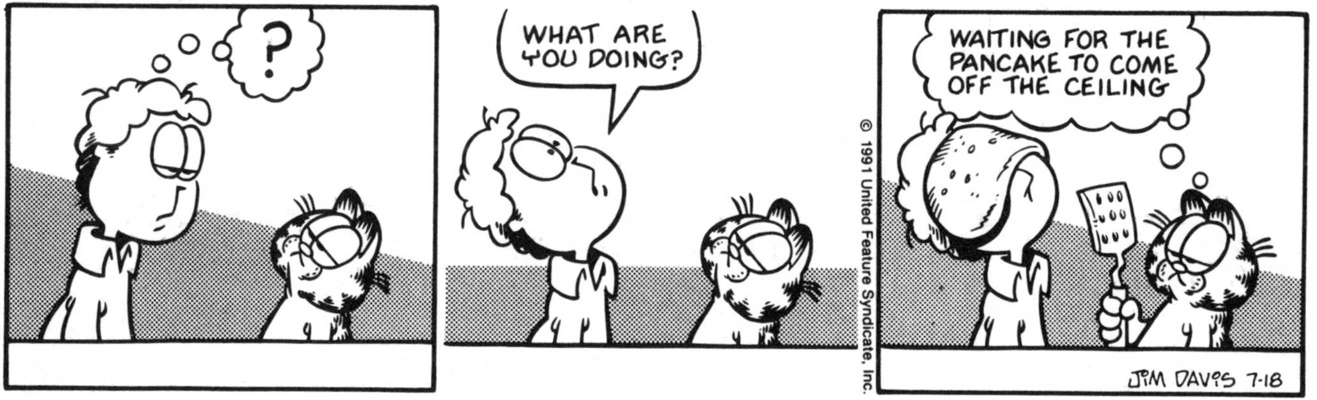
?
WHAT ARE YOU DOING?
© 1991 United Feature Syndicate, Inc.
WAITING FOR THE PANCAKE TO COME OFF THE CEILING
JIM DAVIS 7-18

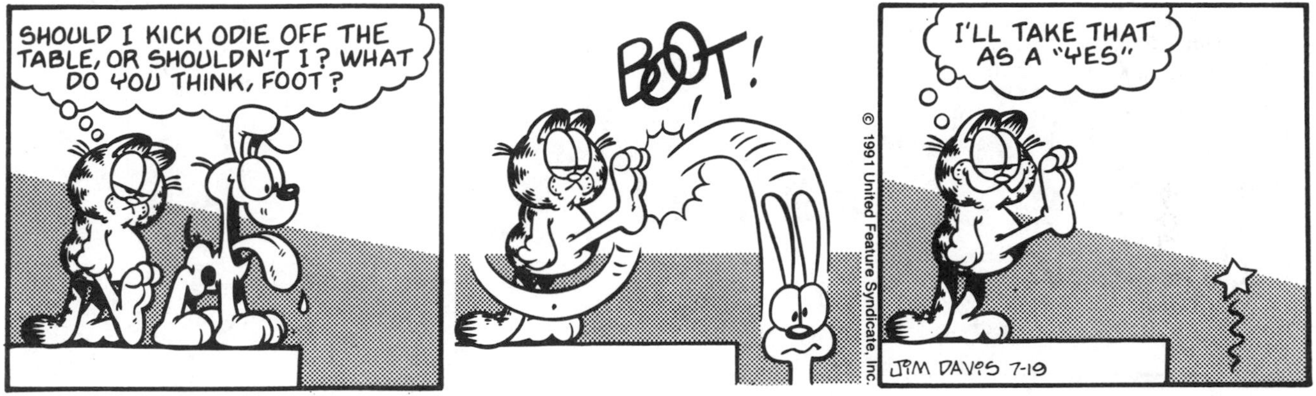
SHOULD I KICK ODIE OFF THE TABLE, OR SHOULDN'T I? WHAT DO YOU THINK, FOOT?
BOOT!
© 1991 United Feature Syndicate, Inc.
I'LL TAKE THAT AS A "YES"
JIM DAVIS 7-19

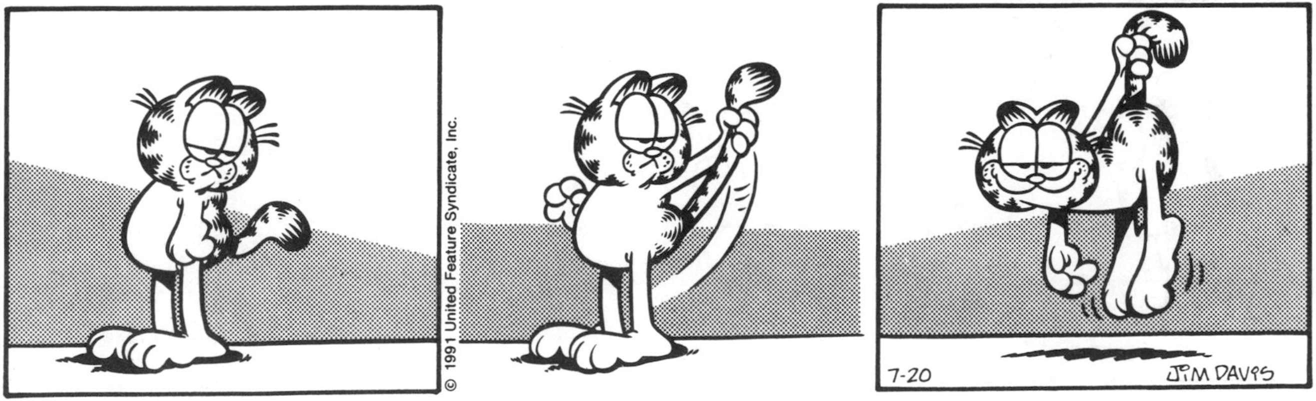
© 1991 United Feature Syndicate, Inc.
7-20
JIM DAVIS

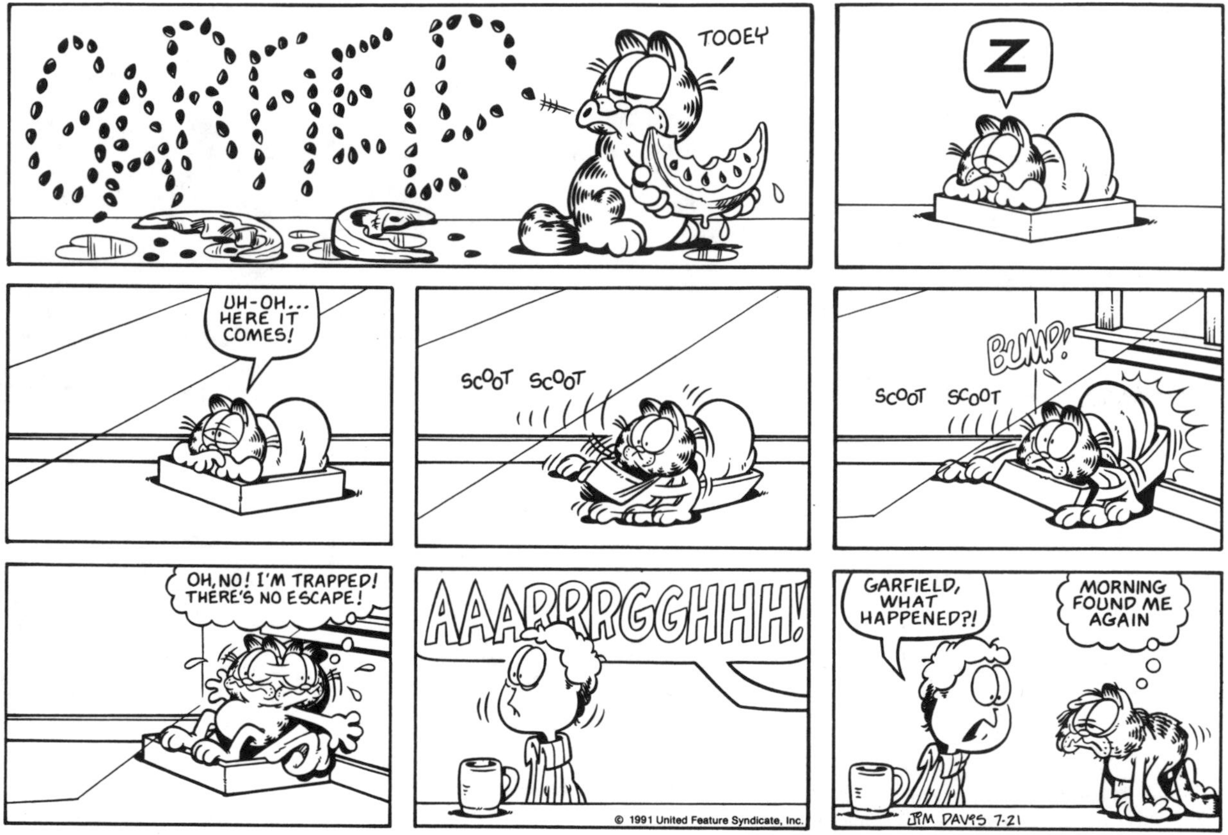
GARFIELD
TOOEY
Z
UH-OH... HERE IT COMES!
SCOOT SCOOT
BUMP!
SCOOT SCOOT
OH, NO! I'M TRAPPED! THERE'S NO ESCAPE!
AAARRRGGHHH!
© 1991 United Feature Syndicate, Inc.
GARFIELD, WHAT HAPPENED?!
MORNING FOUND ME AGAIN
JIM DAVIS 7-21

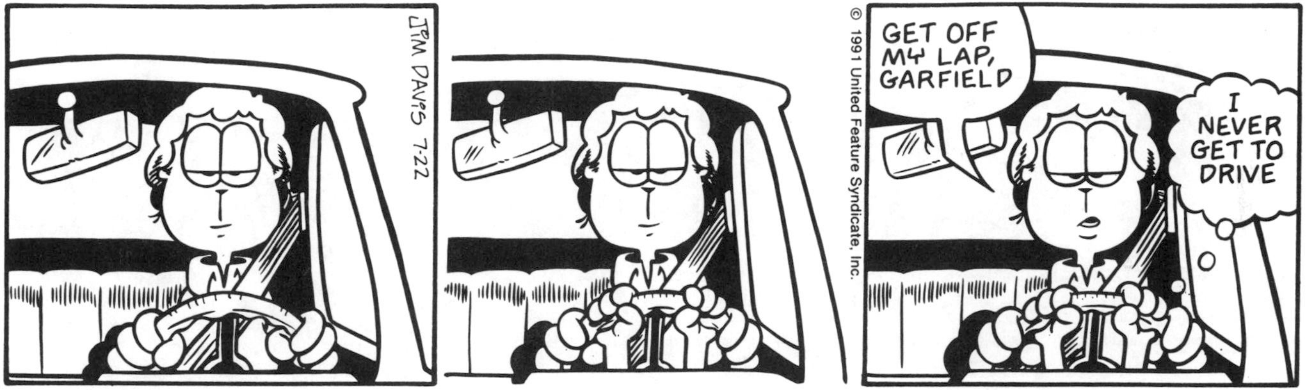
JIM DAVIS 7-22
© 1991 United Feature Syndicate, Inc.
GET OFF MY LAP, GARFIELD
I NEVER GET TO DRIVE

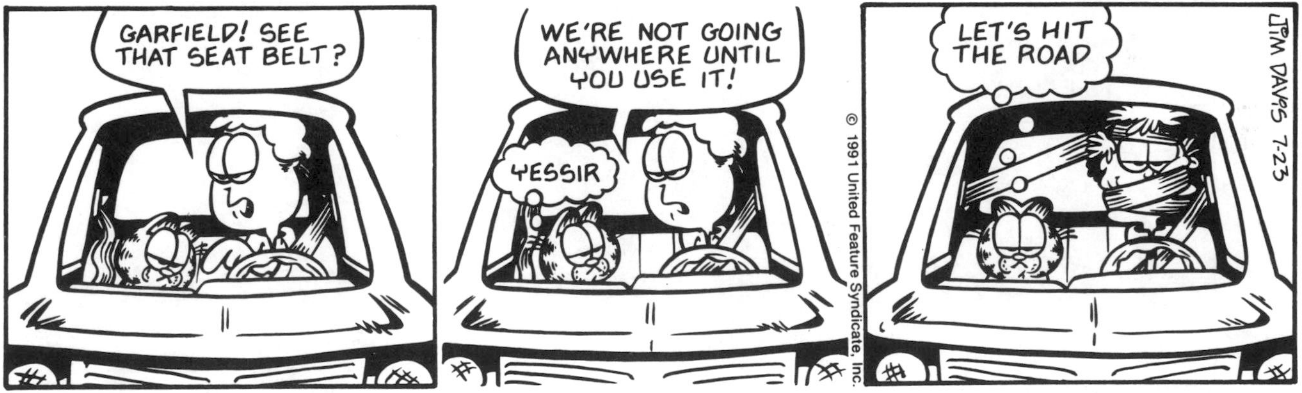
GARFIELD! SEE THAT SEAT BELT?
WE'RE NOT GOING ANYWHERE UNTIL YOU USE IT!
YESSIR
© 1991 United Feature Syndicate, Inc.
LET'S HIT THE ROAD
JIM DAVIS 7-23

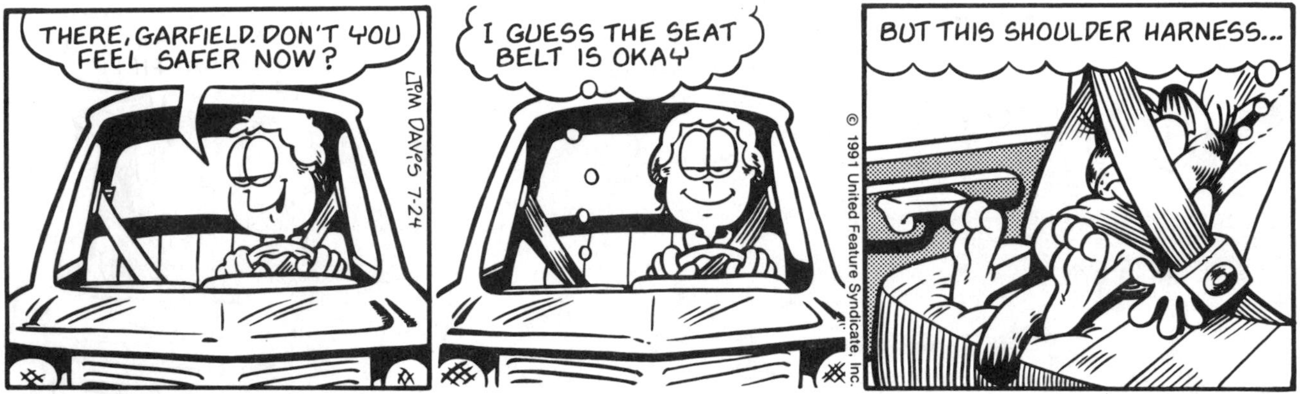
THERE, GARFIELD. DON'T YOU FEEL SAFER NOW?
JIM DAVIS 7-24
I GUESS THE SEAT BELT IS OKAY
© 1991 United Feature Syndicate, Inc.
BUT THIS SHOULDER HARNESS...

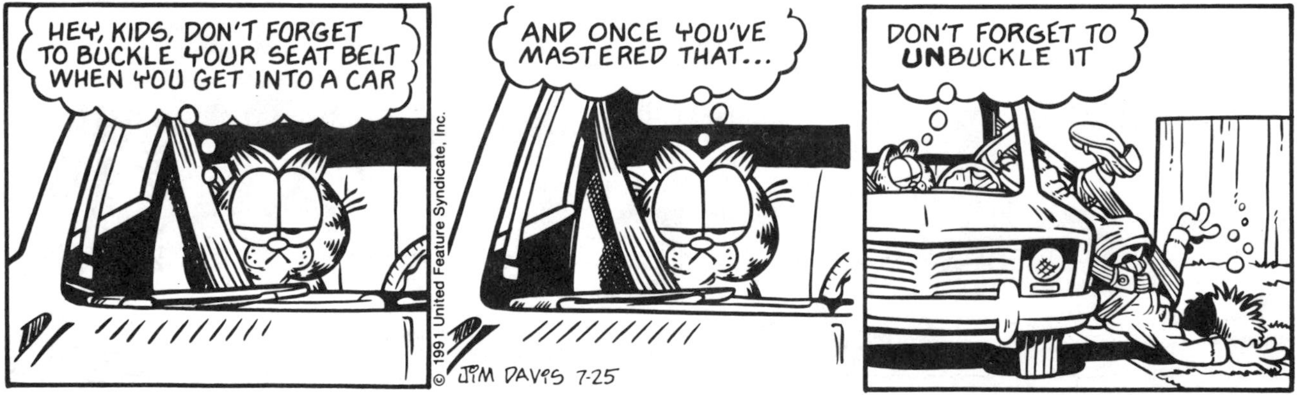
HEY, KIDS, DON'T FORGET TO BUCKLE YOUR SEAT BELT WHEN YOU GET INTO A CAR
© 1991 United Feature Syndicate, Inc.
AND ONCE YOU'VE MASTERED THAT...
JIM DAVIS 7-25
DON'T FORGET TO **UN**BUCKLE IT

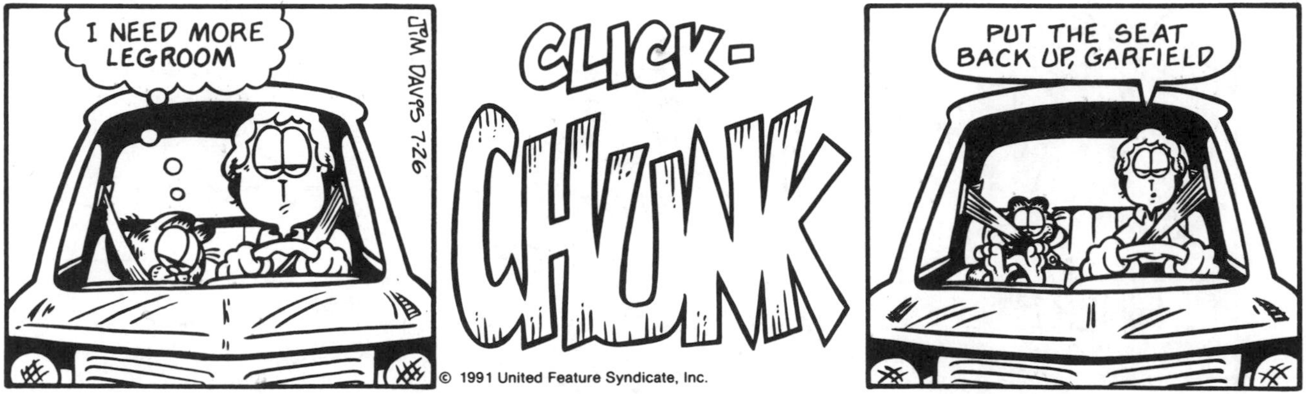
I NEED MORE LEGROOM
JIM DAVIS 7-26
CLICK-CHUNK
PUT THE SEAT BACK UP, GARFIELD
© 1991 United Feature Syndicate, Inc.

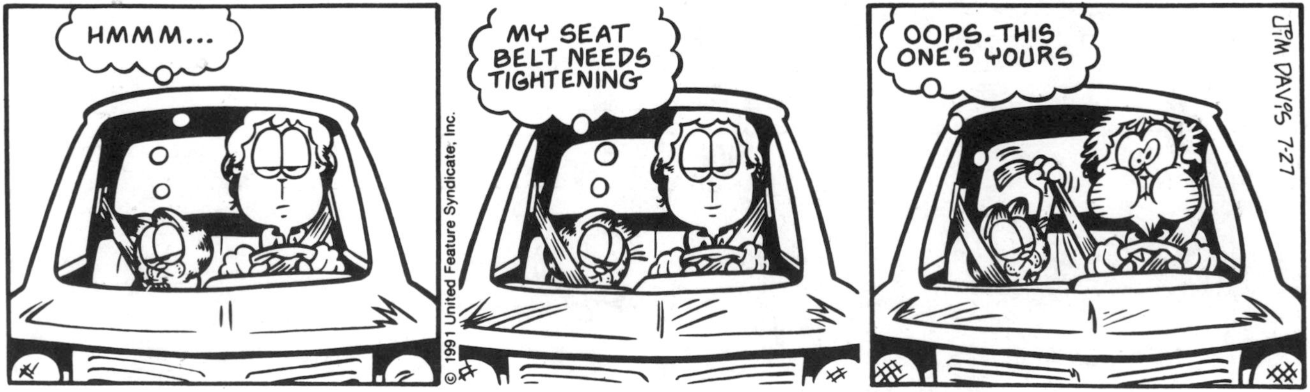
HMMM...
MY SEAT BELT NEEDS TIGHTENING
© 1991 United Feature Syndicate, Inc.
OOPS. THIS ONE'S YOURS
JIM DAVIS 7-27

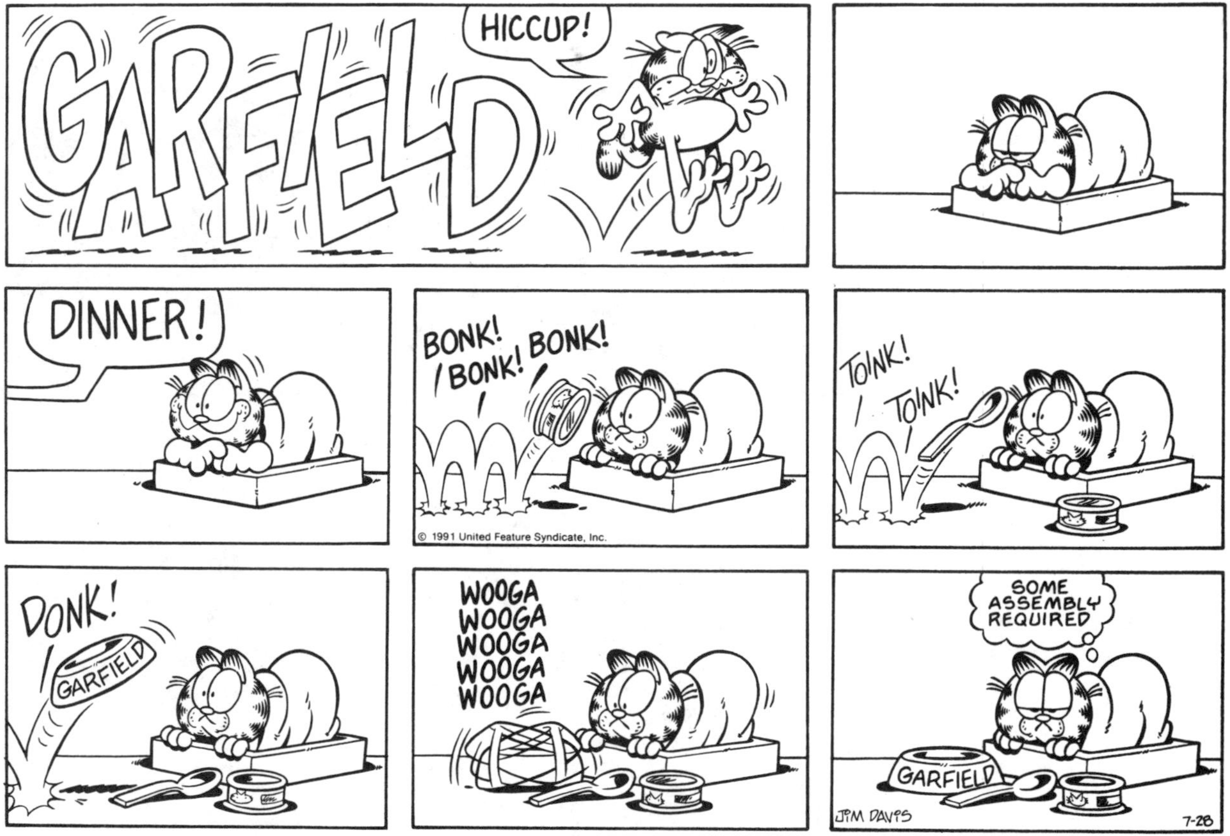
GARFIELD
HICCUP!
DINNER!
BONK! BONK! BONK!
© 1991 United Feature Syndicate, Inc.
TOINK! TOINK!
DONK!
GARFIELD
WOOGA WOOGA WOOGA WOOGA WOOGA
SOME ASSEMBLY REQUIRED
GARFIELD
JIM DAVIS
7-28

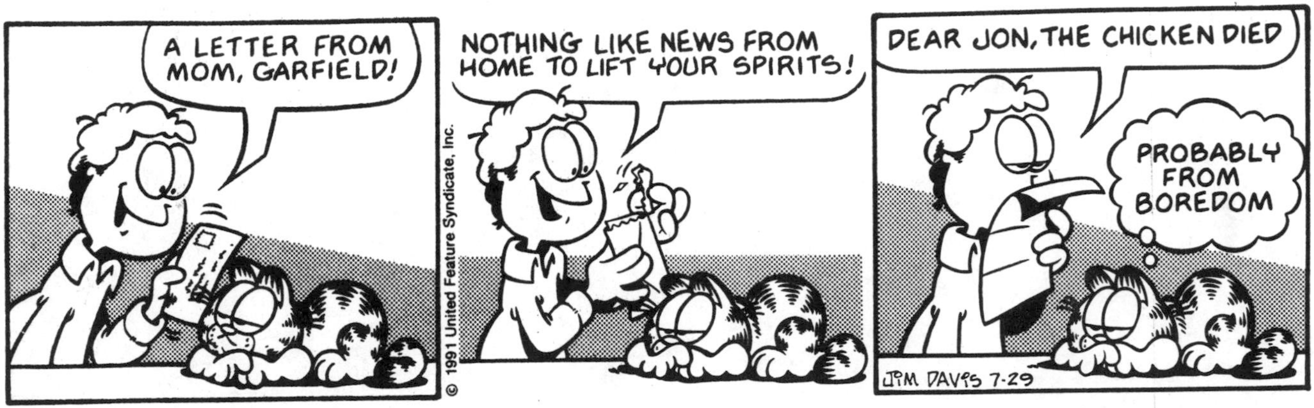
A LETTER FROM MOM, GARFIELD!
NOTHING LIKE NEWS FROM HOME TO LIFT YOUR SPIRITS!
DEAR JON, THE CHICKEN DIED
PROBABLY FROM BOREDOM
© 1991 United Feature Syndicate, Inc.
JIM DAVIS 7-29

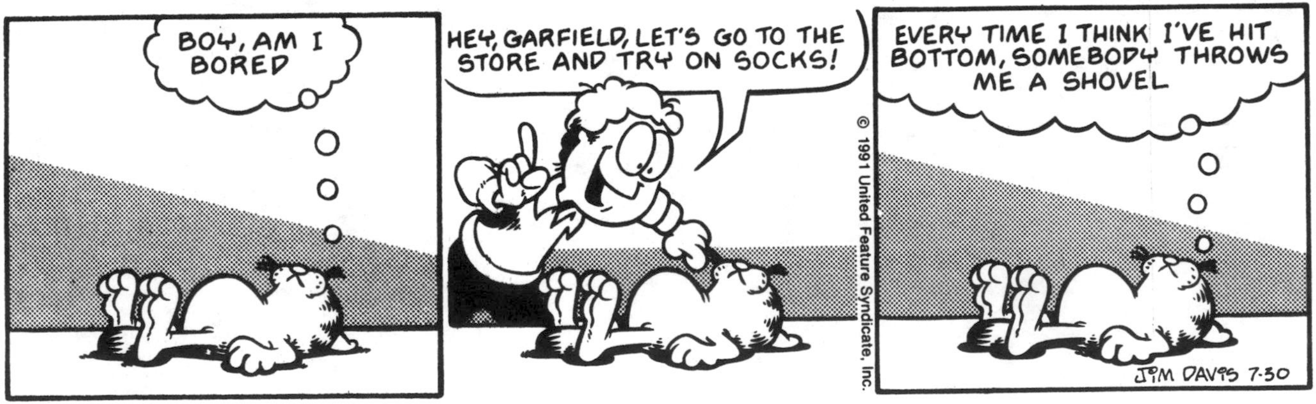
BOY, AM I BORED
HEY, GARFIELD, LET'S GO TO THE STORE AND TRY ON SOCKS!
EVERY TIME I THINK I'VE HIT BOTTOM, SOMEBODY THROWS ME A SHOVEL
© 1991 United Feature Syndicate, Inc.
JIM DAVIS 7-30

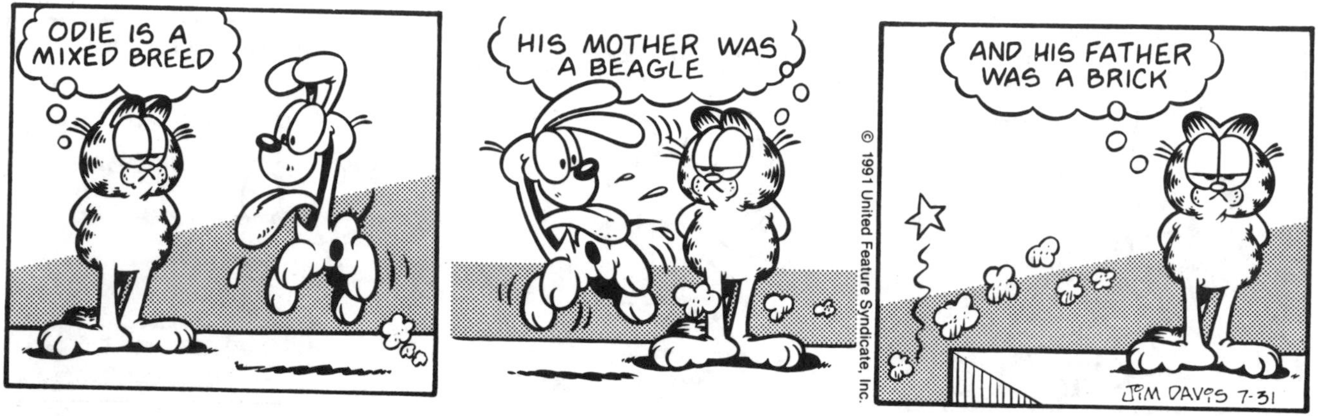
ODIE IS A MIXED BREED
HIS MOTHER WAS A BEAGLE
AND HIS FATHER WAS A BRICK
JIM DAVIS 7-31
© 1991 United Feature Syndicate, Inc.

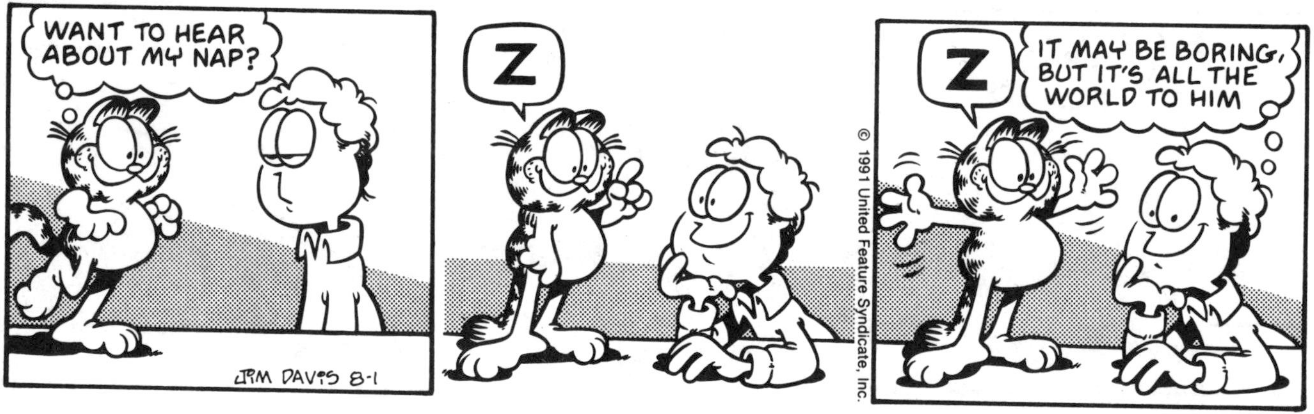
WANT TO HEAR ABOUT MY NAP?
Z
Z
IT MAY BE BORING, BUT IT'S ALL THE WORLD TO HIM
JIM DAVIS 8-1
© 1991 United Feature Syndicate, Inc.

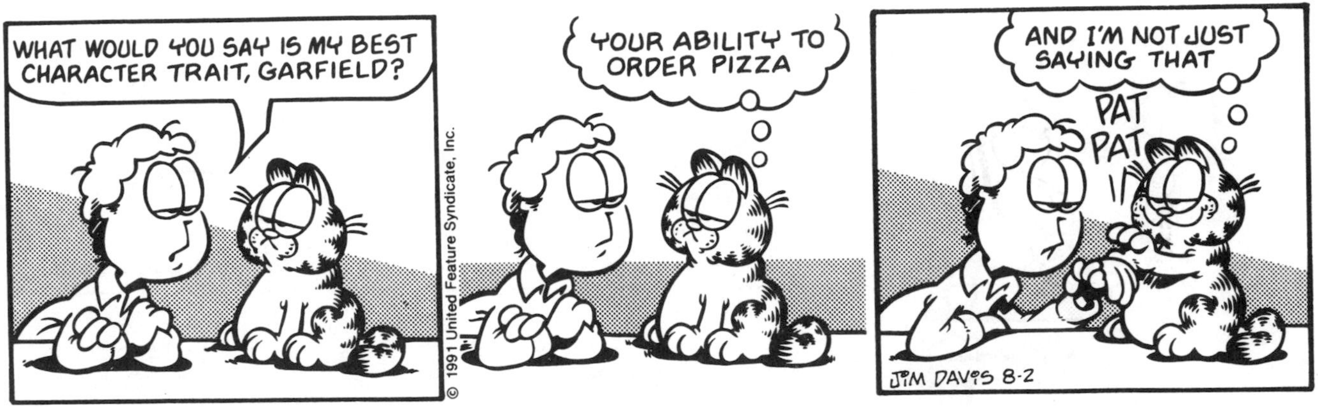
WHAT WOULD YOU SAY IS MY BEST CHARACTER TRAIT, GARFIELD?
© 1991 United Feature Syndicate, Inc.
YOUR ABILITY TO ORDER PIZZA
AND I'M NOT JUST SAYING THAT
PAT PAT
JIM DAVIS 8-2

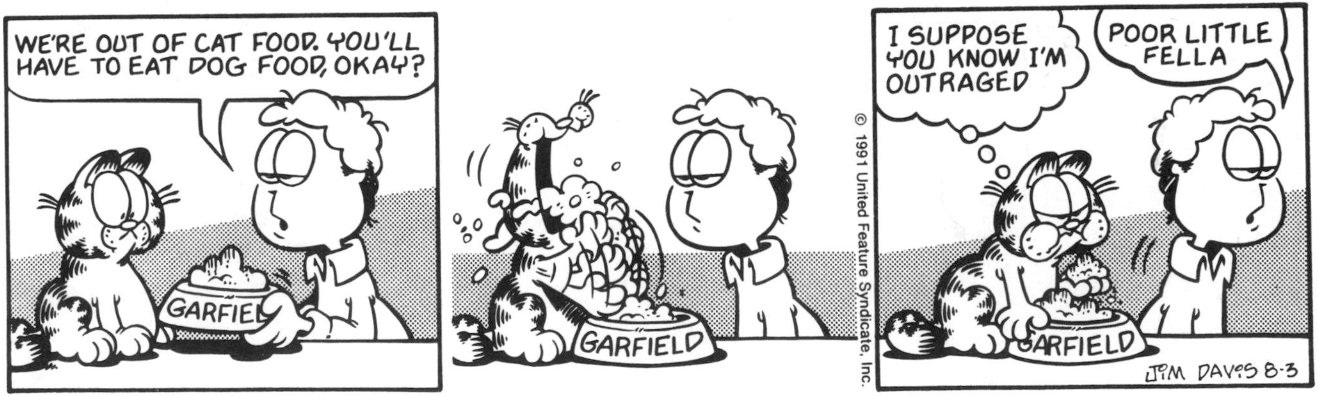
WE'RE OUT OF CAT FOOD. YOU'LL HAVE TO EAT DOG FOOD, OKAY?
GARFIEL
GARFIELD
© 1991 United Feature Syndicate, Inc.
I SUPPOSE YOU KNOW I'M OUTRAGED
POOR LITTLE FELLA
GARFIELD
JIM DAVIS 8-3

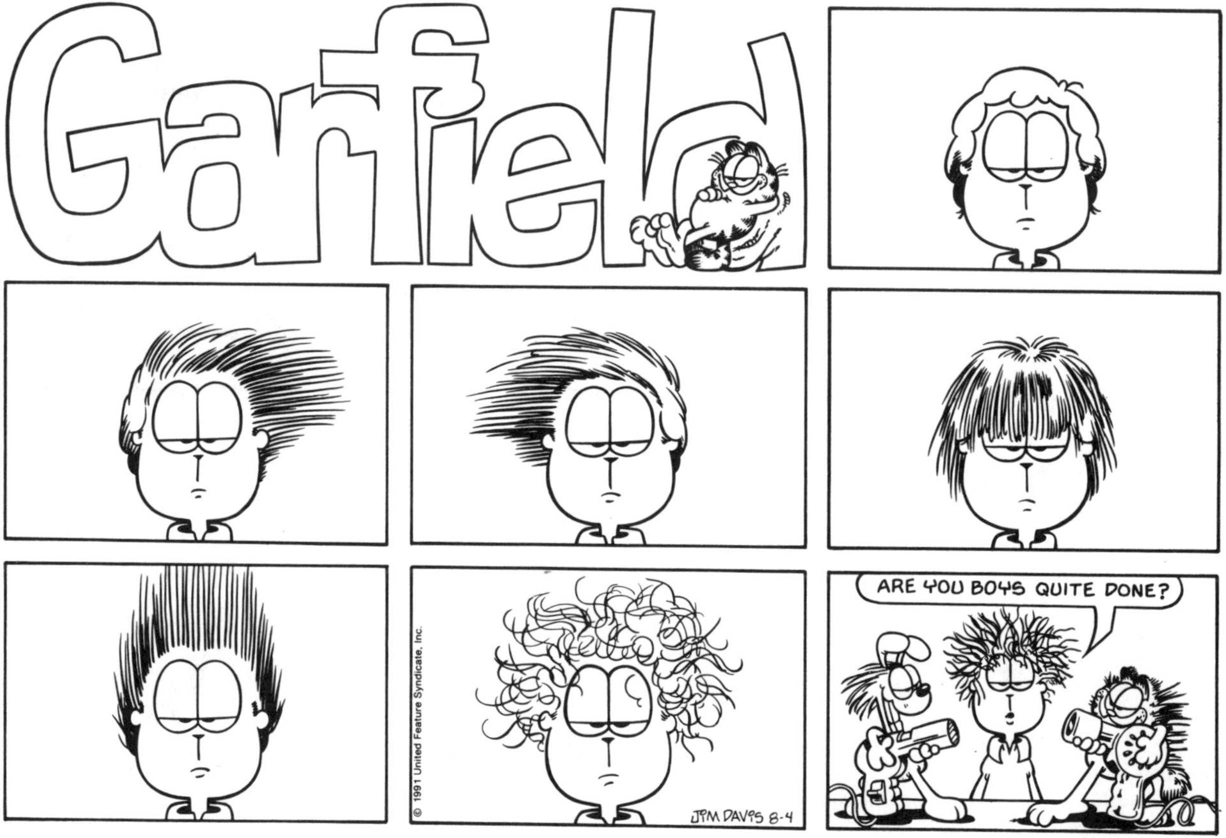
Garfield
© 1991 United Feature Syndicate, Inc.
JIM DAVIS 8-4
ARE YOU BOYS QUITE DONE?

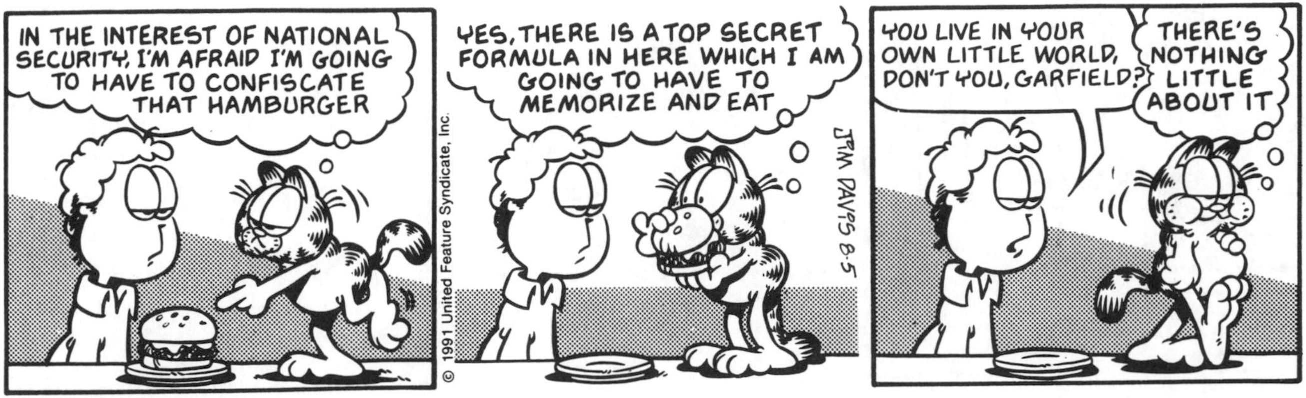
IN THE INTEREST OF NATIONAL SECURITY, I'M AFRAID I'M GOING TO HAVE TO CONFISCATE THAT HAMBURGER
© 1991 United Feature Syndicate, Inc.
YES, THERE IS A TOP SECRET FORMULA IN HERE WHICH I AM GOING TO HAVE TO MEMORIZE AND EAT
JIM DAVIS 8-5
YOU LIVE IN YOUR OWN LITTLE WORLD, DON'T YOU, GARFIELD?
THERE'S NOTHING LITTLE ABOUT IT

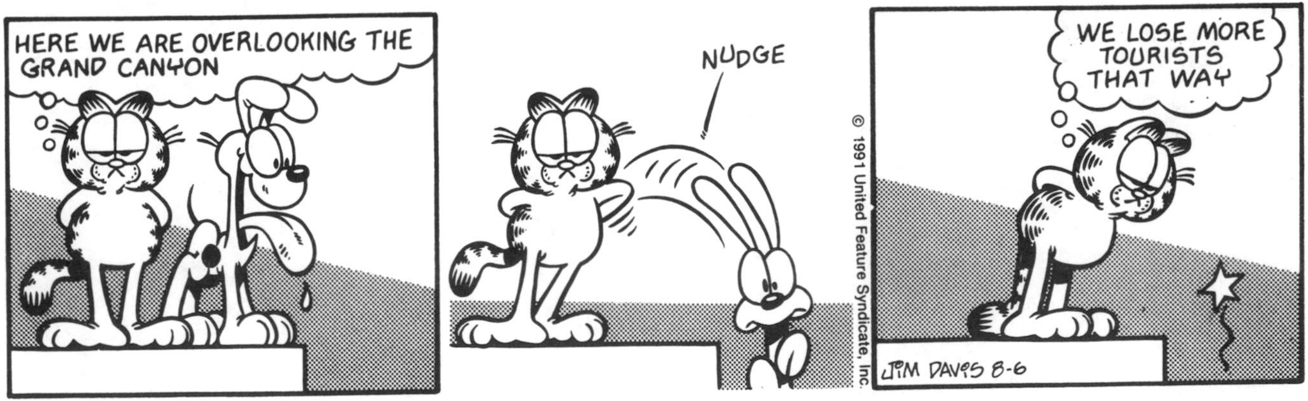
HERE WE ARE OVERLOOKING THE GRAND CANYON
NUDGE
© 1991 United Feature Syndicate, Inc.
WE LOSE MORE TOURISTS THAT WAY
JIM DAVIS 8-6

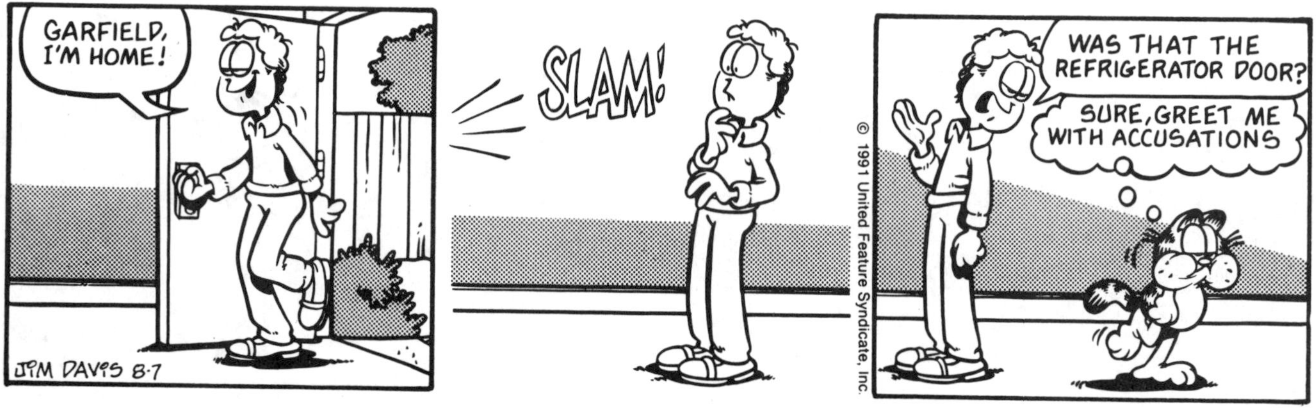
GARFIELD, I'M HOME!
JIM DAVIS 8-7
SLAM!
© 1991 United Feature Syndicate, Inc.
WAS THAT THE REFRIGERATOR DOOR?
SURE, GREET ME WITH ACCUSATIONS

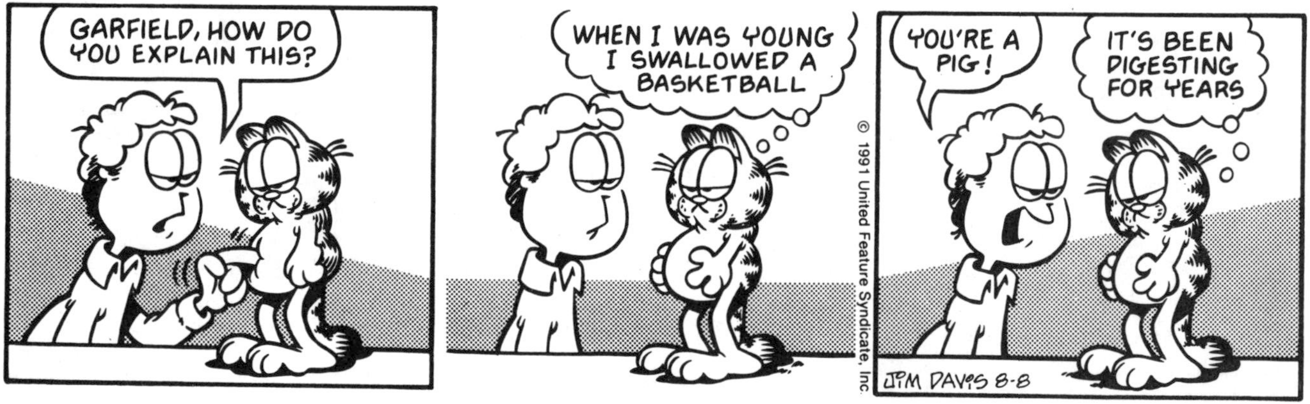
GARFIELD, HOW DO YOU EXPLAIN THIS?
WHEN I WAS YOUNG I SWALLOWED A BASKETBALL
© 1991 United Feature Syndicate, Inc.
YOU'RE A PIG!
IT'S BEEN DIGESTING FOR YEARS
JIM DAVIS 8-8

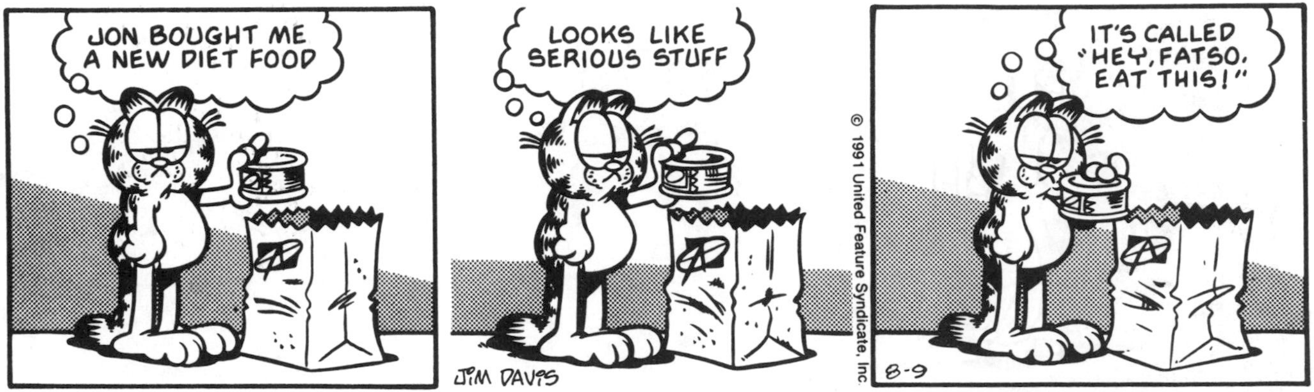
JON BOUGHT ME A NEW DIET FOOD
LOOKS LIKE SERIOUS STUFF
IT'S CALLED "HEY, FATSO, EAT THIS!"
JIM DAVIS
8-9

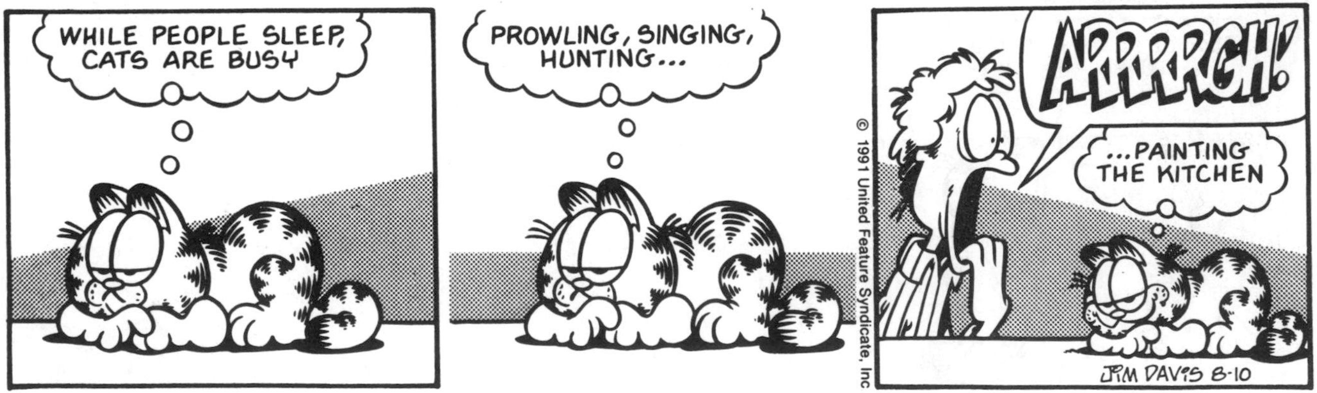
WHILE PEOPLE SLEEP, CATS ARE BUSY
PROWLING, SINGING, HUNTING...
AARRRGH!
...PAINTING THE KITCHEN
JIM DAVIS 8-10

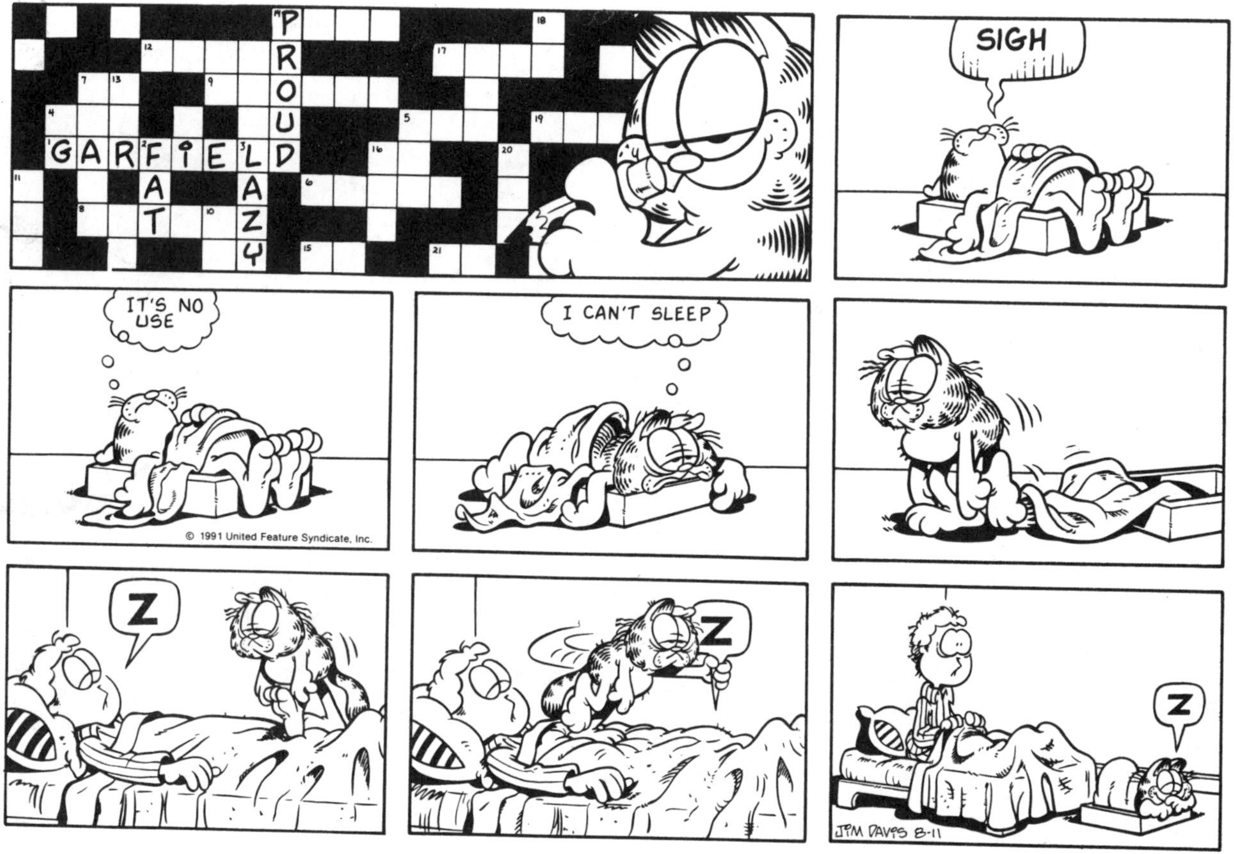
PROUD
GARFIELD
FAT
LAZY
SIGH
IT'S NO USE
I CAN'T SLEEP
Z
Z
Z
JIM DAVIS 8-11

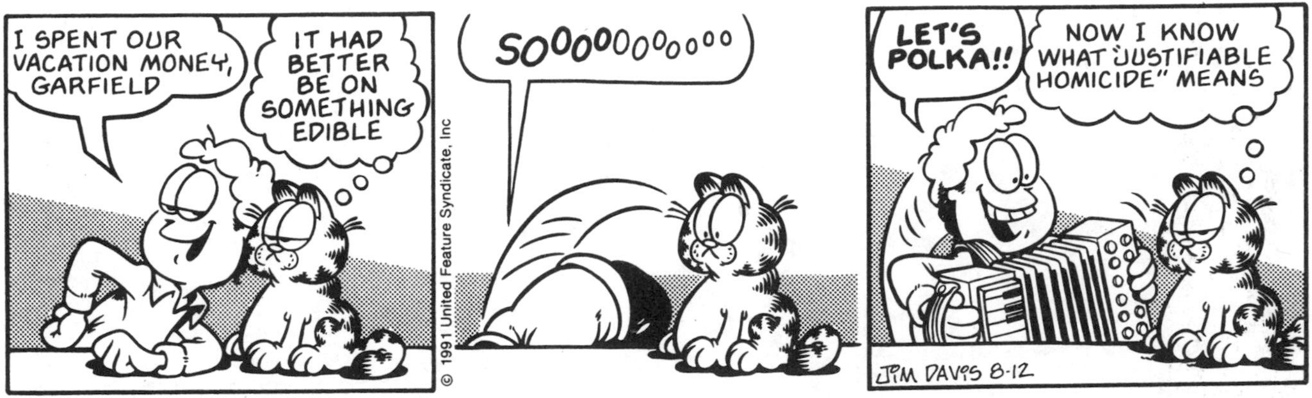
I SPENT OUR VACATION MONEY, GARFIELD
IT HAD BETTER BE ON SOMETHING EDIBLE
© 1991 United Feature Syndicate, Inc
SOOOOOOOOOOO
LET'S POLKA!!
NOW I KNOW WHAT "JUSTIFIABLE HOMICIDE" MEANS
JIM DAVIS 8-12

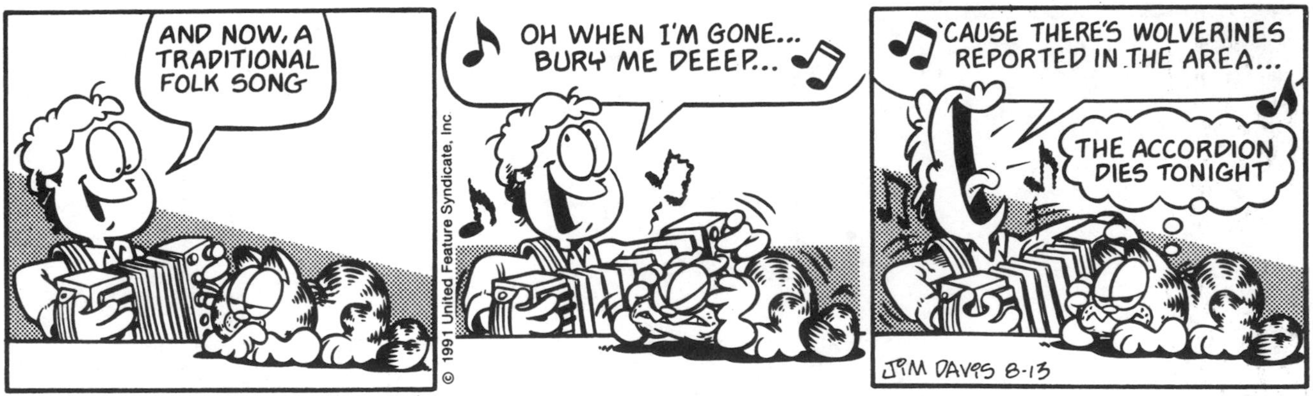
AND NOW, A TRADITIONAL FOLK SONG
© 1991 United Feature Syndicate, Inc
OH WHEN I'M GONE... BURY ME DEEEP...
'CAUSE THERE'S WOLVERINES REPORTED IN THE AREA...
THE ACCORDION DIES TONIGHT
JIM DAVIS 8-13

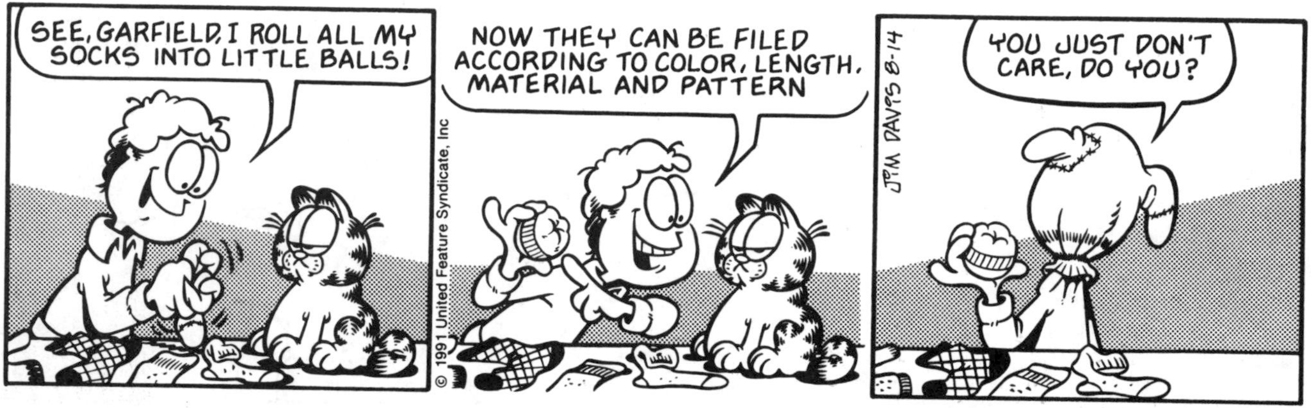
SEE, GARFIELD, I ROLL ALL MY SOCKS INTO LITTLE BALLS!
© 1991 United Feature Syndicate, Inc
NOW THEY CAN BE FILED ACCORDING TO COLOR, LENGTH, MATERIAL AND PATTERN
JIM DAVIS 8-14
YOU JUST DON'T CARE, DO YOU?

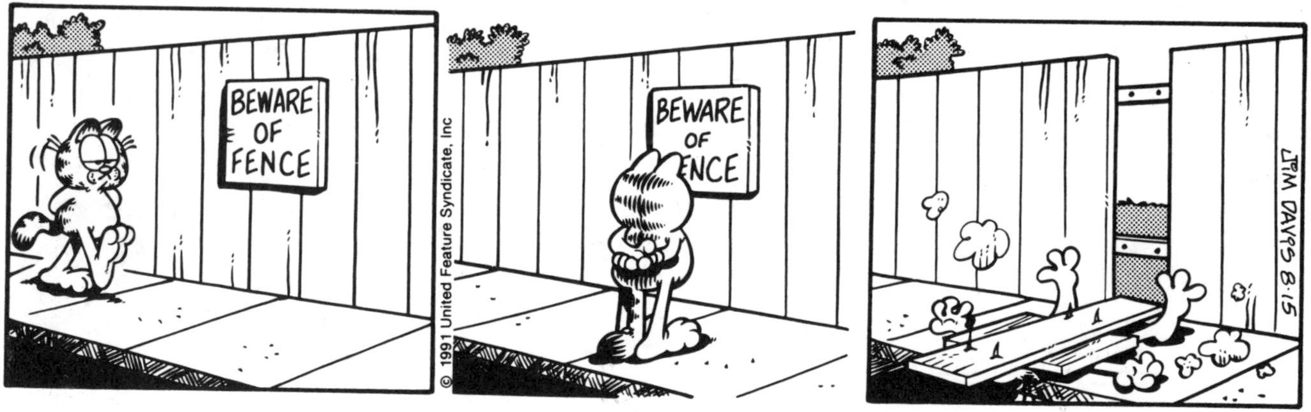
BEWARE OF FENCE
© 1991 United Feature Syndicate, Inc
BEWARE OF
ENCE
JIM DAVIS 8-15

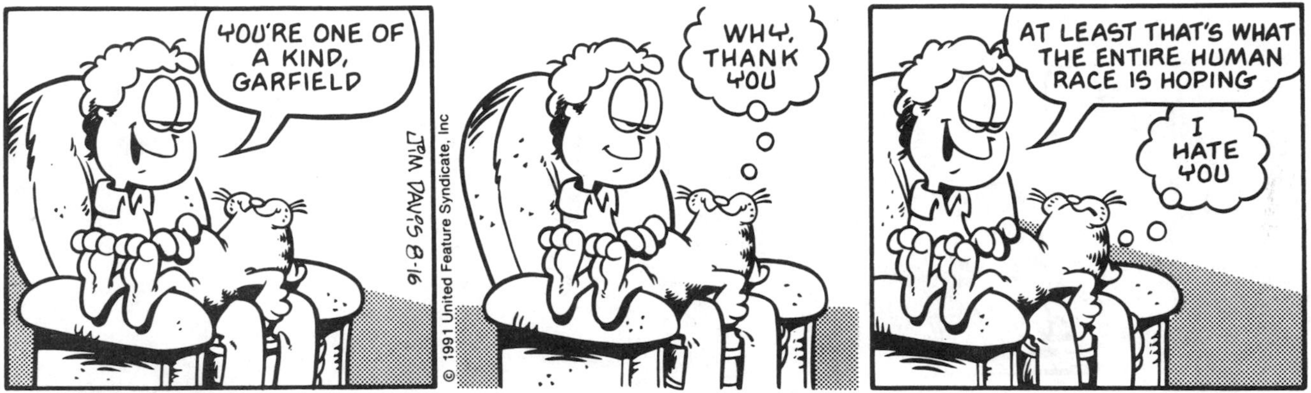
YOU'RE ONE OF A KIND, GARFIELD
JIM DAVIS 8-16
© 1991 United Feature Syndicate, Inc
WHY, THANK YOU
AT LEAST THAT'S WHAT THE ENTIRE HUMAN RACE IS HOPING
I HATE YOU

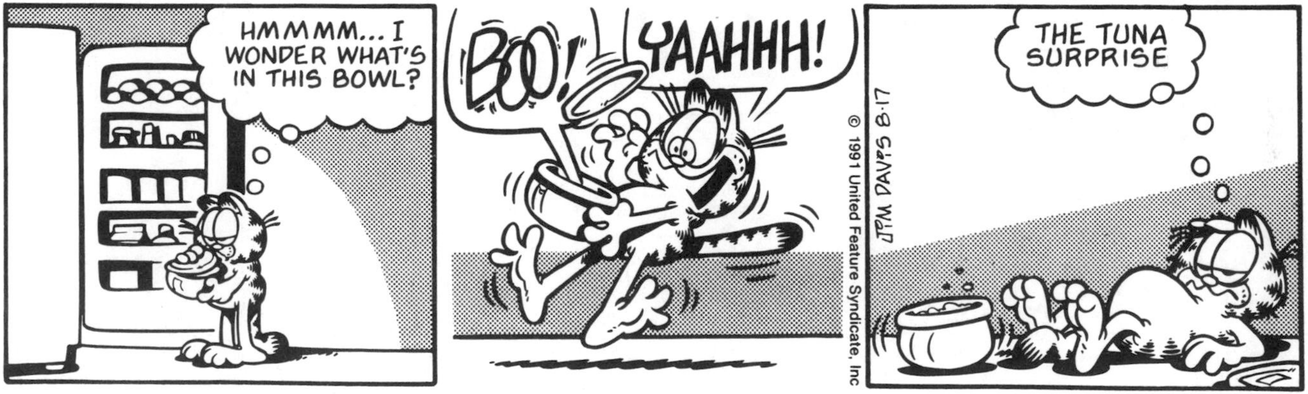
HMMMM... I WONDER WHAT'S IN THIS BOWL?
BOO!
YAAHHH!
© 1991 United Feature Syndicate, Inc
JIM DAVIS 8-17
THE TUNA SURPRISE

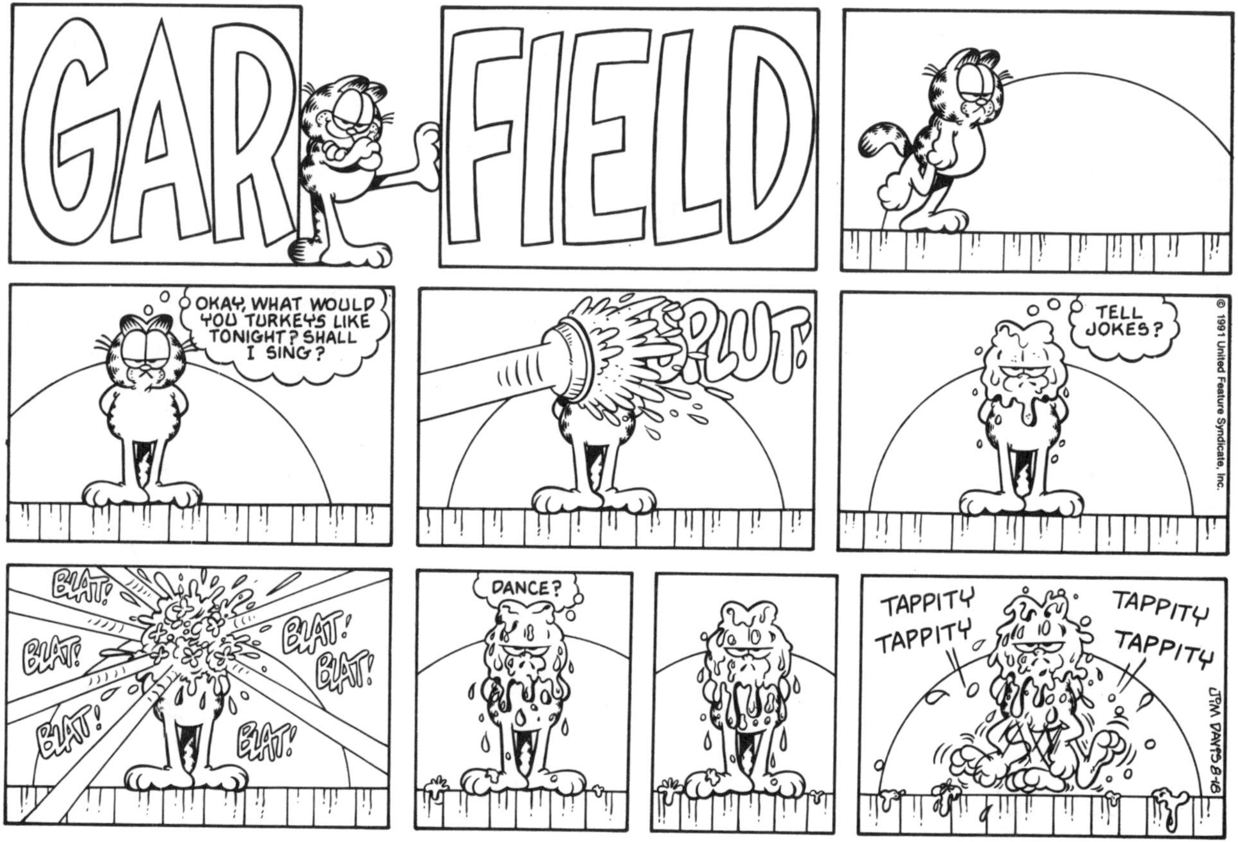
GARFIELD
OKAY, WHAT WOULD YOU TURKEYS LIKE TONIGHT? SHALL I SING?
SPLUT!
TELL JOKES?
© 1991 United Feature Syndicate, Inc.
BLAT!
BLAT!
BLAT!
BLAT!
BLAT!
BLAT!
DANCE?
TAPPITY TAPPITY
TAPPITY TAPPITY
JIM DAVIS 8-18

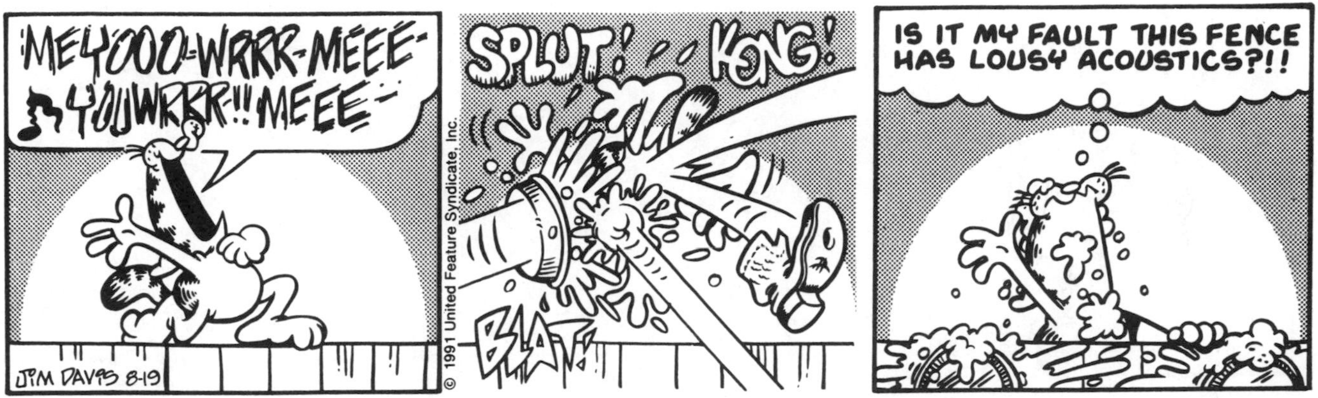
MEYOOO-WRRR-MEEE-YOUWRRR!! MEEE
SPLUT!
KONG!
BLAT!
IS IT MY FAULT THIS FENCE HAS LOUSY ACOUSTICS?!!
JIM DAVIS 8-19
© 1991 United Feature Syndicate, Inc.

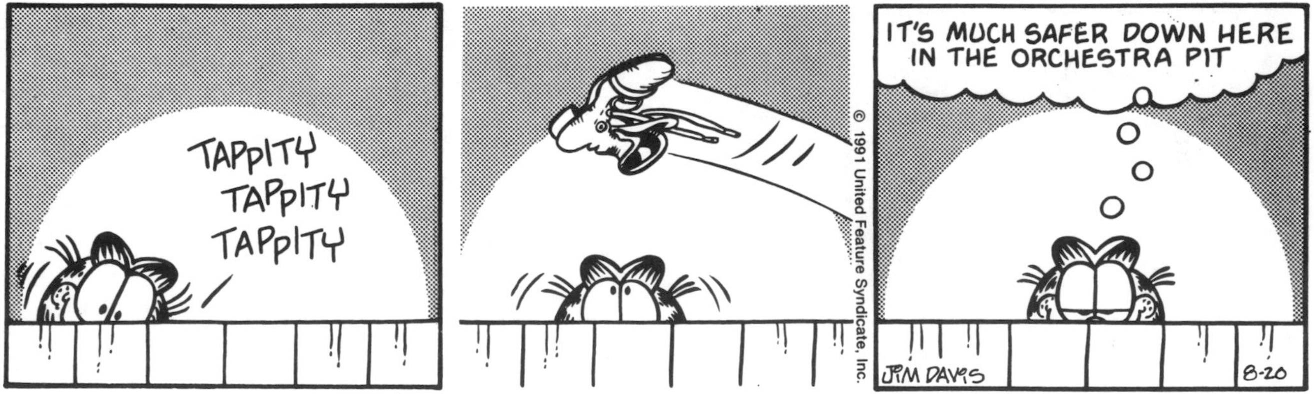
TAPPITY
TAPPITY
TAPPITY
IT'S MUCH SAFER DOWN HERE IN THE ORCHESTRA PIT
JIM DAVIS 8-20
© 1991 United Feature Syndicate, Inc.

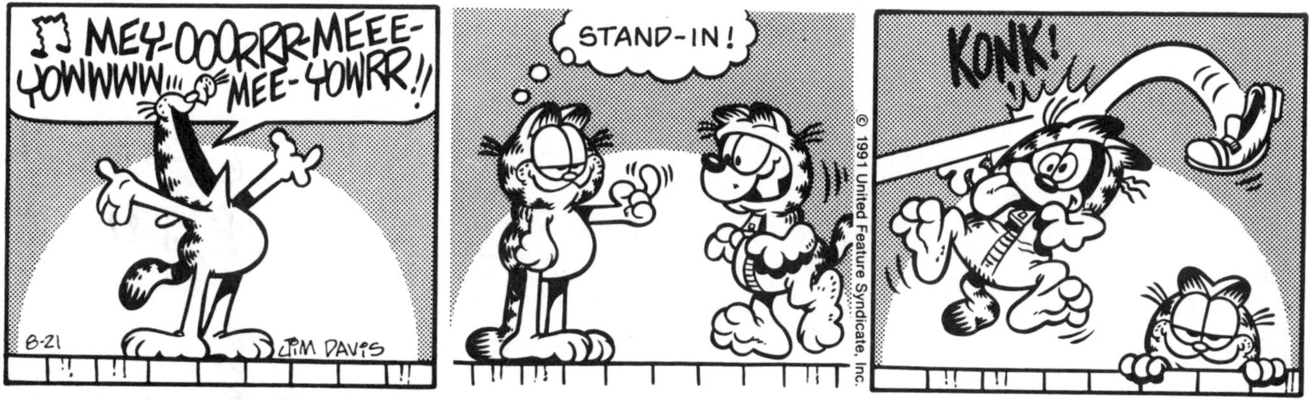
MEY-OOORRR-MEEE-YOWWW MEE-YOWRR!!
8-21
JIM DAVIS
STAND-IN!
© 1991 United Feature Syndicate, Inc.
KONK!

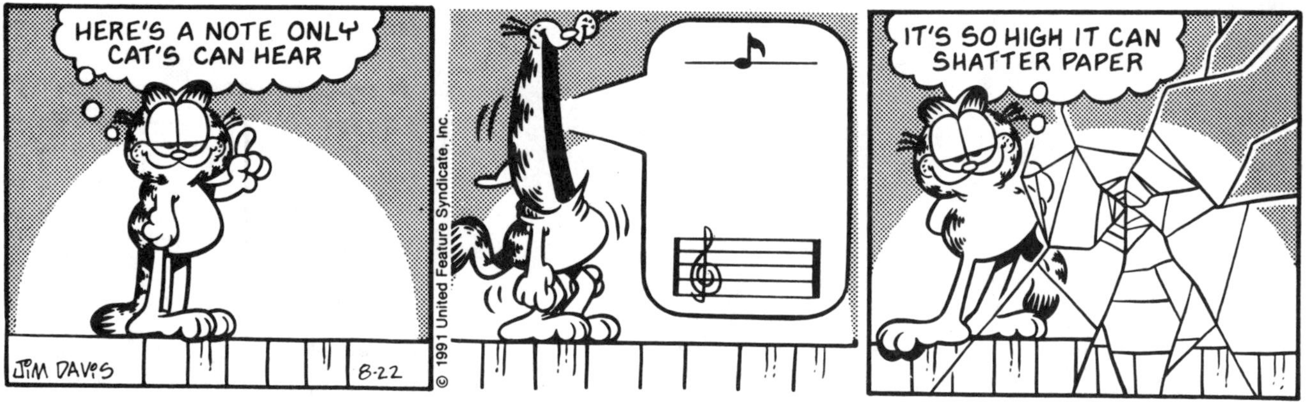
HERE'S A NOTE ONLY CAT'S CAN HEAR
JIM DAVIS
8-22
© 1991 United Feature Syndicate, Inc.
IT'S SO HIGH IT CAN SHATTER PAPER

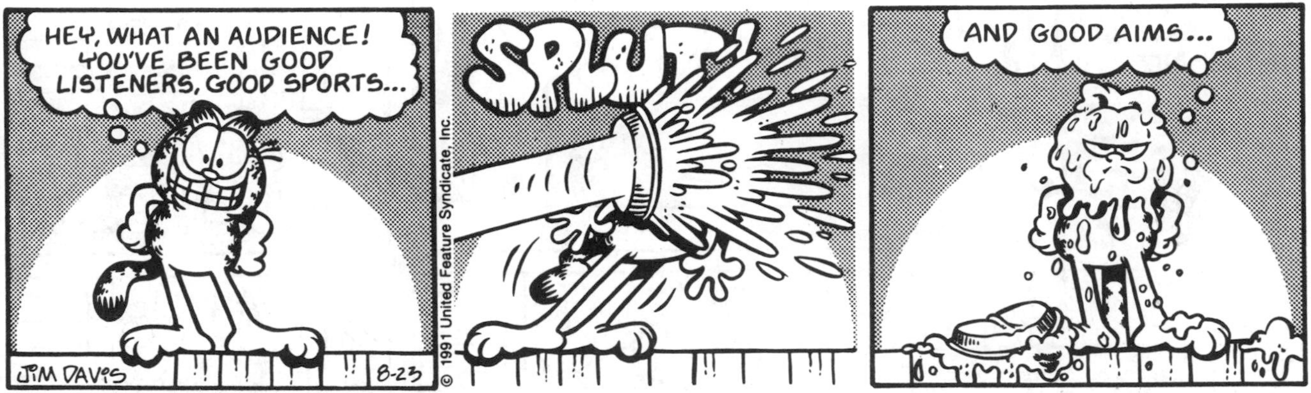
HEY, WHAT AN AUDIENCE! YOU'VE BEEN GOOD LISTENERS, GOOD SPORTS...
JIM DAVIS
8-23
SPLUT!
© 1991 United Feature Syndicate, Inc.
AND GOOD AIMS...

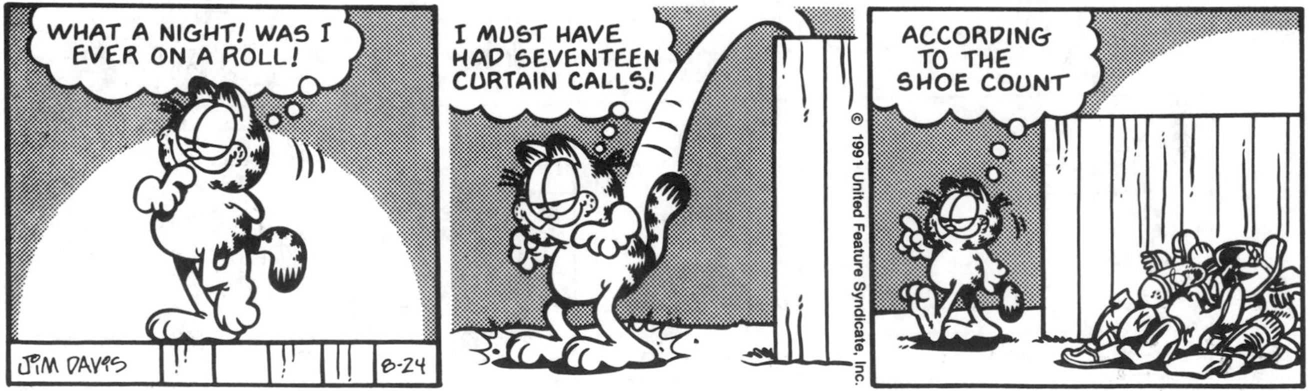
WHAT A NIGHT! WAS I EVER ON A ROLL!
JIM DAVIS
8-24
I MUST HAVE HAD SEVENTEEN CURTAIN CALLS!
© 1991 United Feature Syndicate, Inc.
ACCORDING TO THE SHOE COUNT

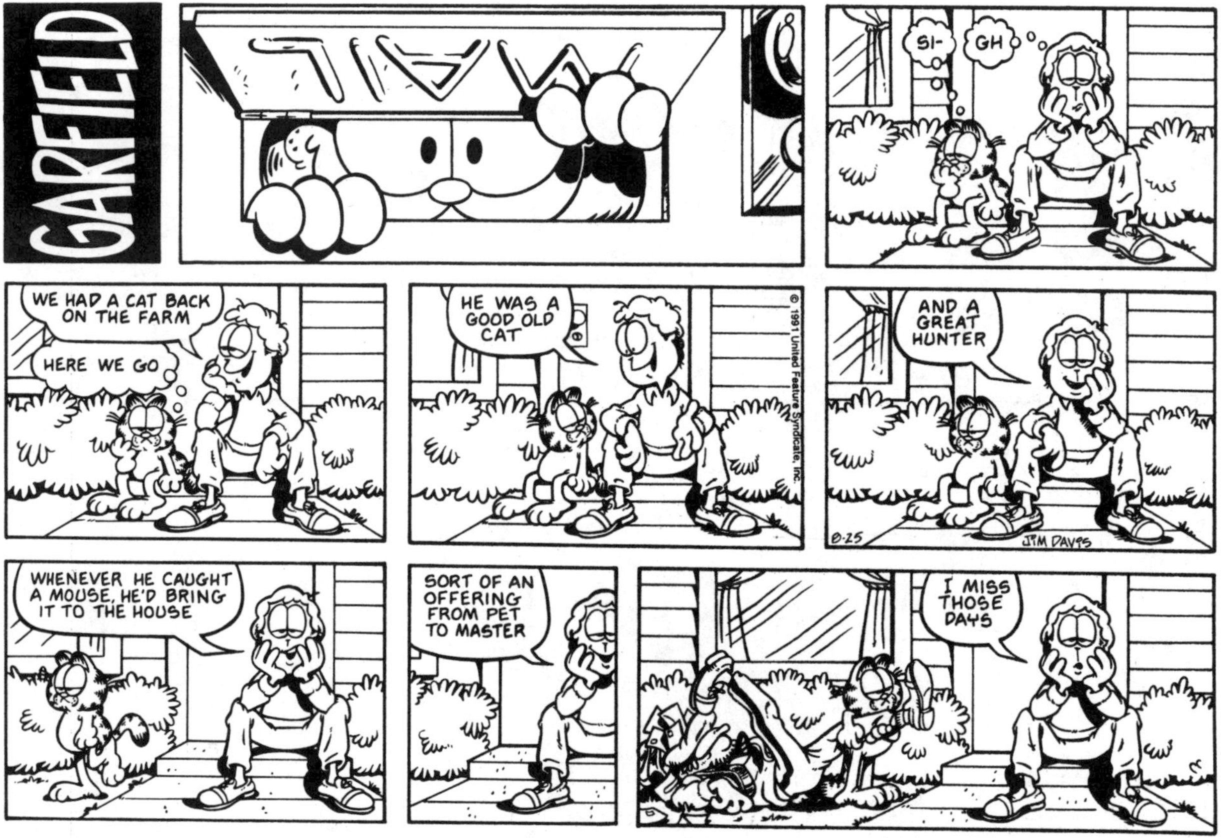
GARFIELD
SI-
GH
WE HAD A CAT BACK ON THE FARM
HERE WE GO
HE WAS A GOOD OLD CAT
© 1991 United Feature Syndicate, Inc.
AND A GREAT HUNTER
8-25
JIM DAVIS
WHENEVER HE CAUGHT A MOUSE, HE'D BRING IT TO THE HOUSE
SORT OF AN OFFERING FROM PET TO MASTER
I MISS THOSE DAYS

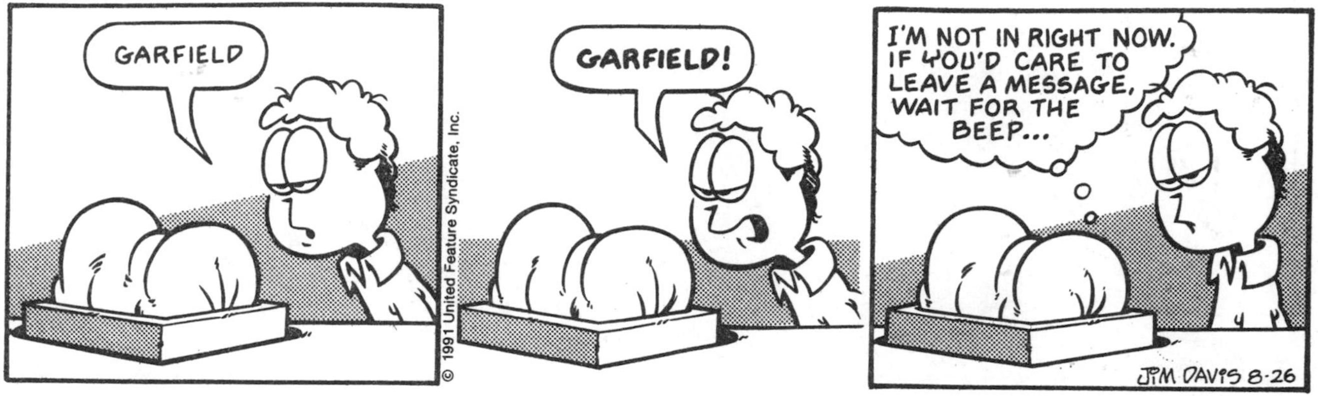
GARFIELD
GARFIELD!
I'M NOT IN RIGHT NOW. IF YOU'D CARE TO LEAVE A MESSAGE, WAIT FOR THE BEEP...
© 1991 United Feature Syndicate, Inc.
JIM DAVIS 8-26

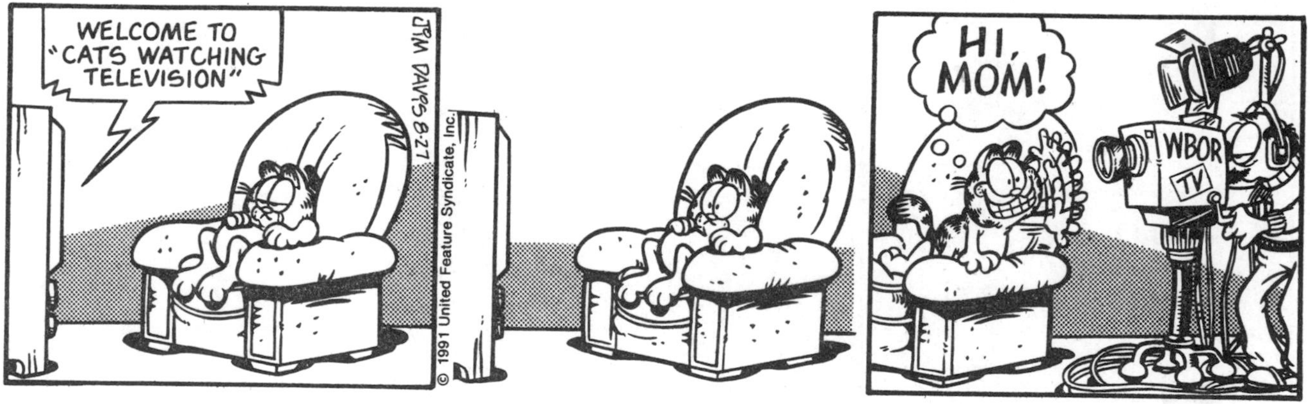
WELCOME TO "CATS WATCHING TELEVISION"
HI, MOM!
WBOR TV
© 1991 United Feature Syndicate, Inc.
JIM DAVIS 8-27

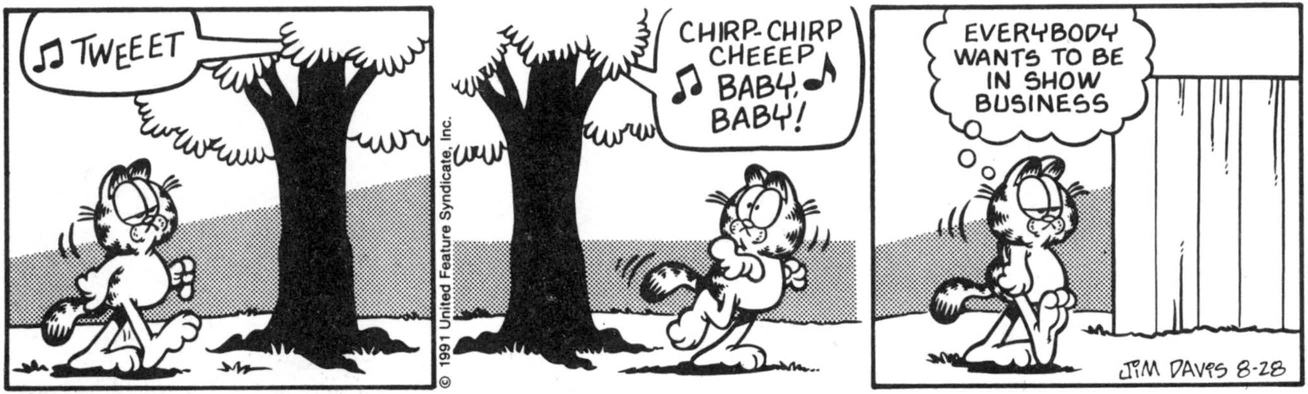

♫ TWEEET
CHIRP-CHIRP CHEEEP ♫ BABY, BABY! ♪
EVERYBODY WANTS TO BE IN SHOW BUSINESS
© 1991 United Feature Syndicate, Inc.
JIM DAVIS 8-28

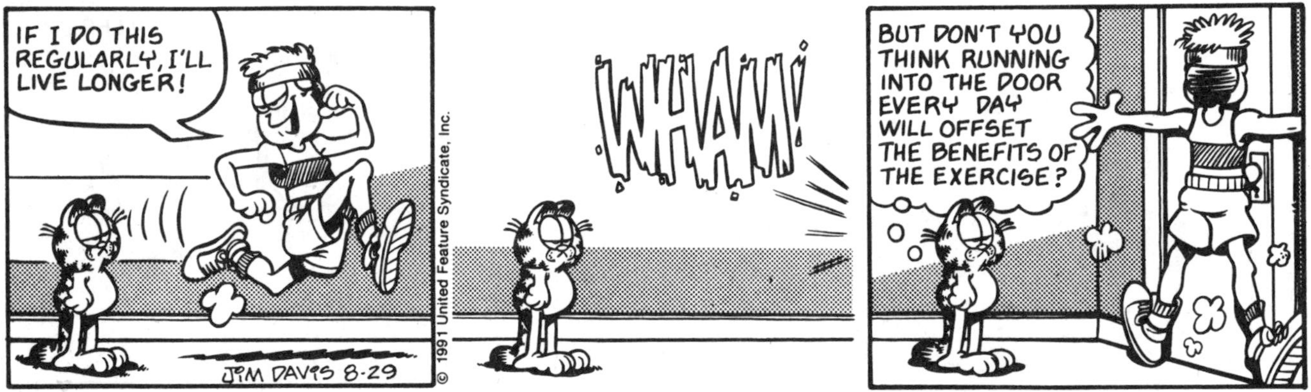

IF I DO THIS REGULARLY, I'LL LIVE LONGER!
WHAM!
BUT DON'T YOU THINK RUNNING INTO THE DOOR EVERY DAY WILL OFFSET THE BENEFITS OF THE EXERCISE?
© 1991 United Feature Syndicate, Inc.
JIM DAVIS 8-29

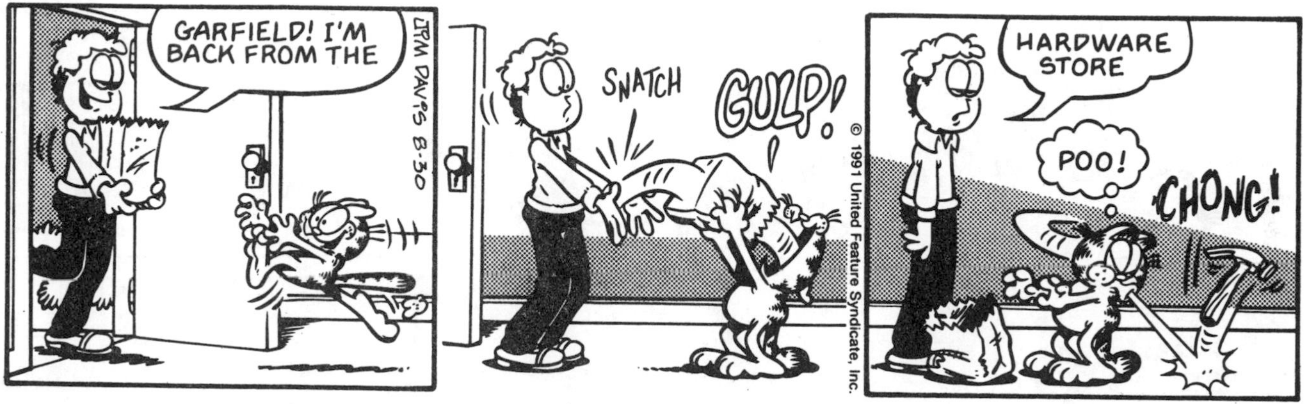
GARFIELD! I'M BACK FROM THE
JIM DAVIS 8-30
SNATCH
GULP!
© 1991 United Feature Syndicate, Inc.
HARDWARE STORE
POO!
CHONG!

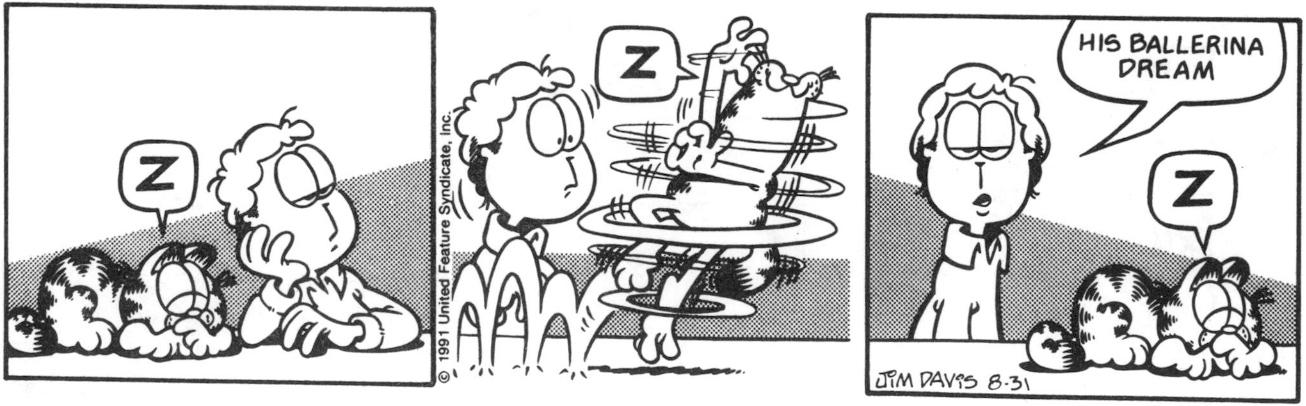
Z
© 1991 United Feature Syndicate, Inc.
Z
HIS BALLERINA DREAM
Z
JIM DAVIS 8-31

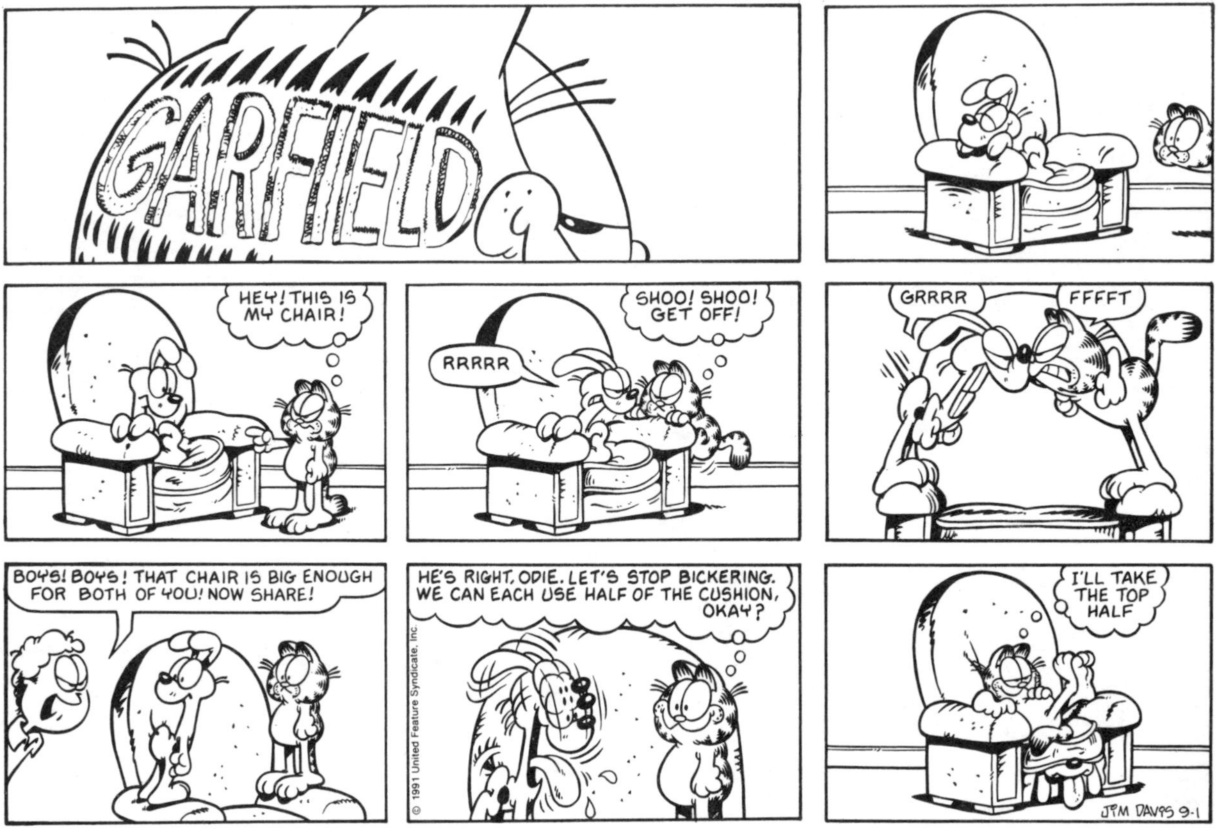
GARFIELD
HEY! THIS IS MY CHAIR!
RRRRR
SHOO! SHOO! GET OFF!
GRRRR
FFFFT
BOYS! BOYS! THAT CHAIR IS BIG ENOUGH FOR BOTH OF YOU! NOW SHARE!
HE'S RIGHT, ODIE. LET'S STOP BICKERING. WE CAN EACH USE HALF OF THE CUSHION, OKAY?
© 1991 United Feature Syndicate, Inc.
I'LL TAKE THE TOP HALF
JIM DAVIS 9-1

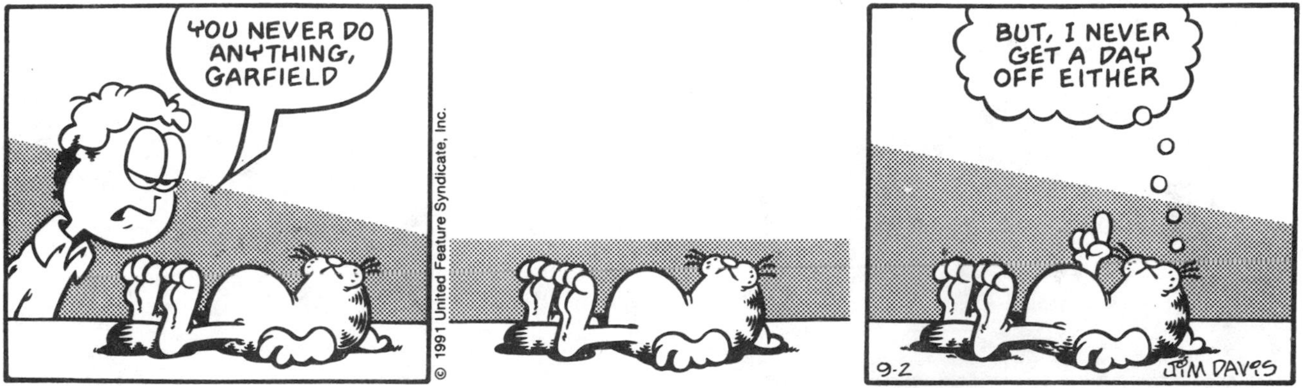
YOU NEVER DO ANYTHING, GARFIELD
BUT, I NEVER GET A DAY OFF EITHER
© 1991 United Feature Syndicate, Inc.
9-2
JIM DAVIS

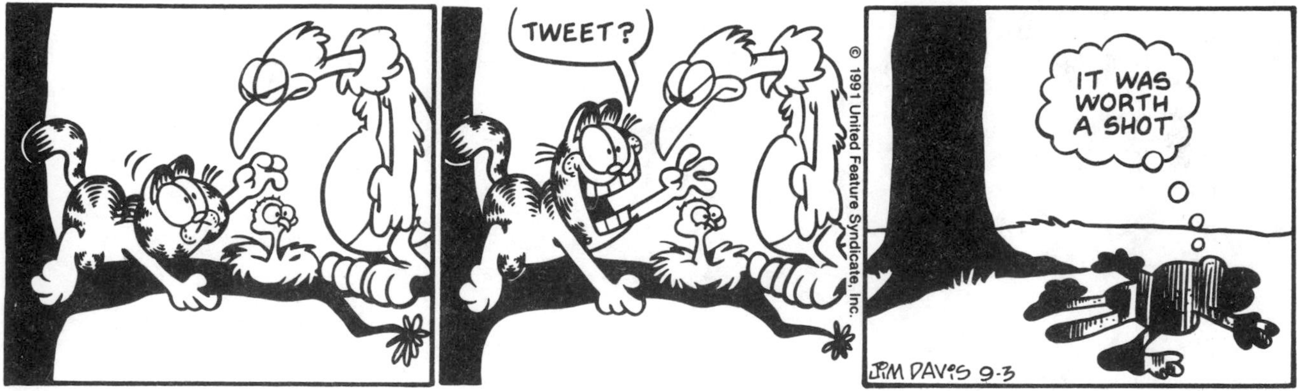
TWEET?
IT WAS WORTH A SHOT
© 1991 United Feature Syndicate, Inc.
JIM DAVIS 9-3

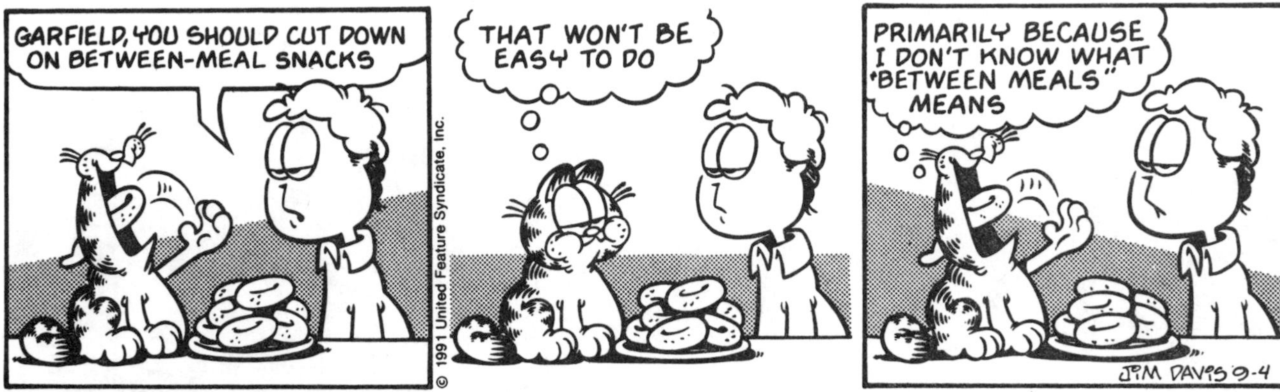
GARFIELD, YOU SHOULD CUT DOWN ON BETWEEN-MEAL SNACKS
THAT WON'T BE EASY TO DO
© 1991 United Feature Syndicate, Inc.
PRIMARILY BECAUSE I DON'T KNOW WHAT "BETWEEN MEALS" MEANS
JIM DAVIS 9-4

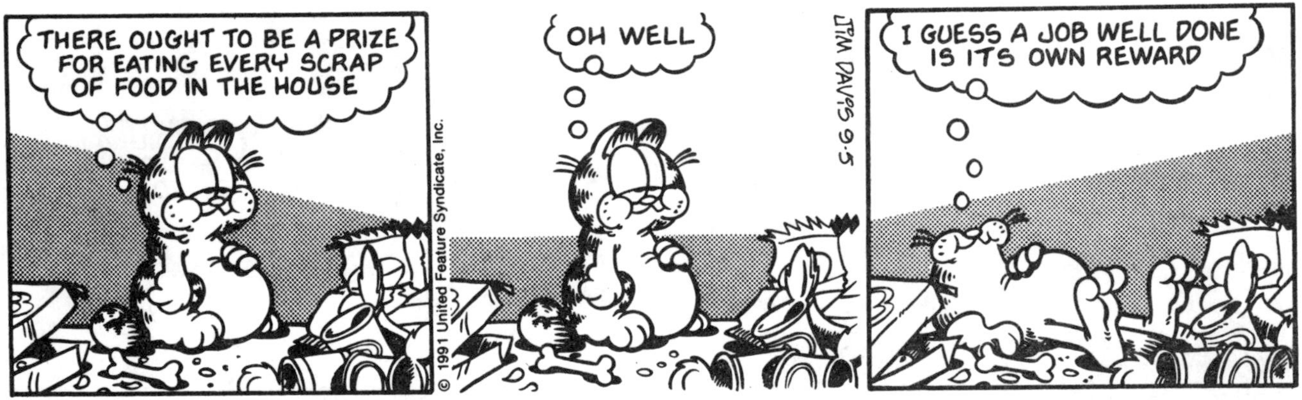
THERE OUGHT TO BE A PRIZE FOR EATING EVERY SCRAP OF FOOD IN THE HOUSE
© 1991 United Feature Syndicate, Inc.
OH WELL
JIM DAVIS 9-5
I GUESS A JOB WELL DONE IS ITS OWN REWARD

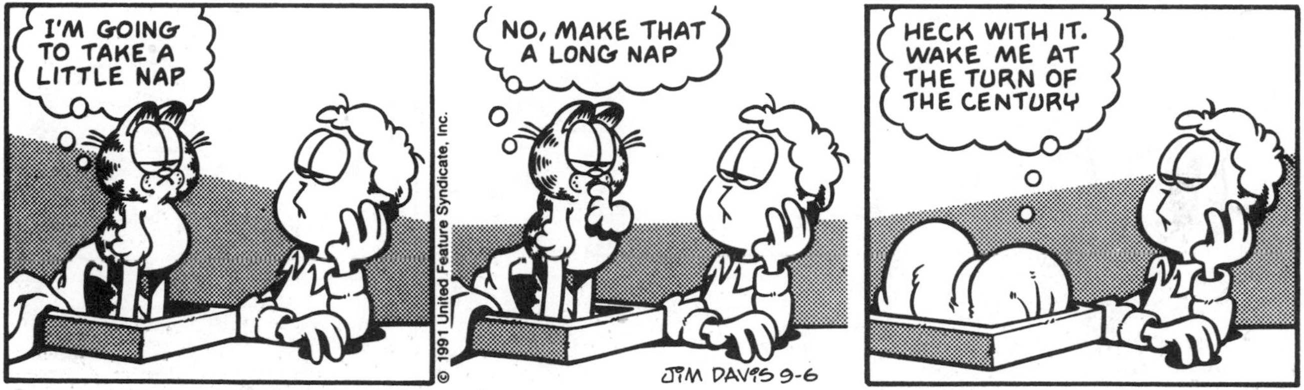
I'M GOING TO TAKE A LITTLE NAP
NO, MAKE THAT A LONG NAP
HECK WITH IT. WAKE ME AT THE TURN OF THE CENTURY
© 1991 United Feature Syndicate, Inc.
JIM DAVIS 9-6

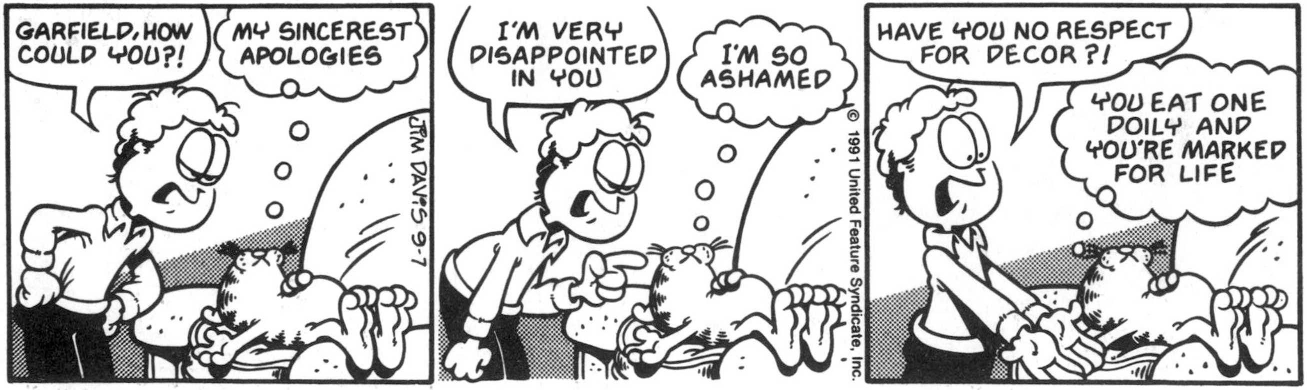
GARFIELD, HOW COULD YOU?!
MY SINCEREST APOLOGIES
JIM DAVIS 9-7
I'M VERY DISAPPOINTED IN YOU
I'M SO ASHAMED
© 1991 United Feature Syndicate, Inc.
HAVE YOU NO RESPECT FOR DECOR?!
YOU EAT ONE DOILY AND YOU'RE MARKED FOR LIFE

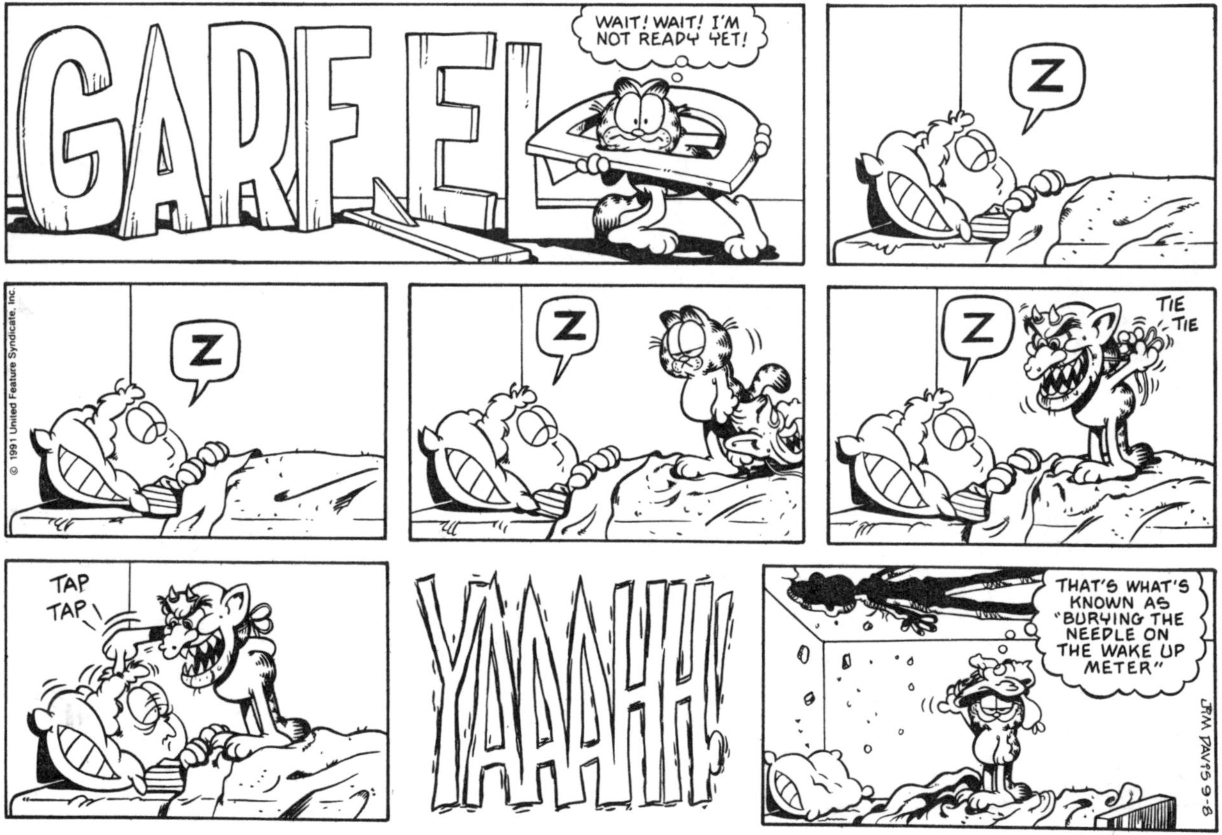

GARFIELD
WAIT! WAIT! I'M NOT READY YET!
Z
© 1991 United Feature Syndicate, Inc.
Z
Z
Z
TIE TIE
TAP TAP
YAAAHH!
THAT'S WHAT'S KNOWN AS "BURYING THE NEEDLE ON THE WAKE UP METER"
JPM DAVPS 9-8

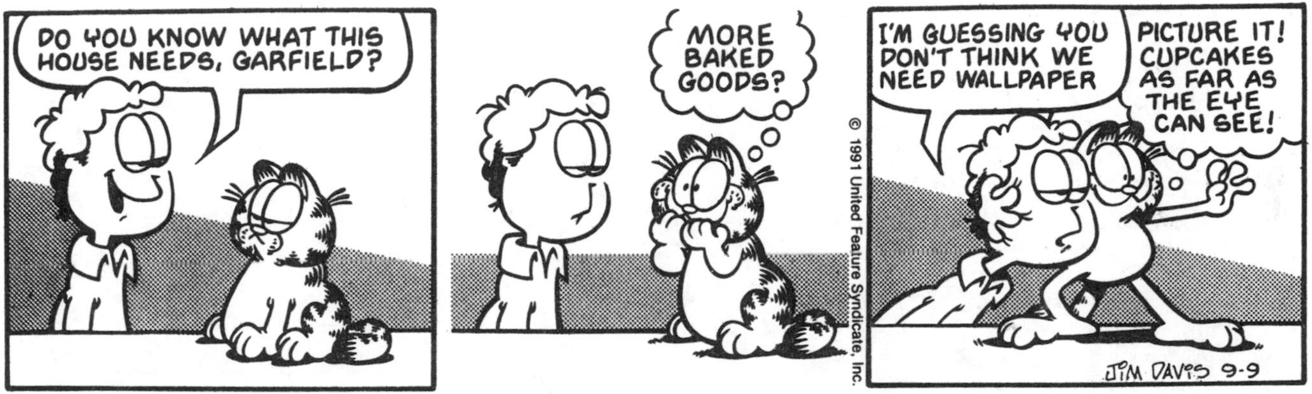
DO YOU KNOW WHAT THIS HOUSE NEEDS, GARFIELD?
MORE BAKED GOODS?
© 1991 United Feature Syndicate, Inc.
I'M GUESSING YOU DON'T THINK WE NEED WALLPAPER
PICTURE IT! CUPCAKES AS FAR AS THE EYE CAN SEE!
JIM DAVIS 9-9

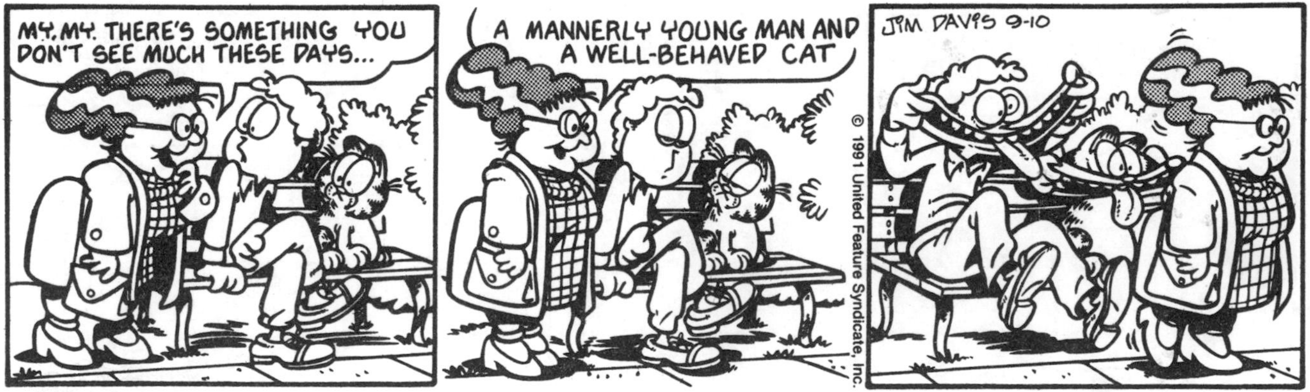
MY, MY. THERE'S SOMETHING YOU DON'T SEE MUCH THESE DAYS...
A MANNERLY YOUNG MAN AND A WELL-BEHAVED CAT
© 1991 United Feature Syndicate, Inc.
JIM DAVIS 9-10

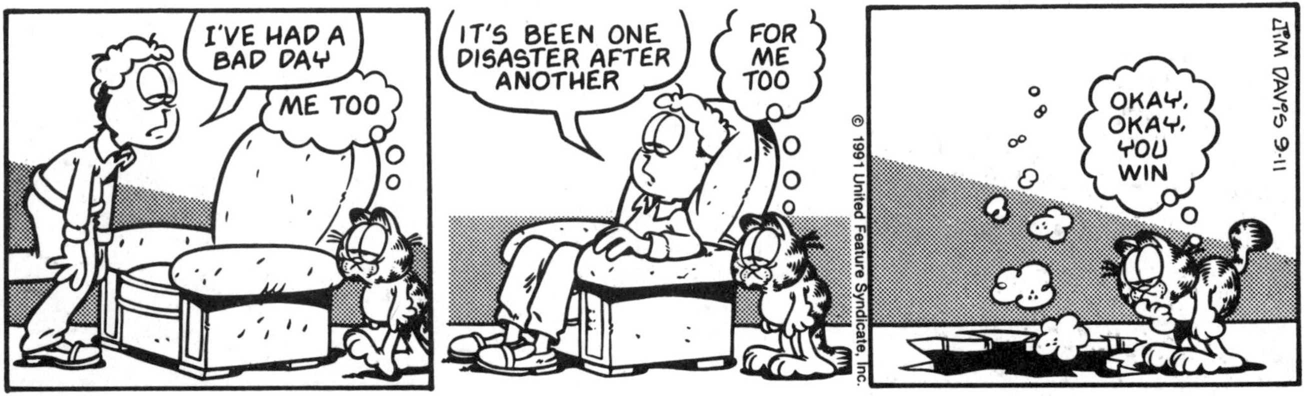
I'VE HAD A BAD DAY
ME TOO
IT'S BEEN ONE DISASTER AFTER ANOTHER
FOR ME TOO
© 1991 United Feature Syndicate, Inc.
OKAY, OKAY, YOU WIN
JIM DAVIS 9-11

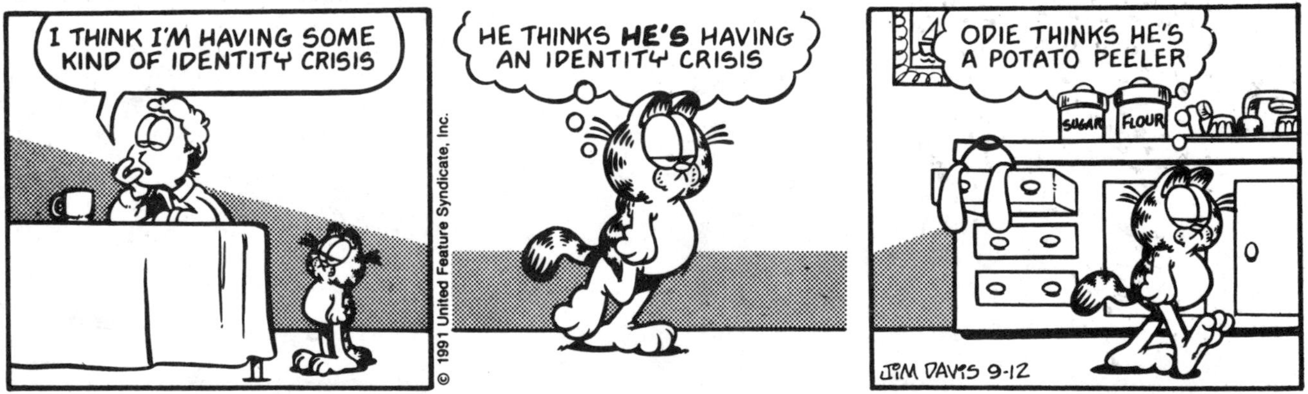
I THINK I'M HAVING SOME KIND OF IDENTITY CRISIS
© 1991 United Feature Syndicate, Inc.
HE THINKS **HE'S** HAVING AN IDENTITY CRISIS
ODIE THINKS HE'S A POTATO PEELER
SUGAR
FLOUR
JIM DAVIS 9-12

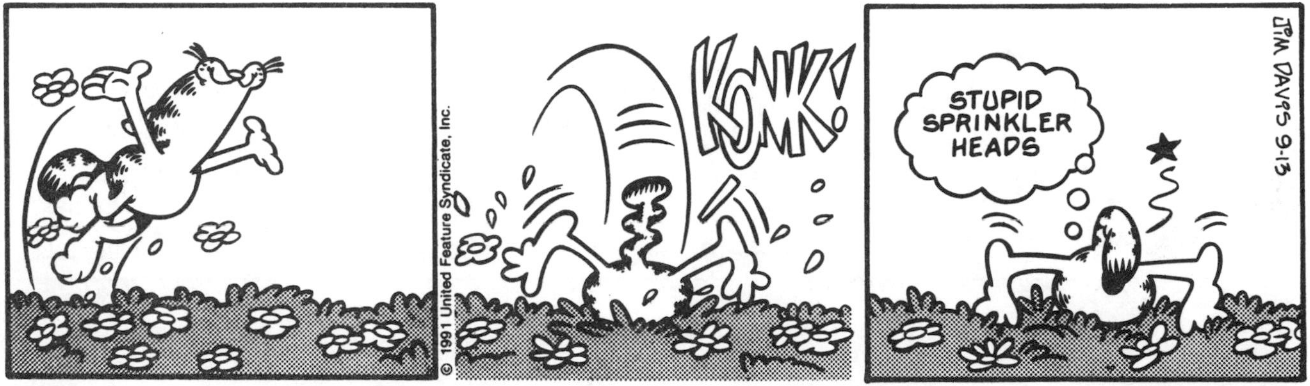
© 1991 United Feature Syndicate, Inc.
KONK!
STUPID SPRINKLER HEADS
JIM DAVIS 9-13

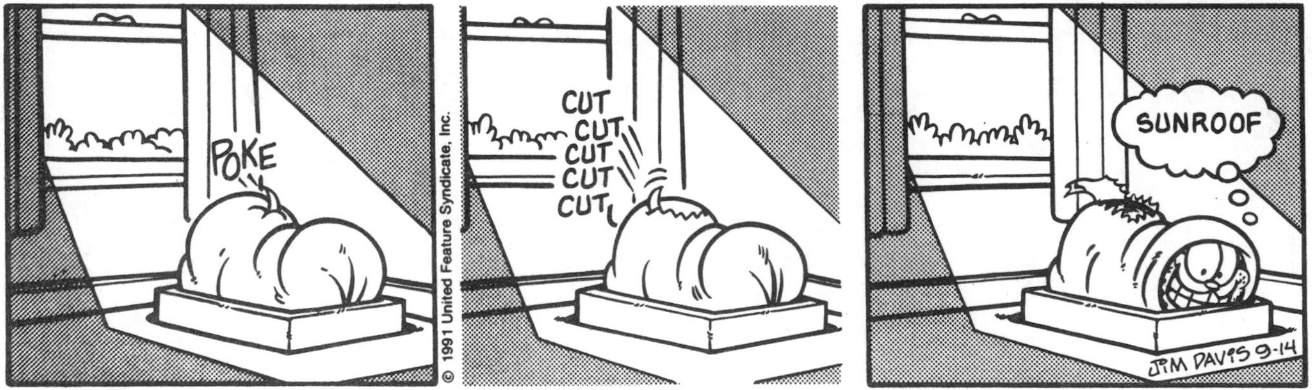
© 1991 United Feature Syndicate, Inc.
POKE
CUT CUT CUT CUT CUT
SUNROOF
JIM DAVIS 9-14

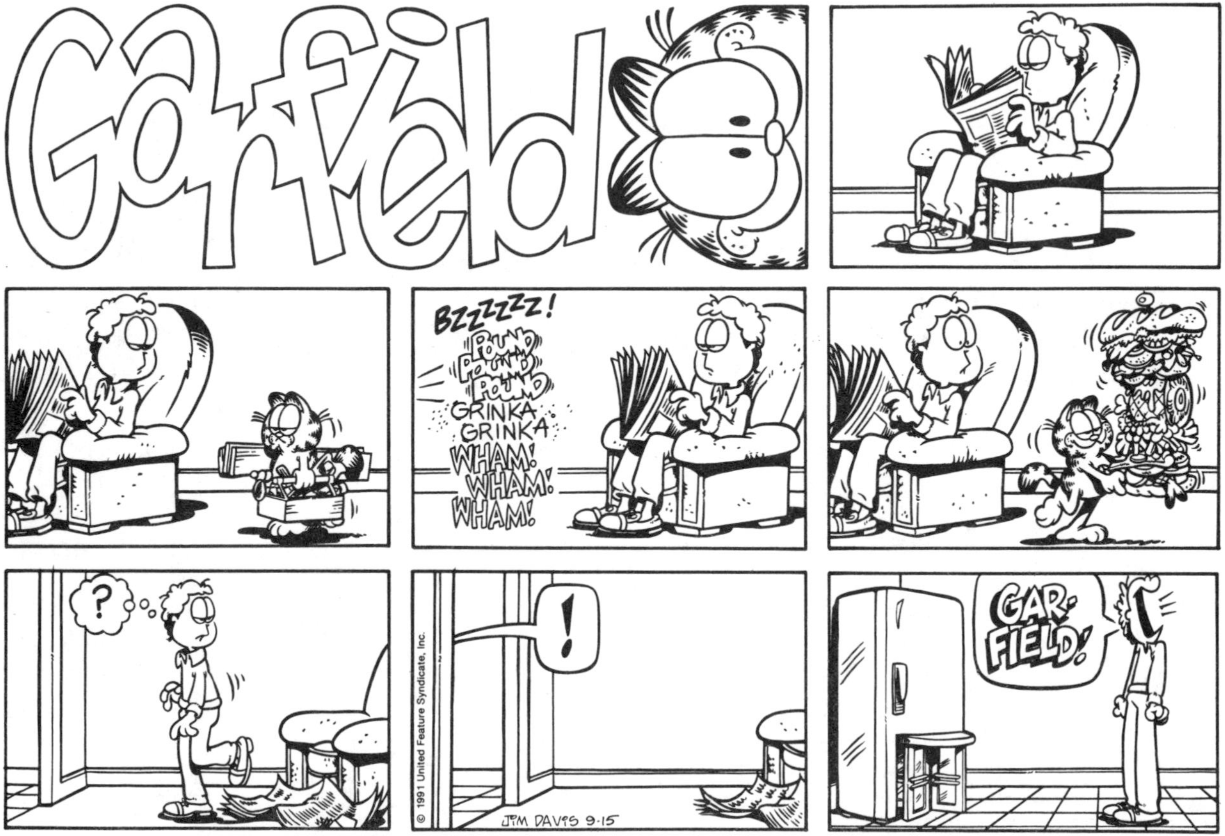
Garfield
BZZZZZZ!
POUND POUND POUND
GRINKA GRINKA
WHAM! WHAM! WHAM!
?
!
GAR-FIELD!
© 1991 United Feature Syndicate, Inc.
JIM DAVIS 9-15

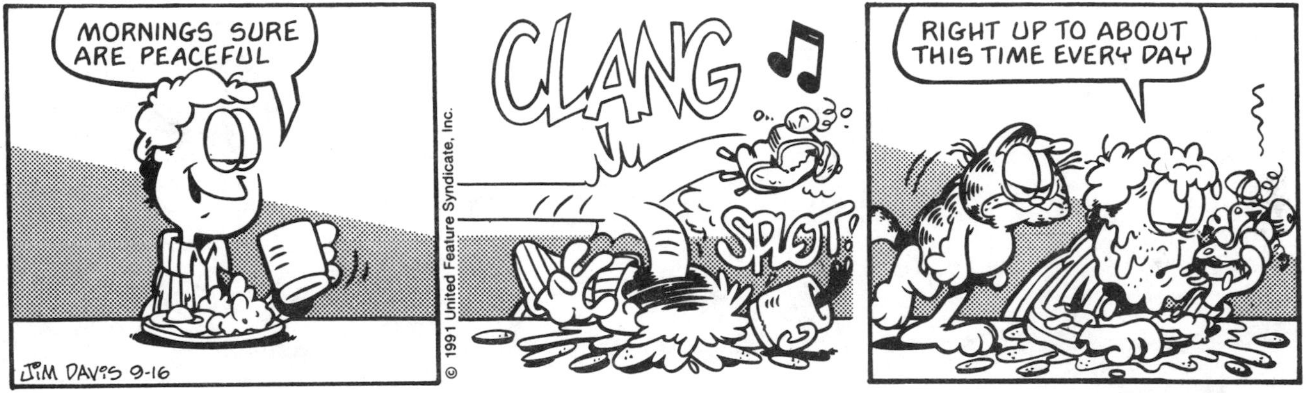
MORNINGS SURE ARE PEACEFUL
JIM DAVIS 9-16
© 1991 United Feature Syndicate, Inc.
CLANG
SPLOT!
RIGHT UP TO ABOUT THIS TIME EVERY DAY

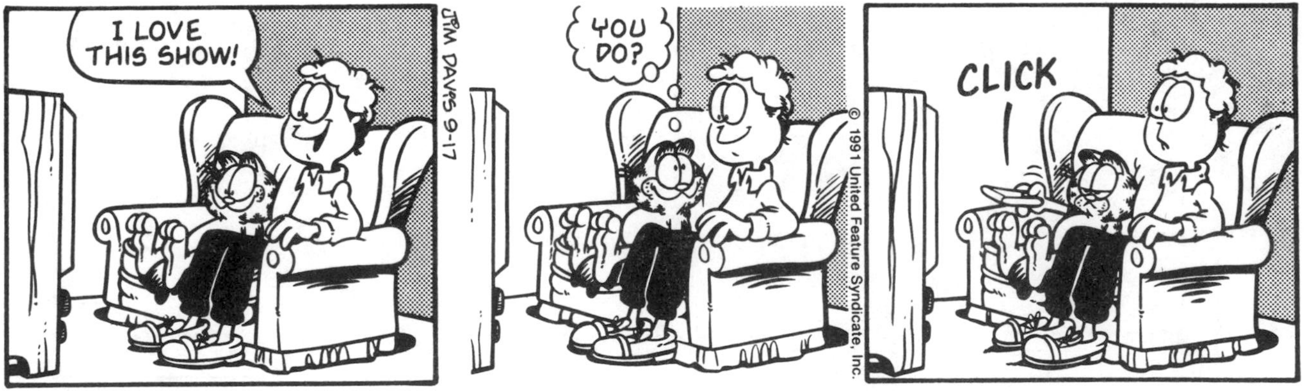
I LOVE THIS SHOW!
JIM DAVIS 9-17
YOU DO?
© 1991 United Feature Syndicate, Inc.
CLICK

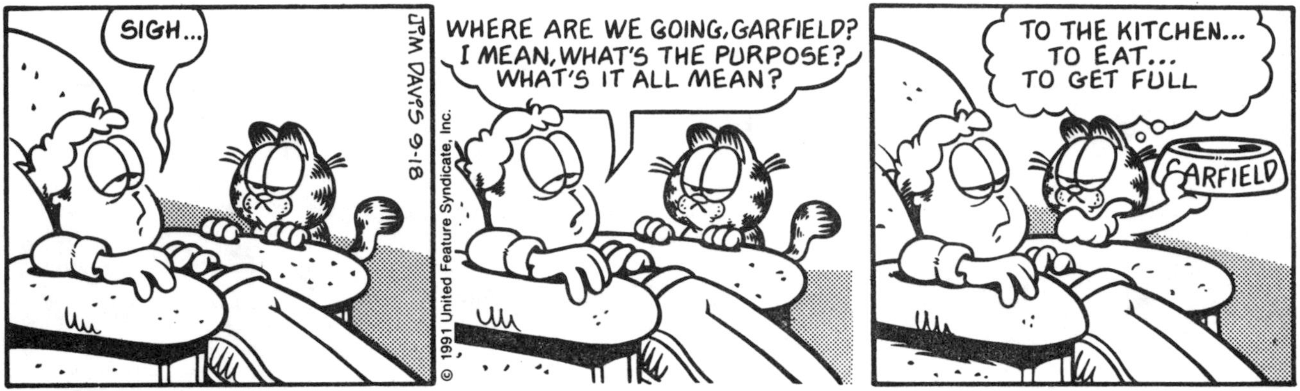
SIGH...
JIM DAVIS 9-18
© 1991 United Feature Syndicate, Inc.
WHERE ARE WE GOING, GARFIELD? I MEAN, WHAT'S THE PURPOSE? WHAT'S IT ALL MEAN?
TO THE KITCHEN... TO EAT... TO GET FULL
GARFIELD

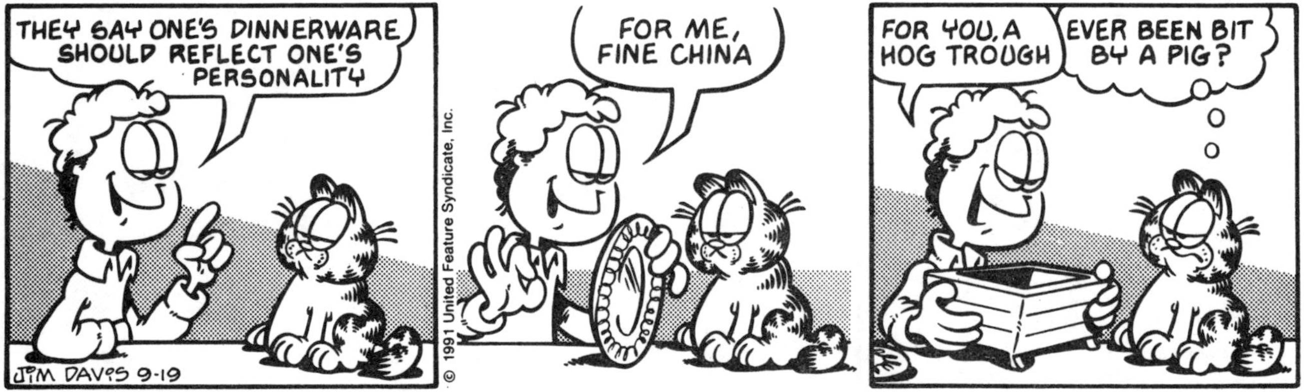
THEY SAY ONE'S DINNERWARE SHOULD REFLECT ONE'S PERSONALITY
JIM DAVIS 9-19
© 1991 United Feature Syndicate, Inc.
FOR ME, FINE CHINA
FOR YOU, A HOG TROUGH
EVER BEEN BIT BY A PIG?

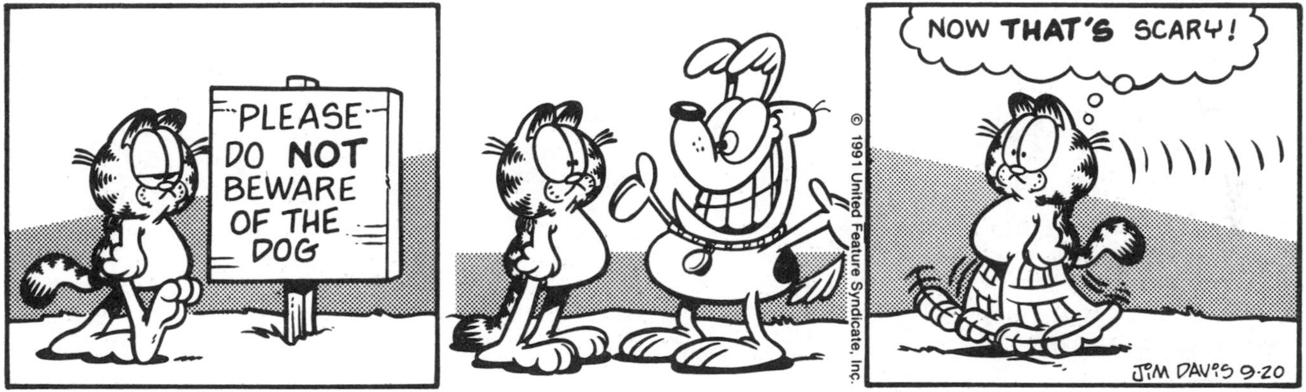
PLEASE DO NOT BEWARE OF THE DOG
© 1991 United Feature Syndicate, Inc.
NOW THAT'S SCARY!
JIM DAVIS 9-20

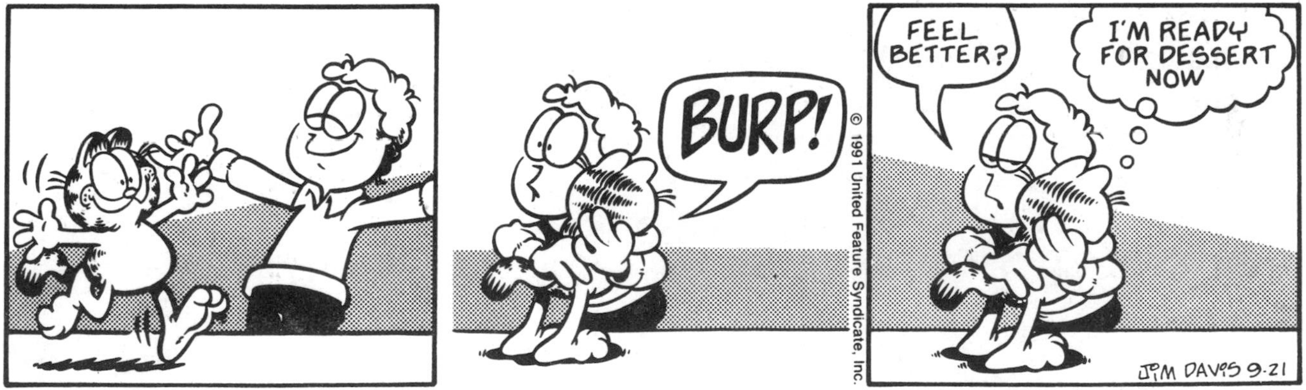
BURP!
© 1991 United Feature Syndicate, Inc.
FEEL BETTER?
I'M READY FOR DESSERT NOW
JIM DAVIS 9-21

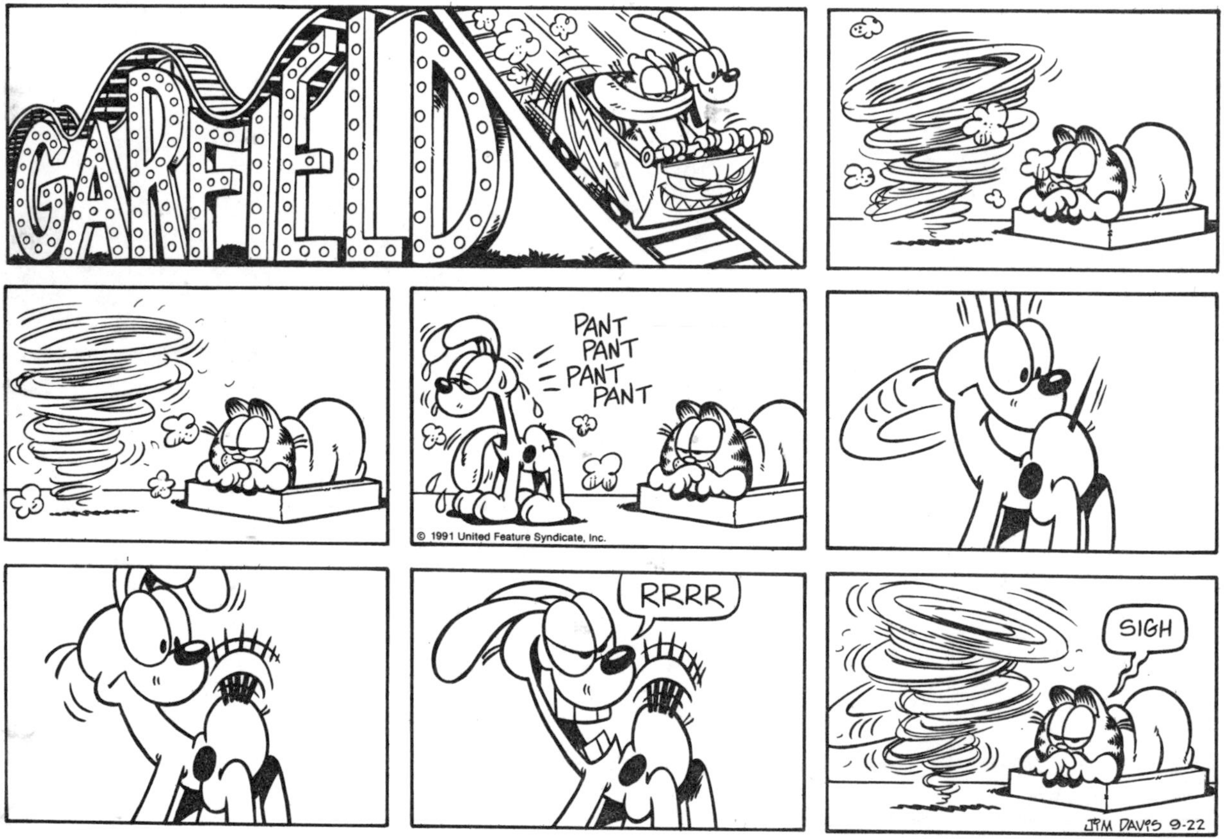
GARFIELD
PANT PANT PANT PANT
© 1991 United Feature Syndicate, Inc.
RRRR
SIGH
JIM DAVIS 9-22

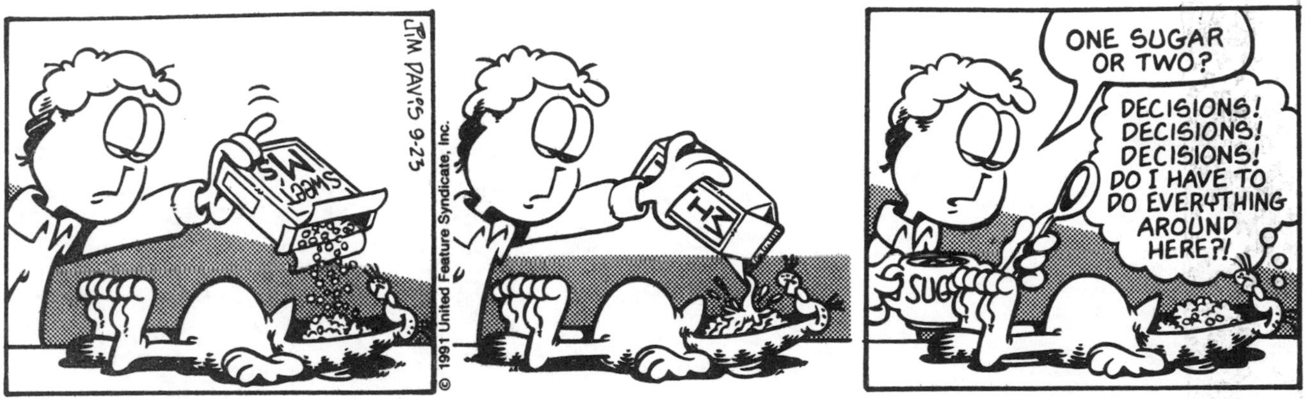
JIM DAVIS 9-23
© 1991 United Feature Syndicate, Inc.
SUG
ONE SUGAR OR TWO?
DECISIONS! DECISIONS! DECISIONS! DO I HAVE TO DO EVERYTHING AROUND HERE?!

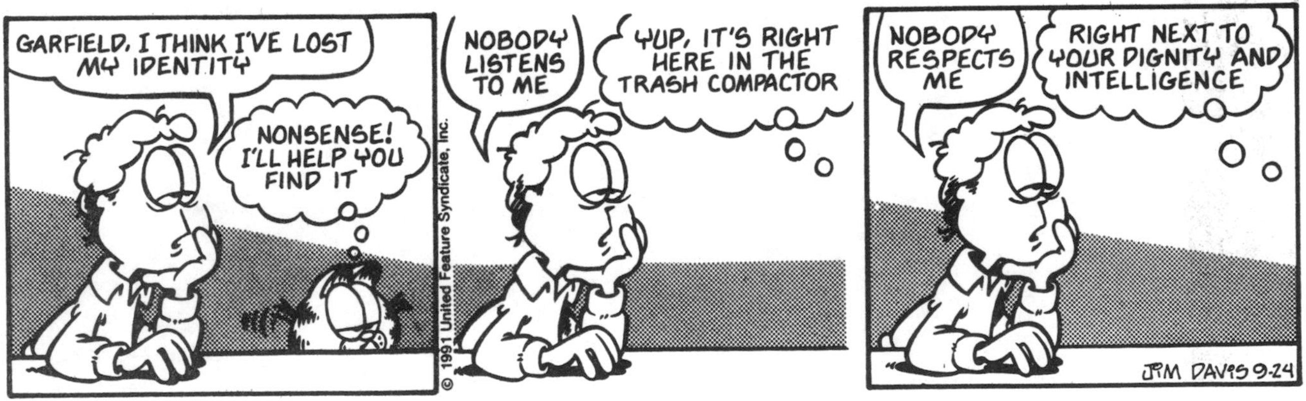
GARFIELD, I THINK I'VE LOST MY IDENTITY
NONSENSE! I'LL HELP YOU FIND IT
© 1991 United Feature Syndicate, Inc.
NOBODY LISTENS TO ME
YUP, IT'S RIGHT HERE IN THE TRASH COMPACTOR
NOBODY RESPECTS ME
RIGHT NEXT TO YOUR DIGNITY AND INTELLIGENCE
JIM DAVIS 9-24

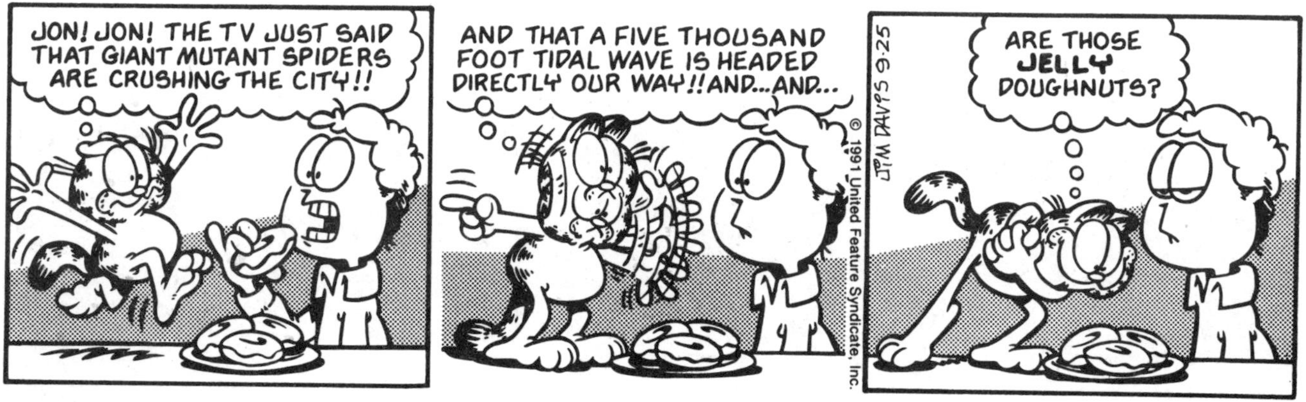
JON! JON! THE TV JUST SAID THAT GIANT MUTANT SPIDERS ARE CRUSHING THE CITY!!
AND THAT A FIVE THOUSAND FOOT TIDAL WAVE IS HEADED DIRECTLY OUR WAY!! AND... AND...
ARE THOSE **JELLY** DOUGHNUTS?
JIM DAVIS 9-25
© 1991 United Feature Syndicate, Inc.

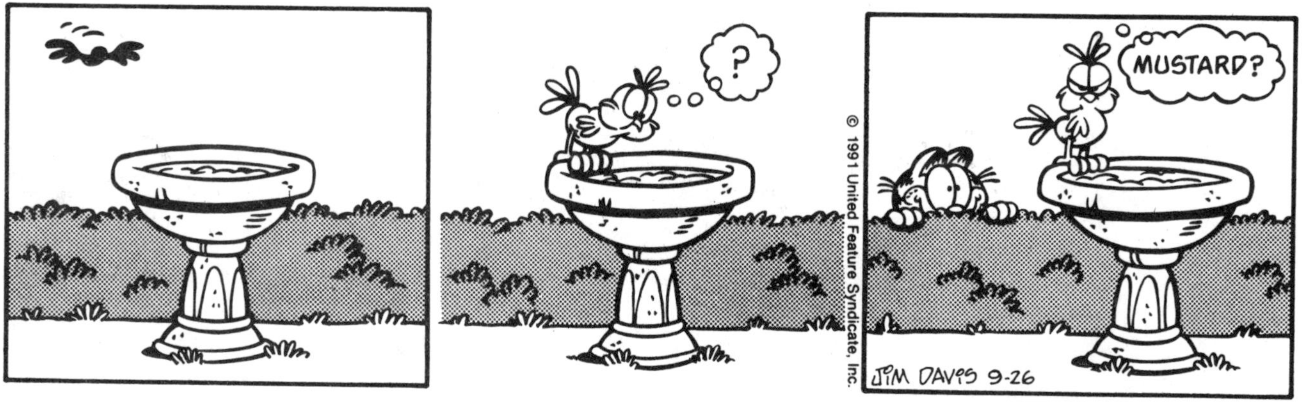
?
MUSTARD?
JIM DAVIS 9-26
© 1991 United Feature Syndicate, Inc.

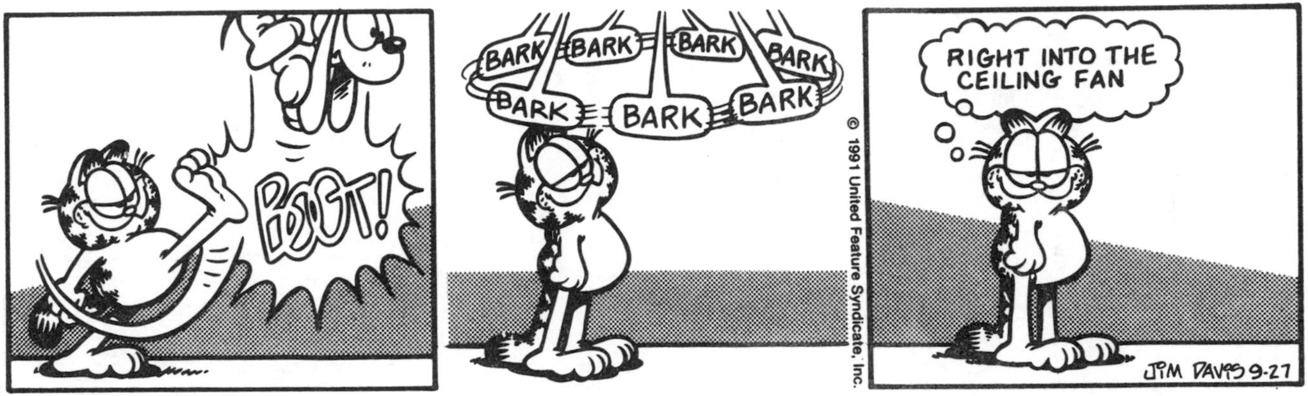
BOOT!
BARK BARK BARK BARK
BARK BARK BARK
© 1991 United Feature Syndicate, Inc.
RIGHT INTO THE CEILING FAN
JIM DAVIS 9-27

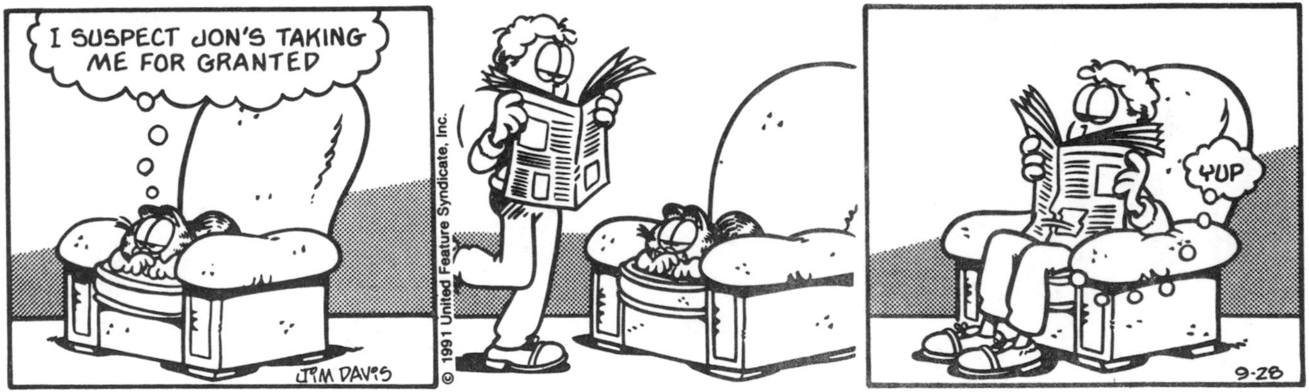
I SUSPECT JON'S TAKING ME FOR GRANTED
JIM DAVIS
© 1991 United Feature Syndicate, Inc.
YUP
9-28

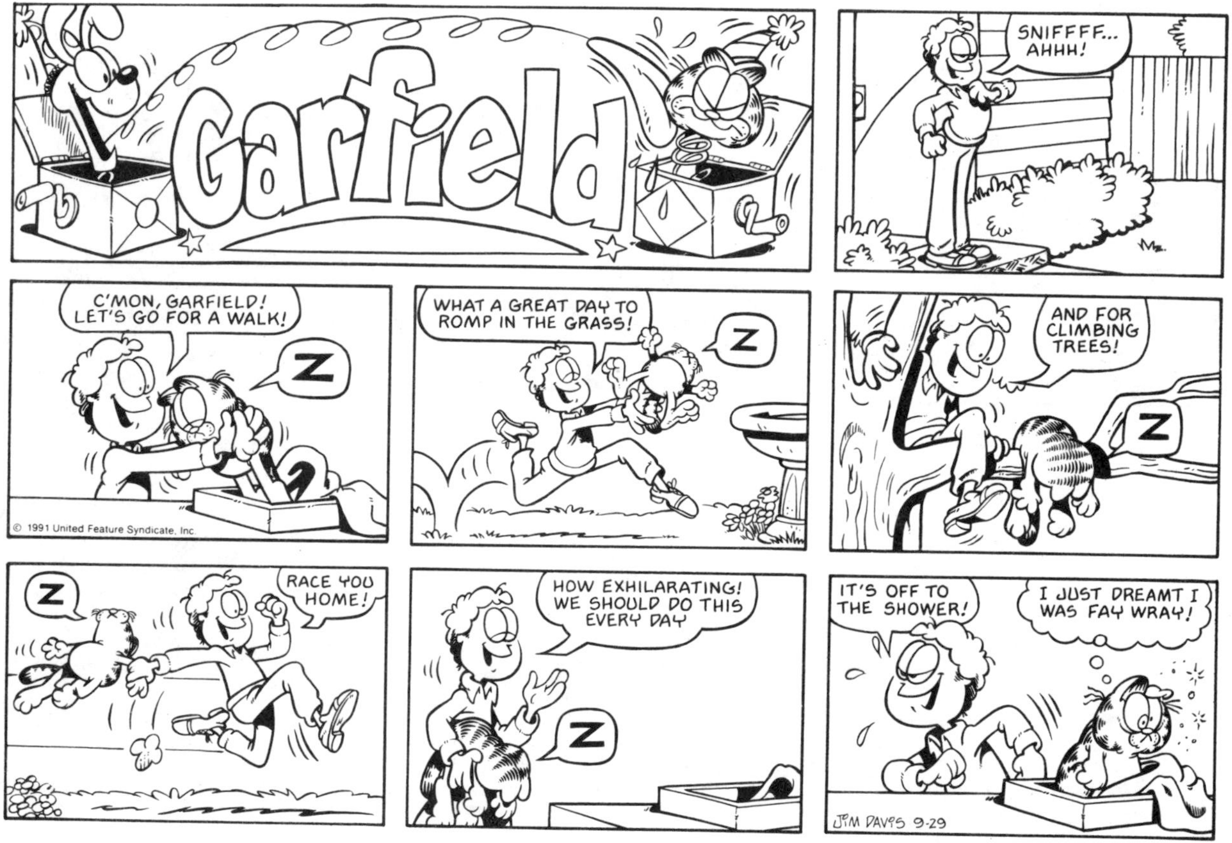
Garfield
SNIFFFF... AHHH!
C'MON, GARFIELD! LET'S GO FOR A WALK!
Z
© 1991 United Feature Syndicate, Inc.
WHAT A GREAT DAY TO ROMP IN THE GRASS!
Z
AND FOR CLIMBING TREES!
Z
Z
RACE YOU HOME!
HOW EXHILARATING! WE SHOULD DO THIS EVERY DAY
Z
IT'S OFF TO THE SHOWER!
I JUST DREAMT I WAS FAY WRAY!
JIM DAVIS 9-29

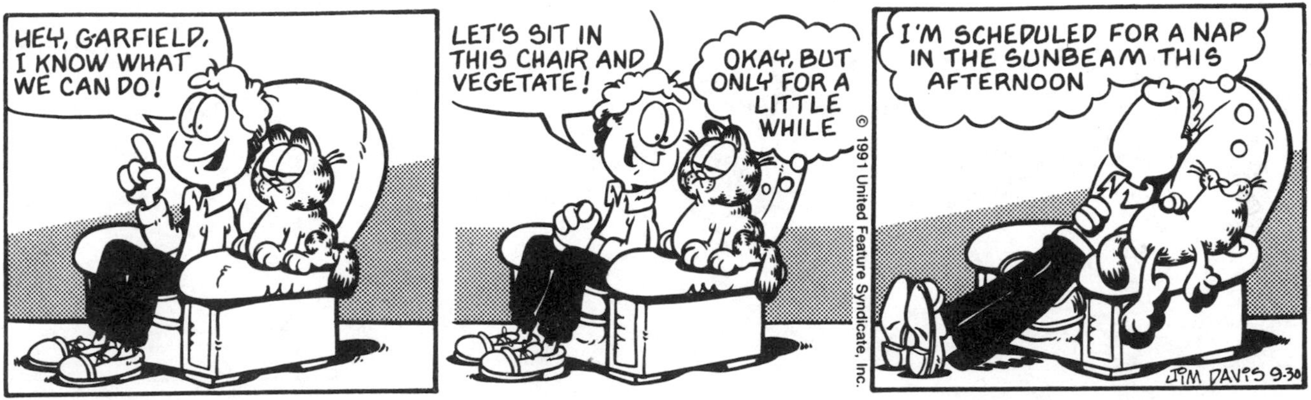
HEY, GARFIELD, I KNOW WHAT WE CAN DO!
LET'S SIT IN THIS CHAIR AND VEGETATE!
OKAY, BUT ONLY FOR A LITTLE WHILE
I'M SCHEDULED FOR A NAP IN THE SUNBEAM THIS AFTERNOON
© 1991 United Feature Syndicate, Inc.
JIM DAVIS 9-30

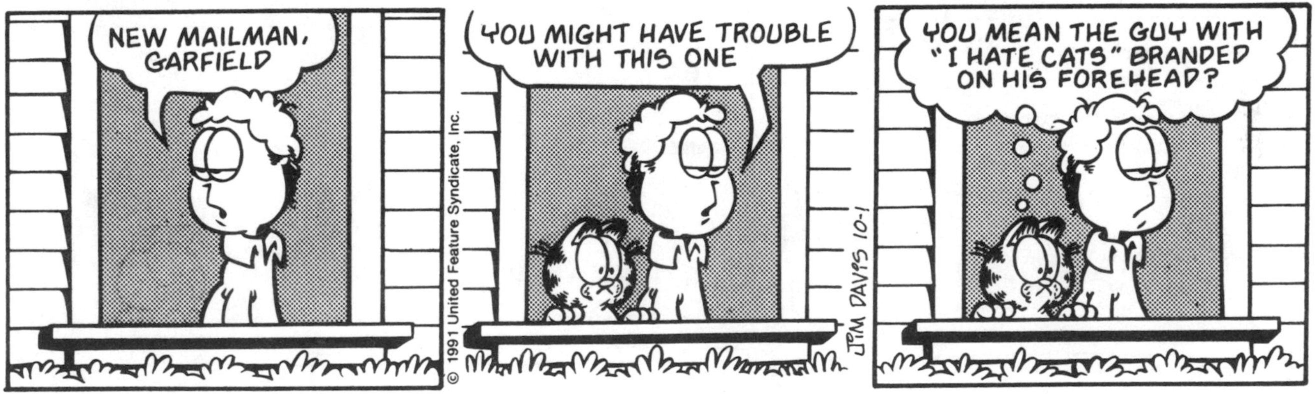
NEW MAILMAN, GARFIELD
YOU MIGHT HAVE TROUBLE WITH THIS ONE
YOU MEAN THE GUY WITH "I HATE CATS" BRANDED ON HIS FOREHEAD?
© 1991 United Feature Syndicate, Inc.
JIM DAVIS 10-1

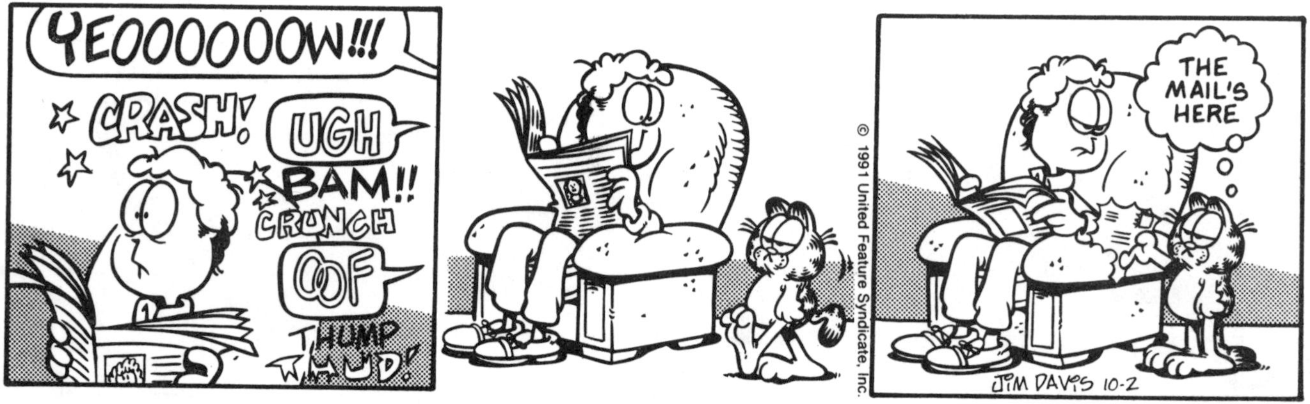
YEOOOOOOW!!!
CRASH!
UGH
BAM!!
CRUNCH
OOF
THUMP
THUD!
© 1991 United Feature Syndicate, Inc.
THE MAIL'S HERE
JIM DAVIS 10-2

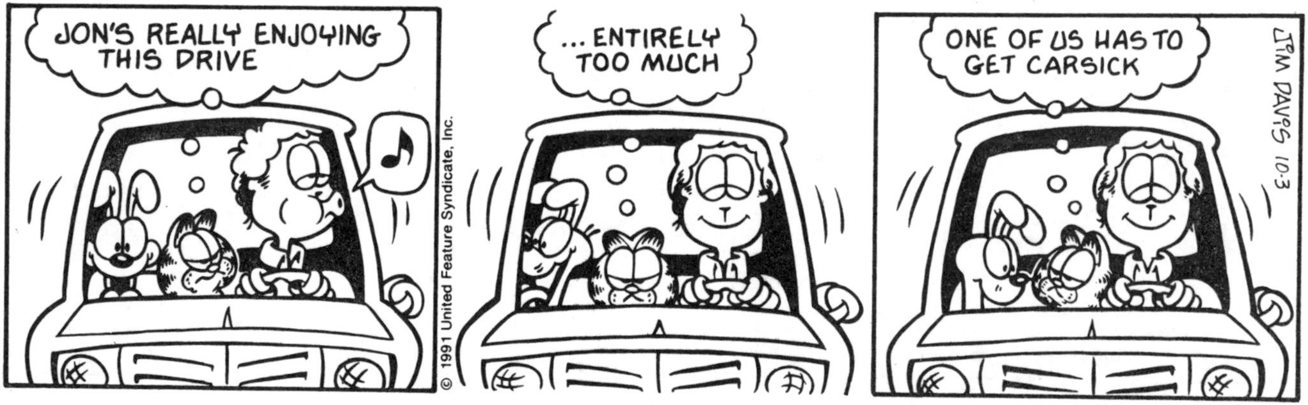
JON'S REALLY ENJOYING THIS DRIVE
♪
© 1991 United Feature Syndicate, Inc.
... ENTIRELY TOO MUCH
ONE OF US HAS TO GET CARSICK
JIM DAVIS 10-3

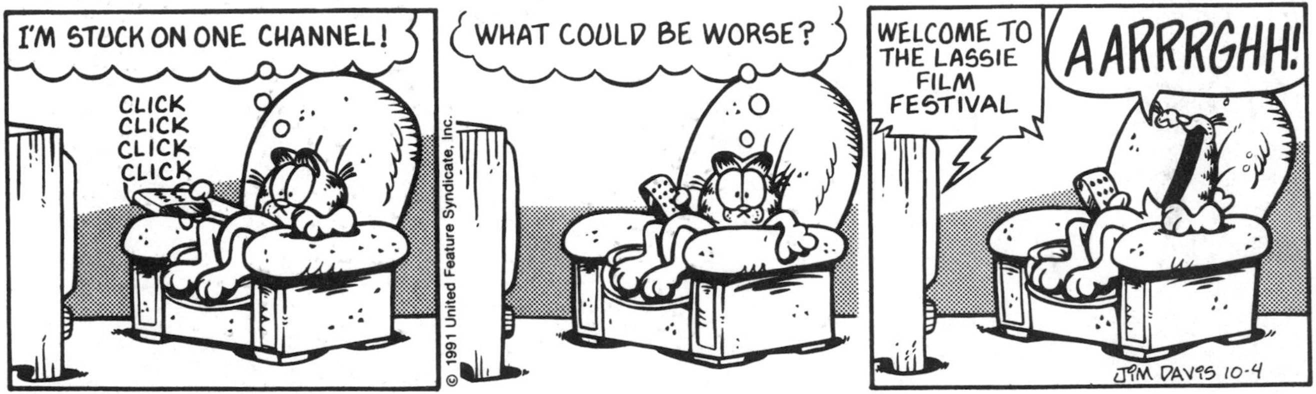
I'M STUCK ON ONE CHANNEL!
CLICK CLICK CLICK CLICK
© 1991 United Feature Syndicate, Inc.
WHAT COULD BE WORSE?
WELCOME TO THE LASSIE FILM FESTIVAL
AARRRGHH!
JIM DAVIS 10-4

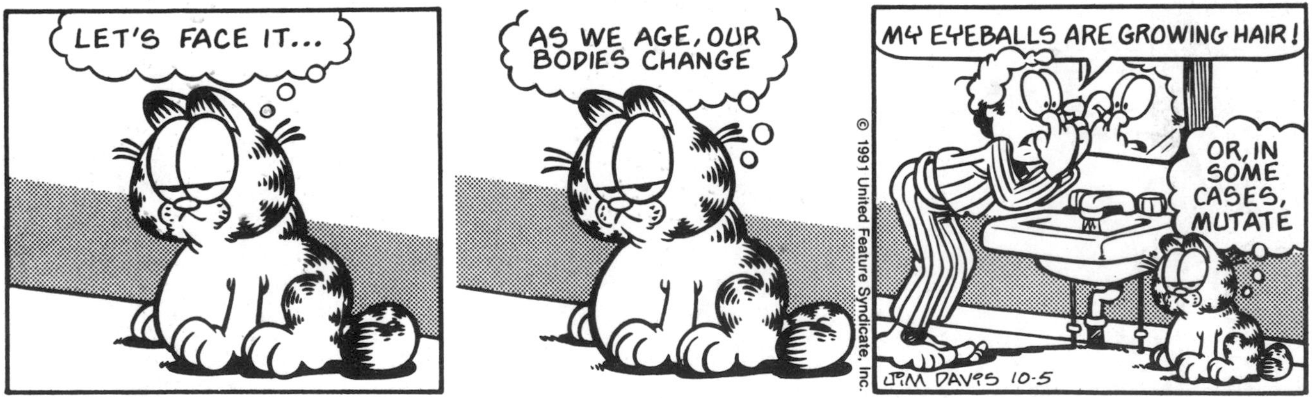
LET'S FACE IT...
AS WE AGE, OUR BODIES CHANGE
© 1991 United Feature Syndicate, Inc.
MY EYEBALLS ARE GROWING HAIR!
OR, IN SOME CASES, MUTATE
JIM DAVIS 10-5

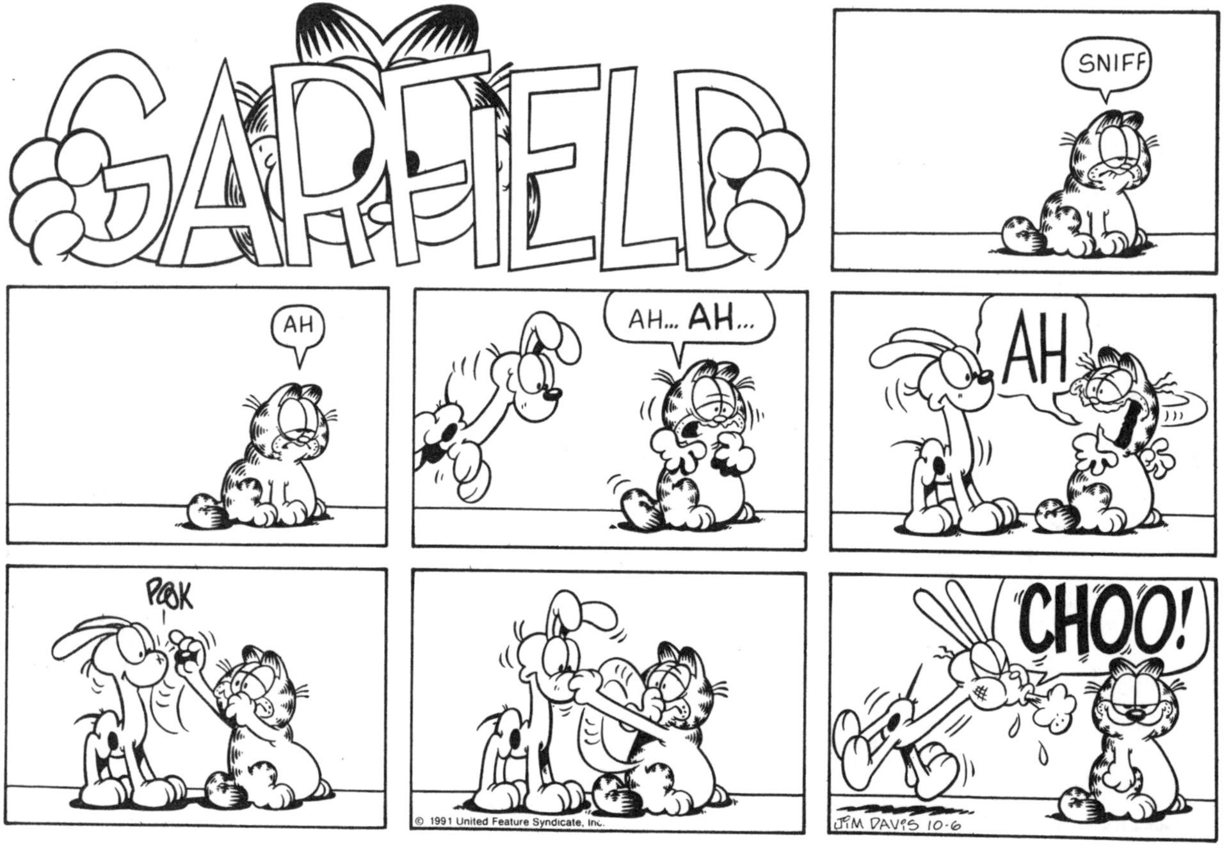
GARFIELD
SNIFF
AH
AH... AH...
AH
POOK
© 1991 United Feature Syndicate, Inc.
CHOO!
JIM DAVIS 10-6

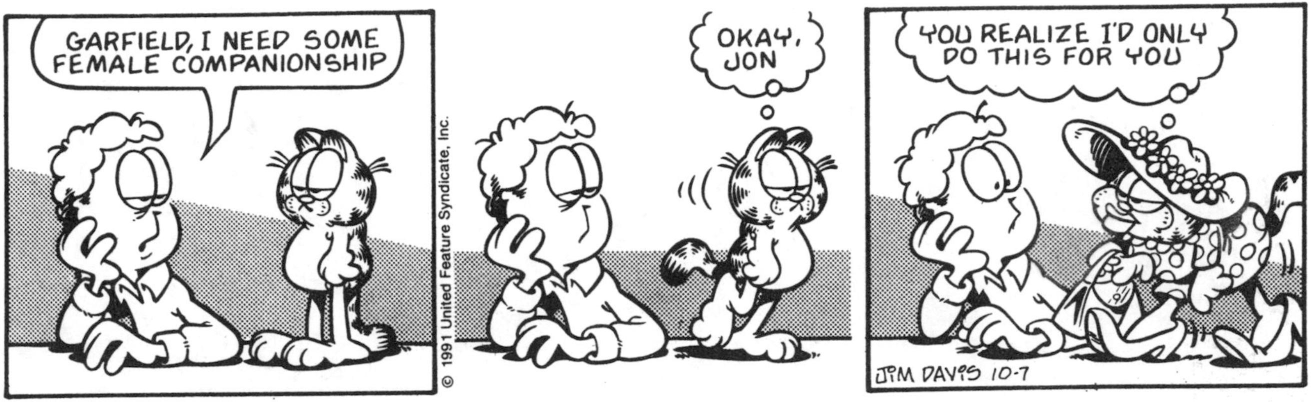

GARFIELD, I NEED SOME FEMALE COMPANIONSHIP
© 1991 United Feature Syndicate, Inc.
OKAY, JON
YOU REALIZE I'D ONLY DO THIS FOR YOU
JIM DAVIS 10-7

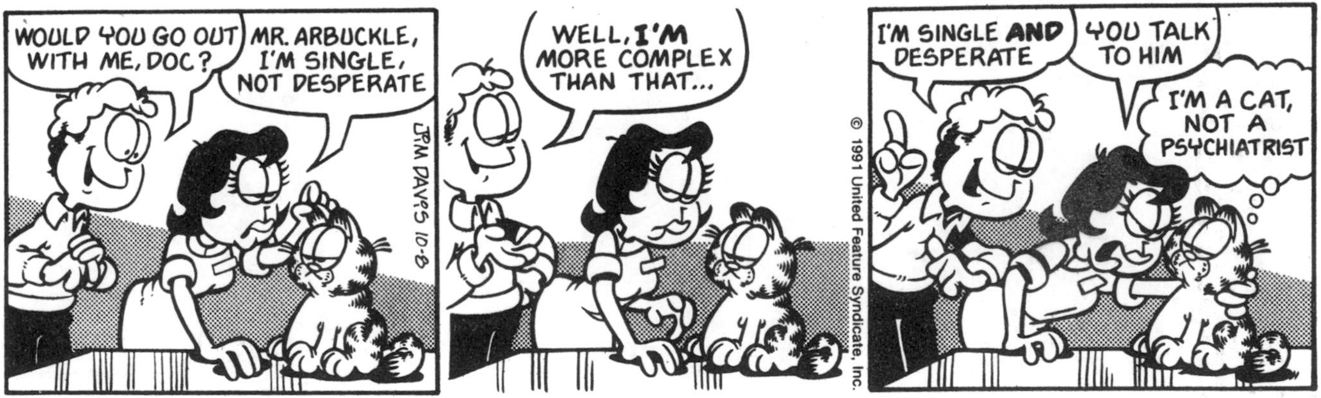

WOULD YOU GO OUT WITH ME, DOC?
MR. ARBUCKLE, I'M SINGLE, NOT DESPERATE
JIM DAVIS 10-8
WELL, **I'M** MORE COMPLEX THAN THAT...
© 1991 United Feature Syndicate, Inc.
I'M SINGLE **AND** DESPERATE
YOU TALK TO HIM
I'M A CAT, NOT A PSYCHIATRIST

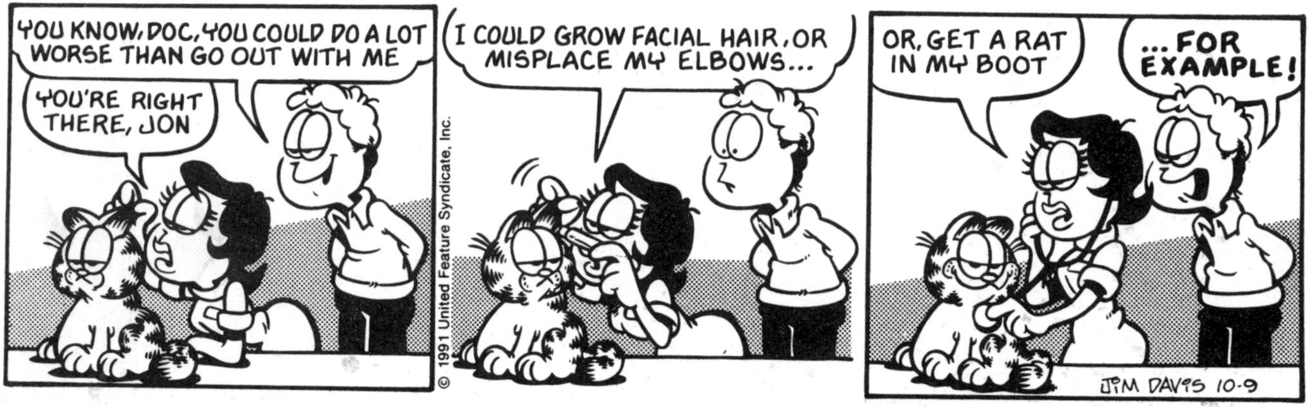
YOU KNOW, DOC, YOU COULD DO A LOT WORSE THAN GO OUT WITH ME
YOU'RE RIGHT THERE, JON
I COULD GROW FACIAL HAIR, OR MISPLACE MY ELBOWS...
OR, GET A RAT IN MY BOOT
...FOR EXAMPLE!
© 1991 United Feature Syndicate, Inc.
JIM DAVIS 10-9

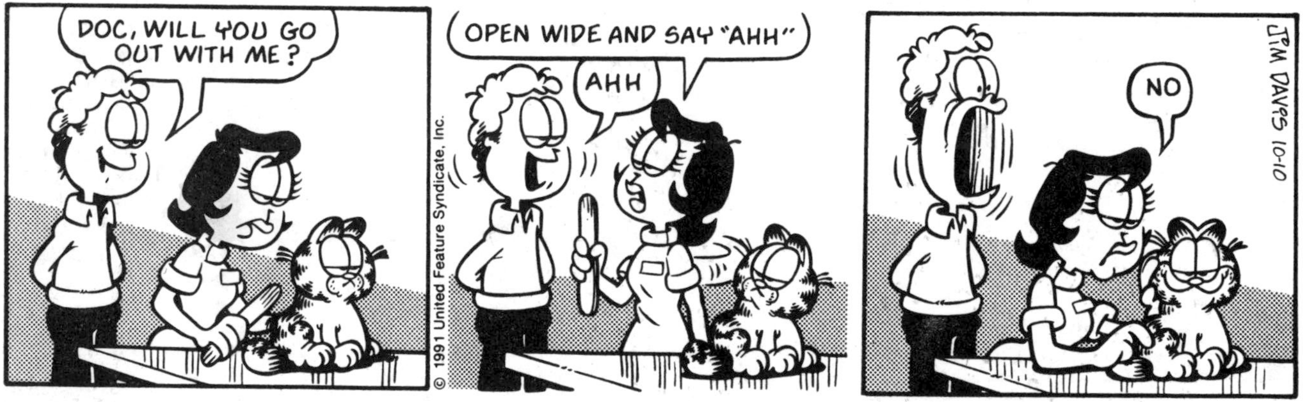
DOC, WILL YOU GO OUT WITH ME?
OPEN WIDE AND SAY "AHH"
AHH
NO
© 1991 United Feature Syndicate, Inc.
JIM DAVIS 10-10

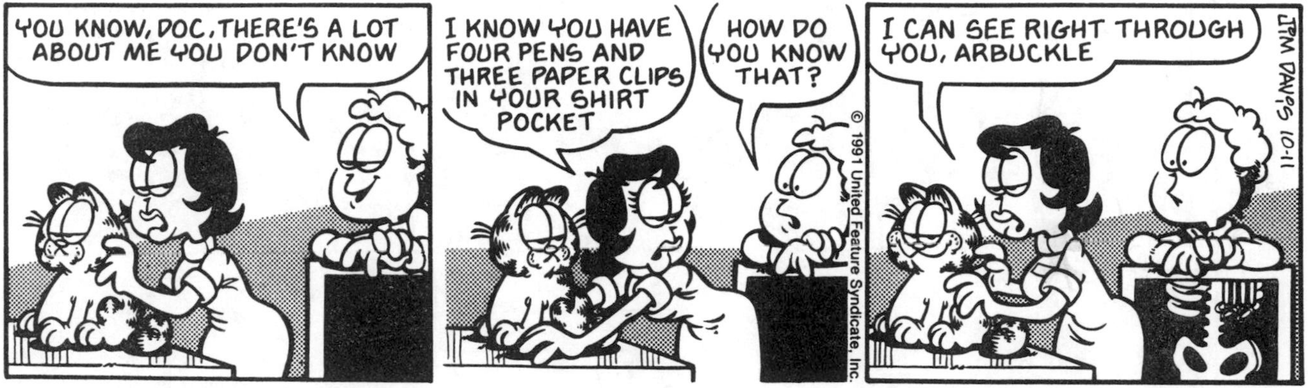
YOU KNOW, DOC, THERE'S A LOT ABOUT ME YOU DON'T KNOW
I KNOW YOU HAVE FOUR PENS AND THREE PAPER CLIPS IN YOUR SHIRT POCKET
HOW DO YOU KNOW THAT?
© 1991 United Feature Syndicate, Inc.
I CAN SEE RIGHT THROUGH YOU, ARBUCKLE
JIM DAVIS 10-11

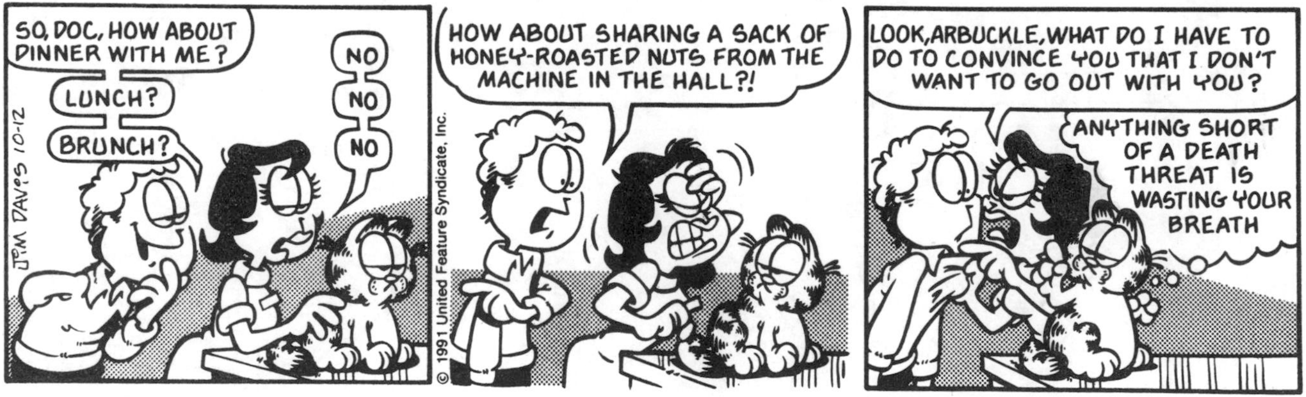
SO, DOC, HOW ABOUT DINNER WITH ME?
LUNCH?
BRUNCH?
NO
NO
NO
JIM DAVIS 10-12
© 1991 United Feature Syndicate, Inc.
HOW ABOUT SHARING A SACK OF HONEY-ROASTED NUTS FROM THE MACHINE IN THE HALL?!
LOOK, ARBUCKLE, WHAT DO I HAVE TO DO TO CONVINCE YOU THAT I DON'T WANT TO GO OUT WITH YOU?
ANYTHING SHORT OF A DEATH THREAT IS WASTING YOUR BREATH

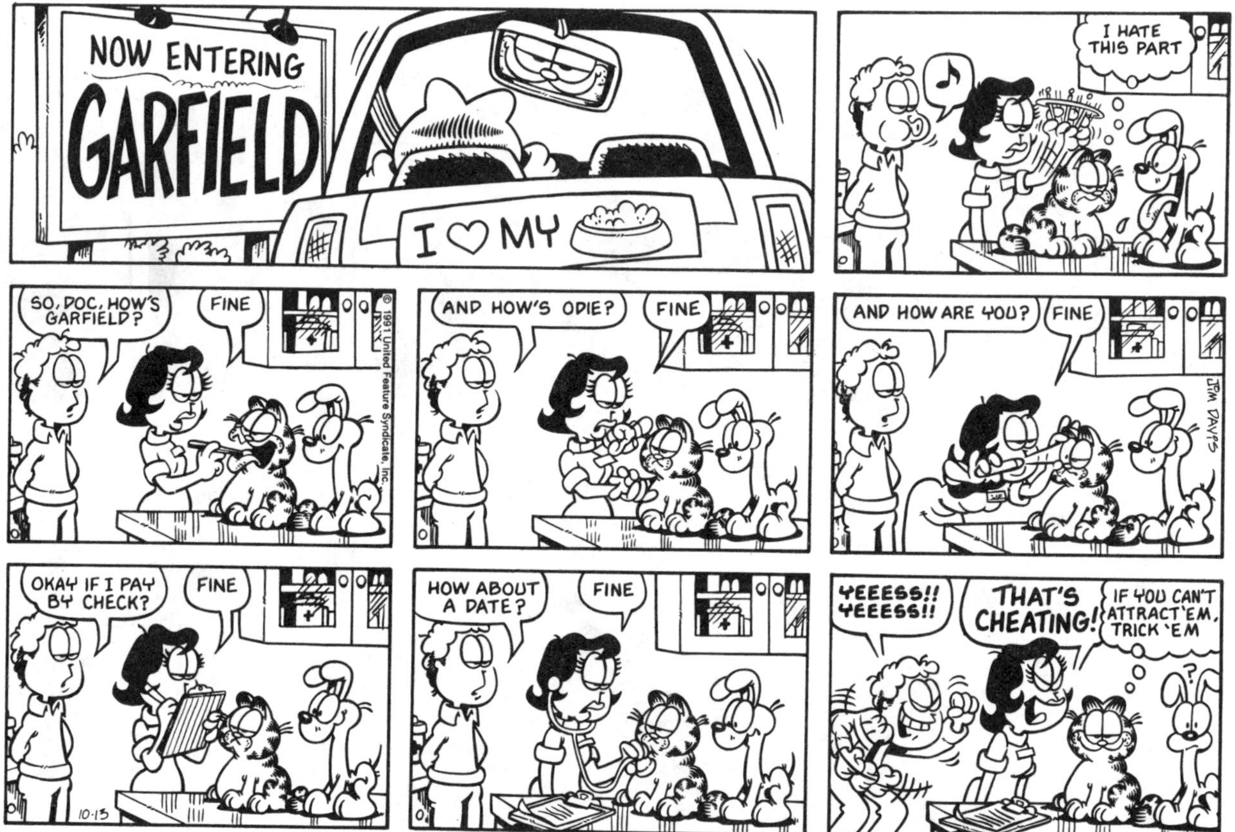

NOW ENTERING
GARFIELD
I ♡ MY
I HATE THIS PART
SO, DOC, HOW'S GARFIELD?
FINE
© 1991 United Feature Syndicate, Inc.
AND HOW'S ODIE?
FINE
AND HOW ARE YOU?
FINE
JIM DAVIS
OKAY IF I PAY BY CHECK?
FINE
10-13
HOW ABOUT A DATE?
FINE
YEEESS!! YEEESS!!
THAT'S CHEATING!
IF YOU CAN'T ATTRACT 'EM, TRICK 'EM

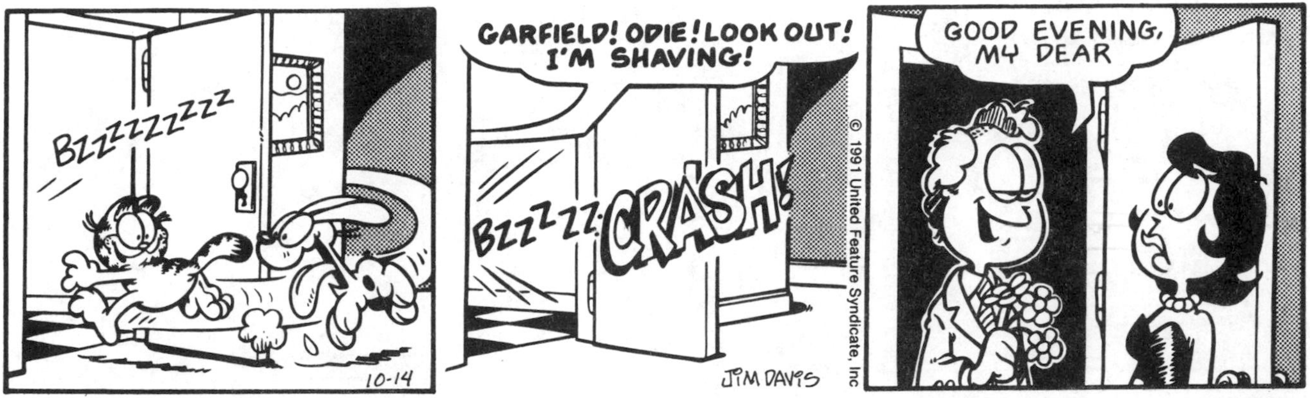
BZZZZZZZZZ
10-14
GARFIELD! ODIE! LOOK OUT! I'M SHAVING!
BZZZZZ CRASH!
JIM DAVIS
© 1991 United Feature Syndicate, Inc
GOOD EVENING, MY DEAR

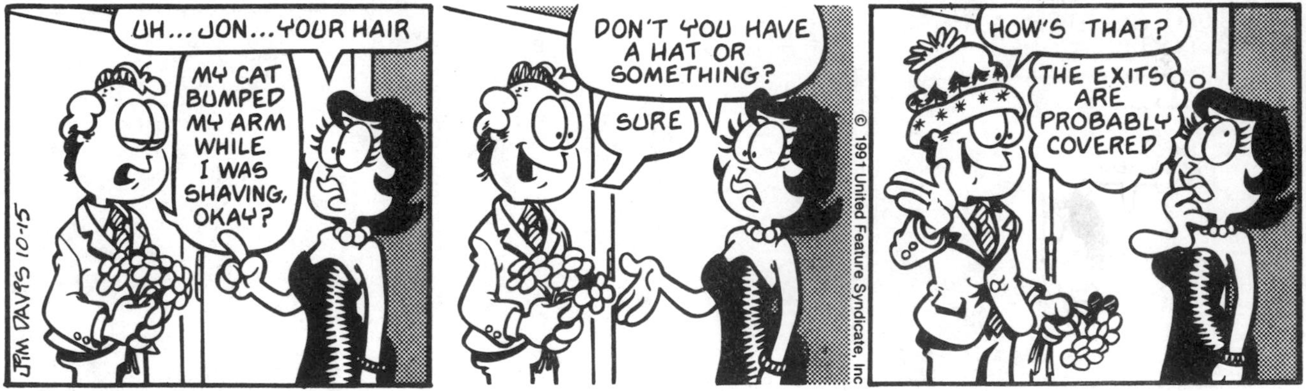
UH... JON... YOUR HAIR
MY CAT BUMPED MY ARM WHILE I WAS SHAVING, OKAY?
JIM DAVIS 10-15
DON'T YOU HAVE A HAT OR SOMETHING?
SURE
© 1991 United Feature Syndicate, Inc
HOW'S THAT?
THE EXITS ARE PROBABLY COVERED

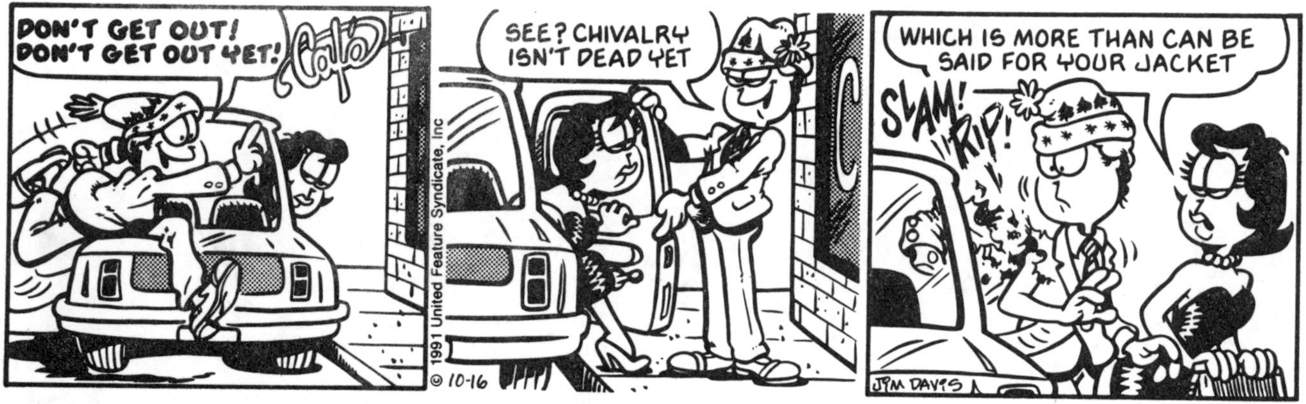
DON'T GET OUT! DON'T GET OUT YET!
© 1991 United Feature Syndicate, Inc
10-16
SEE? CHIVALRY ISN'T DEAD YET
WHICH IS MORE THAN CAN BE SAID FOR YOUR JACKET
SLAM!
RIP!
JIM DAVIS

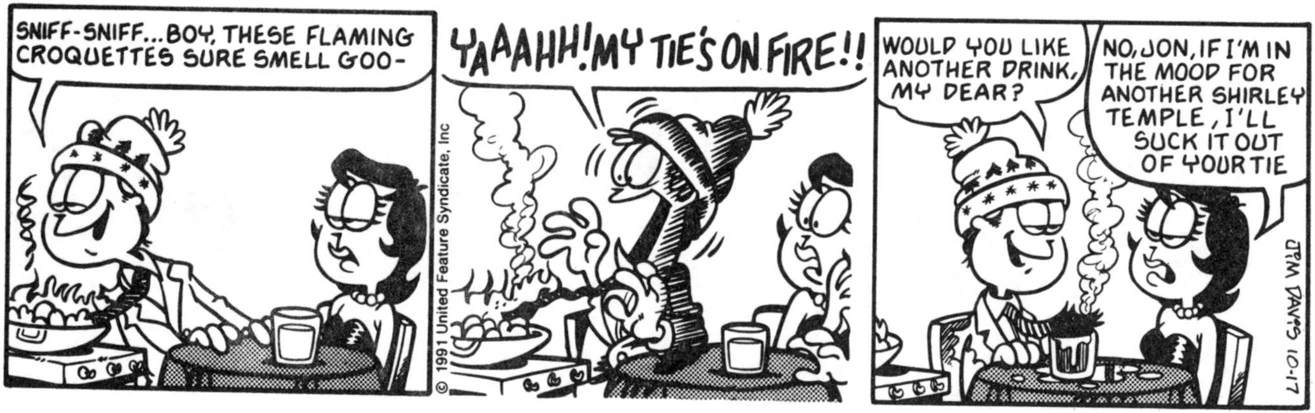
SNIFF-SNIFF...BOY, THESE FLAMING CROQUETTES SURE SMELL GOO-
© 1991 United Feature Syndicate, Inc
YAAAHH! MY TIE'S ON FIRE!!
WOULD YOU LIKE ANOTHER DRINK, MY DEAR?
NO, JON, IF I'M IN THE MOOD FOR ANOTHER SHIRLEY TEMPLE, I'LL SUCK IT OUT OF YOUR TIE
JIM DAVIS 10-17

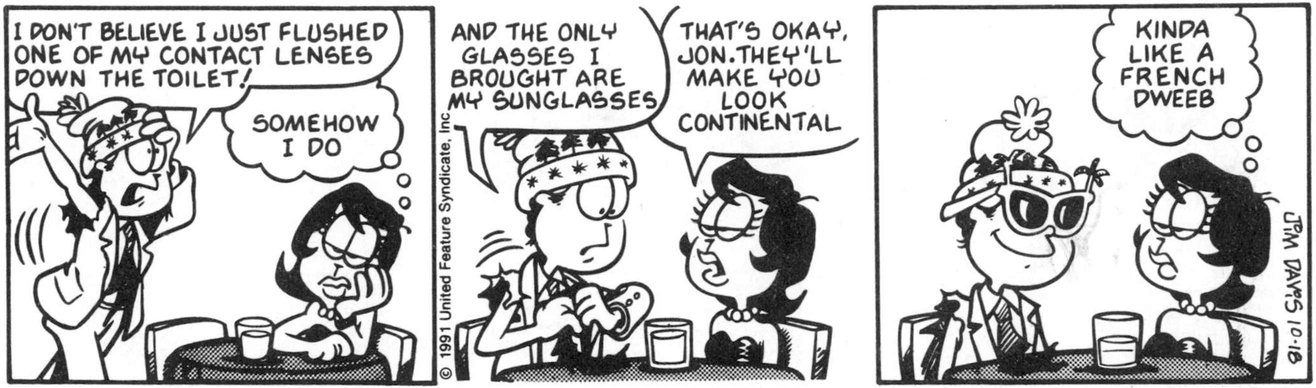
I DON'T BELIEVE I JUST FLUSHED ONE OF MY CONTACT LENSES DOWN THE TOILET!
SOMEHOW I DO
© 1991 United Feature Syndicate, Inc
AND THE ONLY GLASSES I BROUGHT ARE MY SUNGLASSES
THAT'S OKAY, JON. THEY'LL MAKE YOU LOOK CONTINENTAL
KINDA LIKE A FRENCH DWEEB
JIM DAVIS 10-18

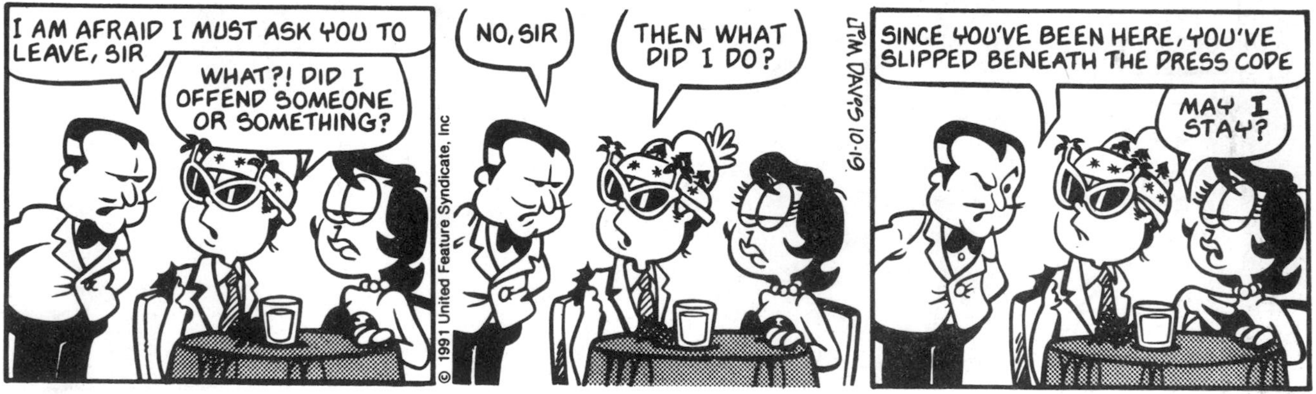
I AM AFRAID I MUST ASK YOU TO LEAVE, SIR
WHAT?! DID I OFFEND SOMEONE OR SOMETHING?
© 1991 United Feature Syndicate, Inc
NO, SIR
THEN WHAT DID I DO?
JIM DAVIS 10-19
SINCE YOU'VE BEEN HERE, YOU'VE SLIPPED BENEATH THE DRESS CODE
MAY I STAY?

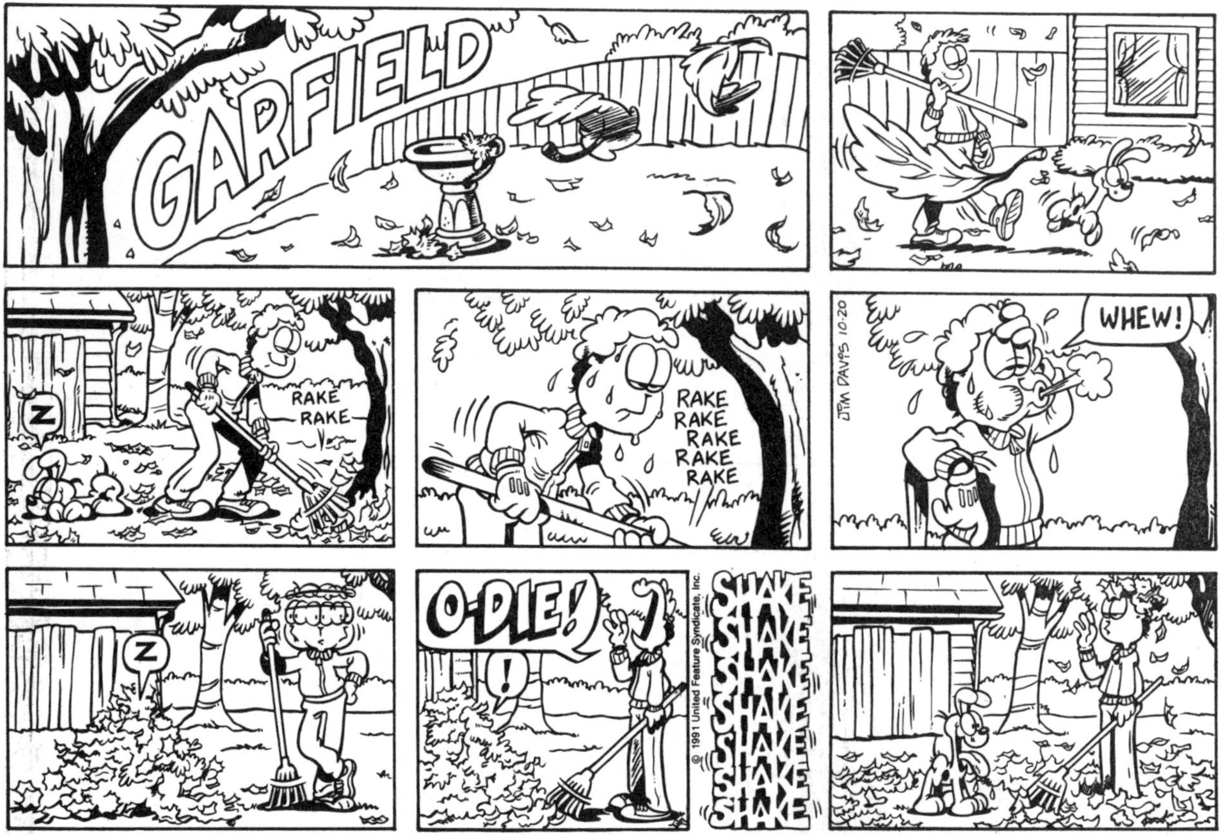
GARFIELD
Z
RAKE
RAKE
RAKE
RAKE
RAKE
RAKE
RAKE
JIM DAVIS 10-20
WHEW!
Z
O-DIE!
!
© 1991 United Feature Syndicate, Inc.
SHAKE
SHAKE
SHAKE
SHAKE
SHAKE
SHAKE
SHAKE
SHAKE

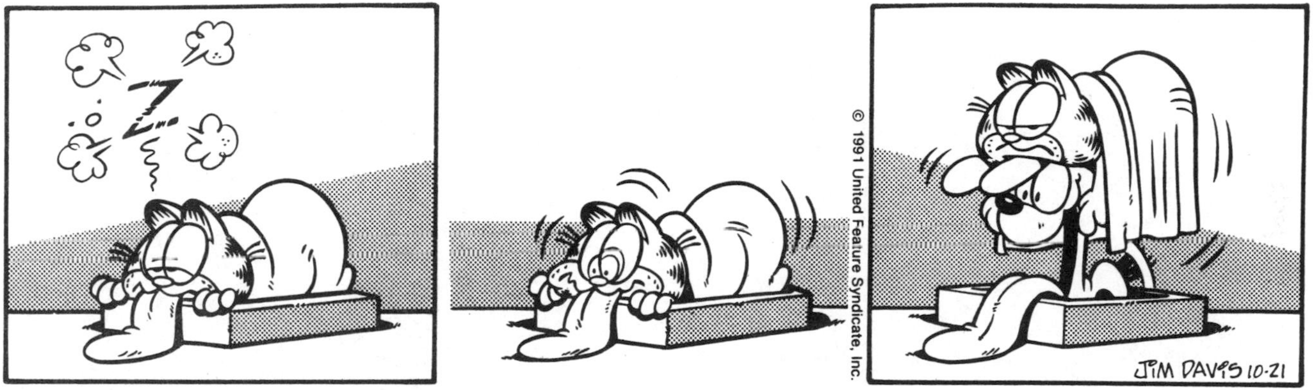
Z
© 1991 United Feature Syndicate, Inc.
JIM DAVIS 10-21

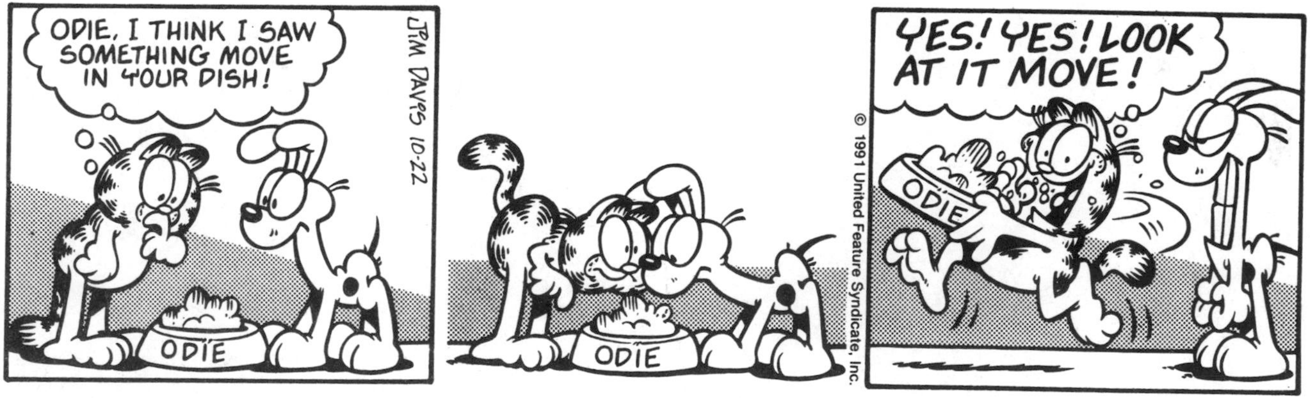
ODIE, I THINK I SAW SOMETHING MOVE IN YOUR DISH!
JIM DAVIS 10-22
ODIE
ODIE
© 1991 United Feature Syndicate, Inc.
YES! YES! LOOK AT IT MOVE!
ODIE

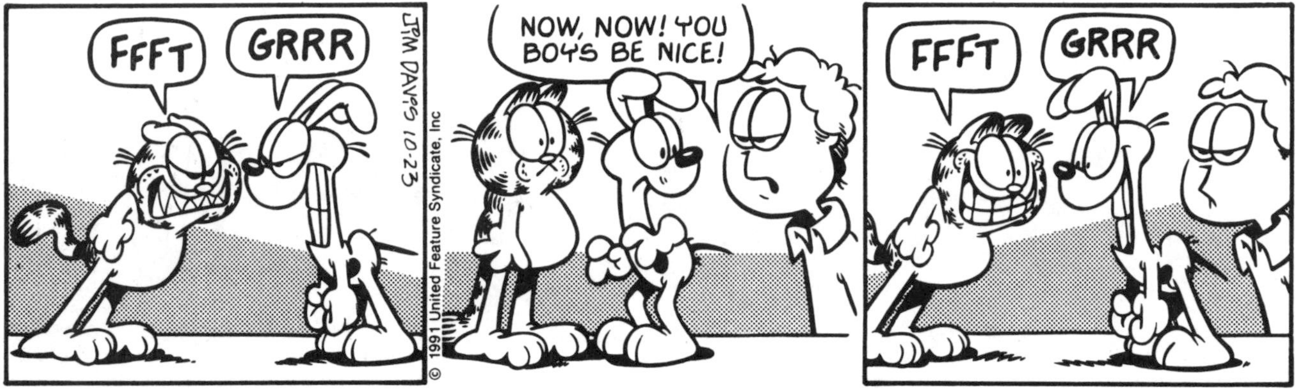
FFFT
GRRR
JIM DAVIS 10-23
© 1991 United Feature Syndicate, Inc
NOW, NOW! YOU BOYS BE NICE!
FFFT
GRRR

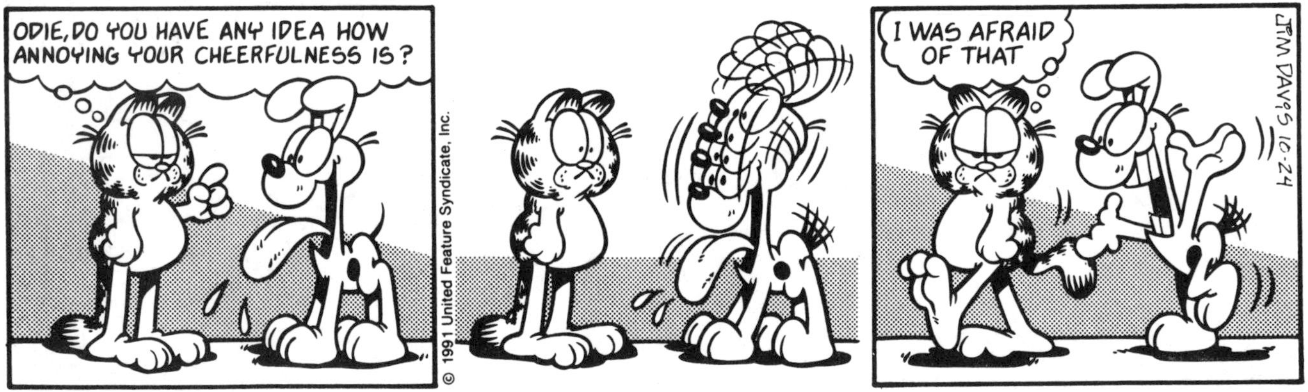
ODIE, DO YOU HAVE ANY IDEA HOW ANNOYING YOUR CHEERFULNESS IS?
© 1991 United Feature Syndicate, Inc.
I WAS AFRAID OF THAT
JIM DAVIS 10-24

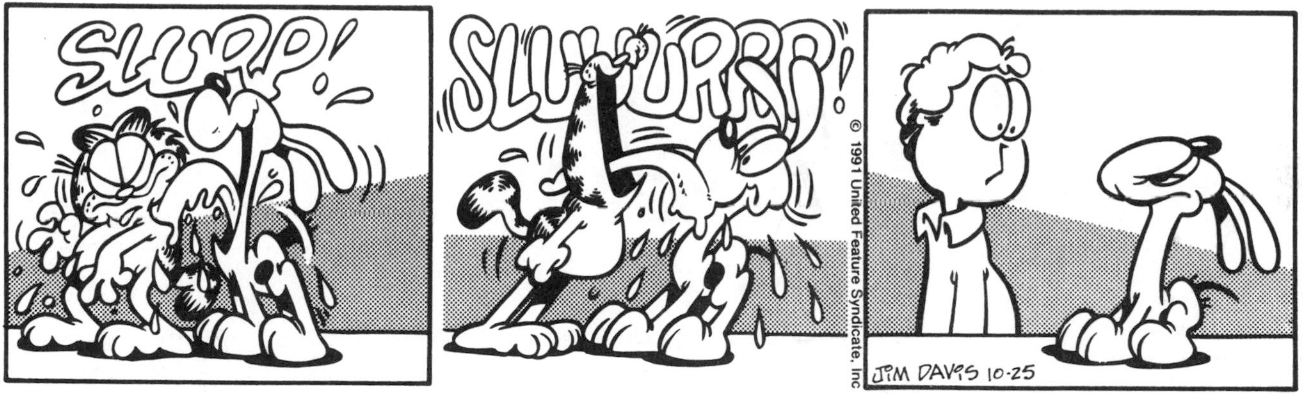
SLURP!
SLUUURRP!
© 1991 United Feature Syndicate, Inc
JIM DAVIS 10-25

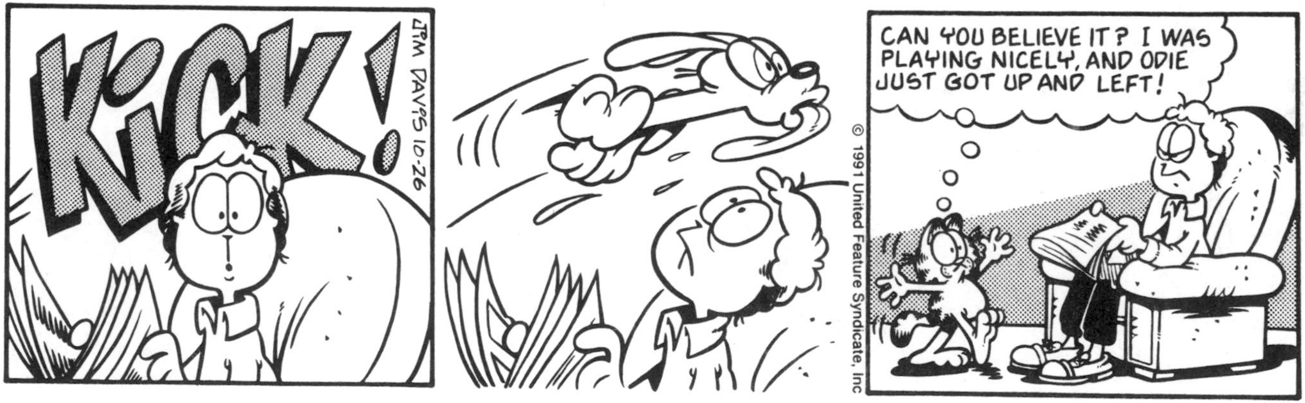
KICK!
JIM DAVIS 10-26
© 1991 United Feature Syndicate, Inc
CAN YOU BELIEVE IT? I WAS PLAYING NICELY, AND ODIE JUST GOT UP AND LEFT!

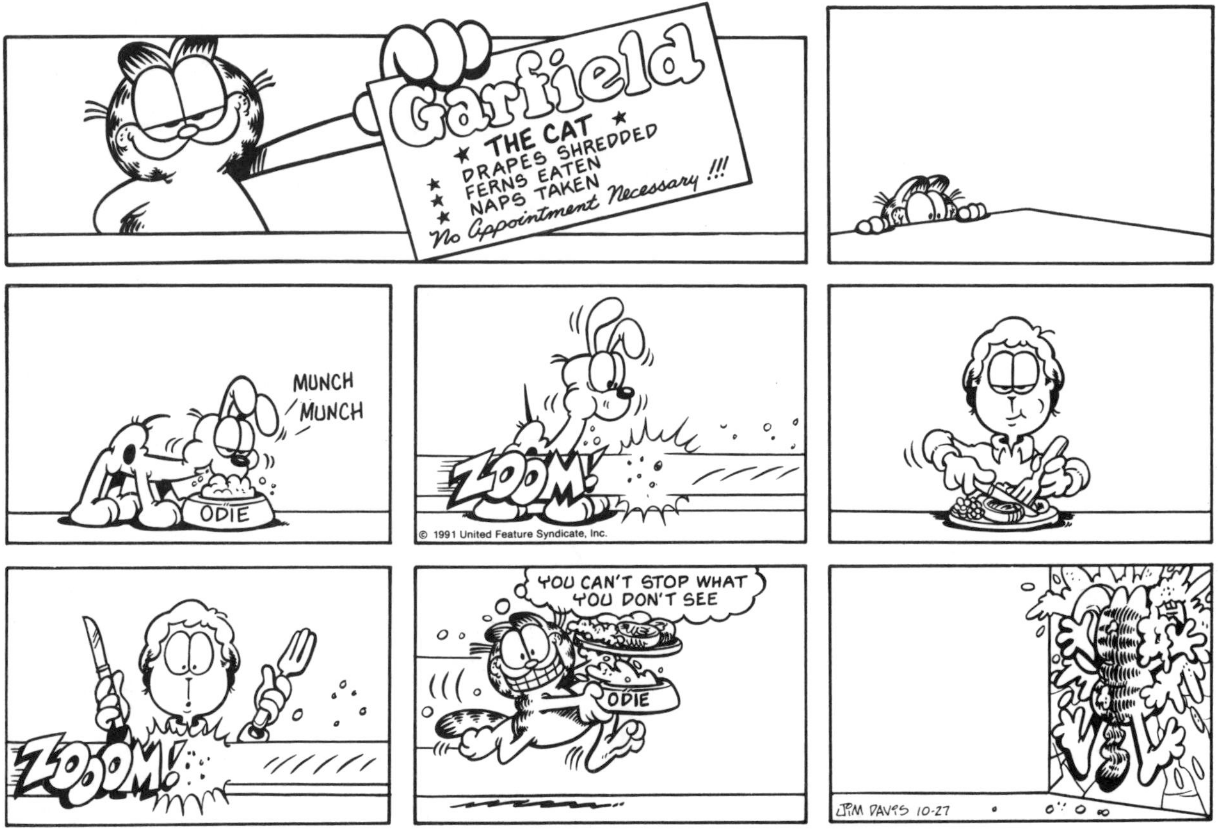
Garfield
THE CAT
DRAPES SHREDDED
FERNS EATEN
NAPS TAKEN
No Appointment Necessary !!!
MUNCH MUNCH
ZOOM!
© 1991 United Feature Syndicate, Inc.
ODIE
ZOOOM!
YOU CAN'T STOP WHAT YOU DON'T SEE
ODIE
JIM DAVIS 10-27

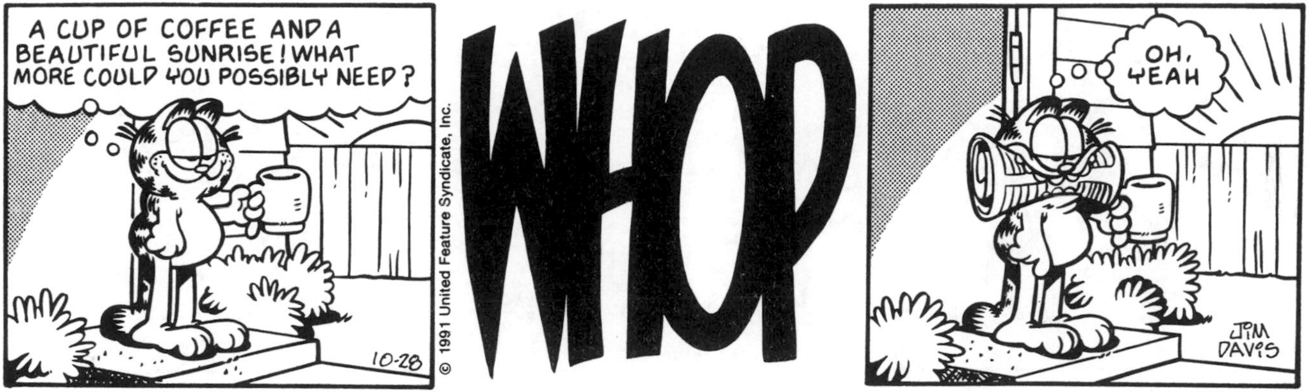
A CUP OF COFFEE AND A BEAUTIFUL SUNRISE! WHAT MORE COULD YOU POSSIBLY NEED?
10-28
© 1991 United Feature Syndicate, Inc.
WHOP
OH, YEAH
JIM DAVIS

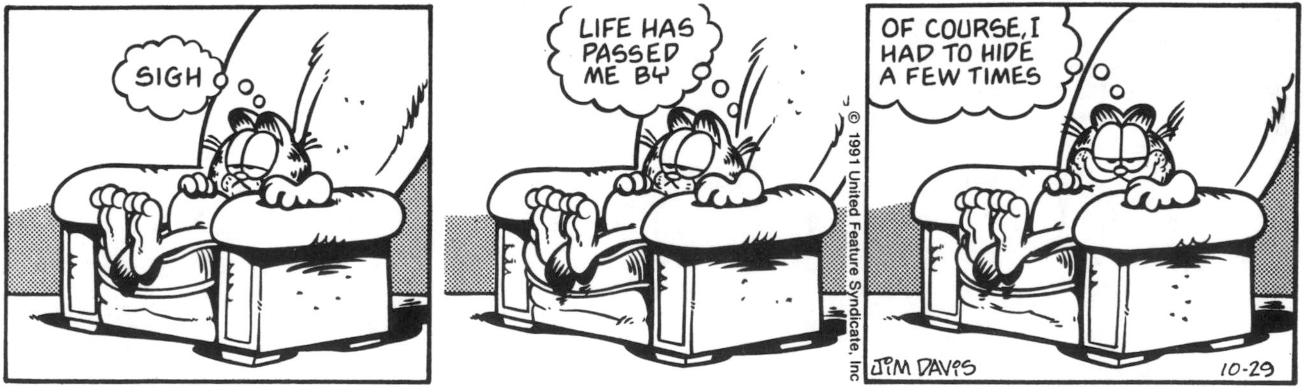
SIGH
LIFE HAS PASSED ME BY
© 1991 United Feature Syndicate, Inc.
OF COURSE, I HAD TO HIDE A FEW TIMES
JIM DAVIS
10-29

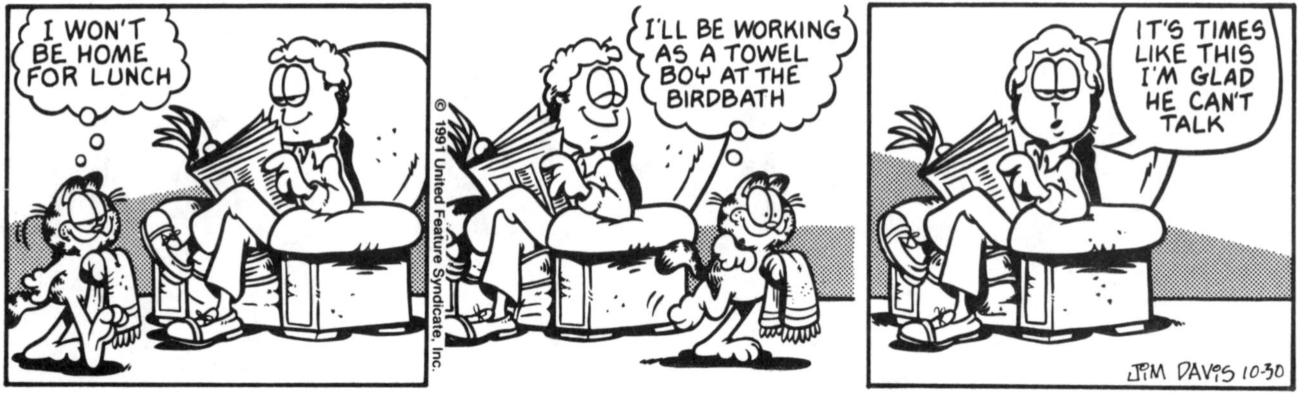
I WON'T BE HOME FOR LUNCH
© 1991 United Feature Syndicate, Inc.
I'LL BE WORKING AS A TOWEL BOY AT THE BIRDBATH
IT'S TIMES LIKE THIS I'M GLAD HE CAN'T TALK
JIM DAVIS 10-30

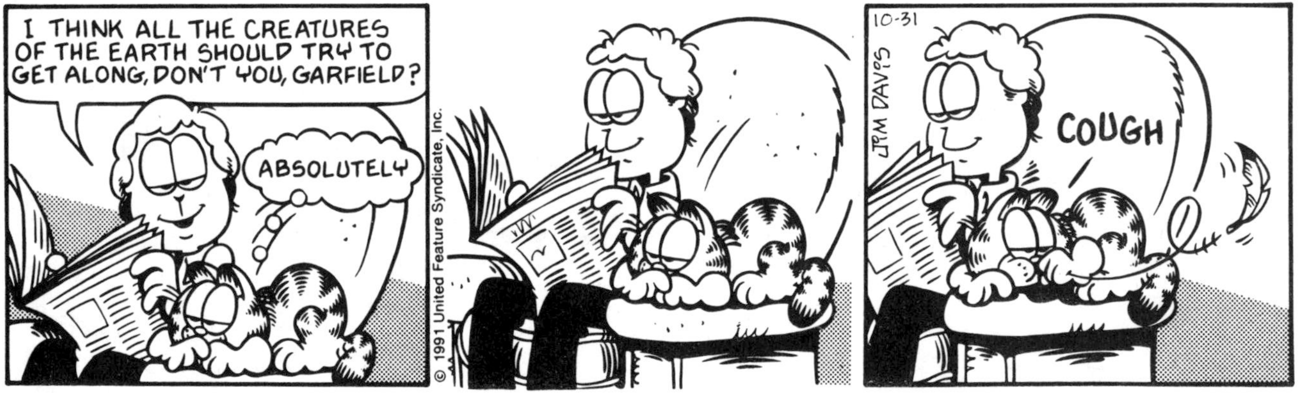
I THINK ALL THE CREATURES OF THE EARTH SHOULD TRY TO GET ALONG, DON'T YOU, GARFIELD?
ABSOLUTELY
© 1991 United Feature Syndicate, Inc.
10-31
JIM DAVIS
COUGH

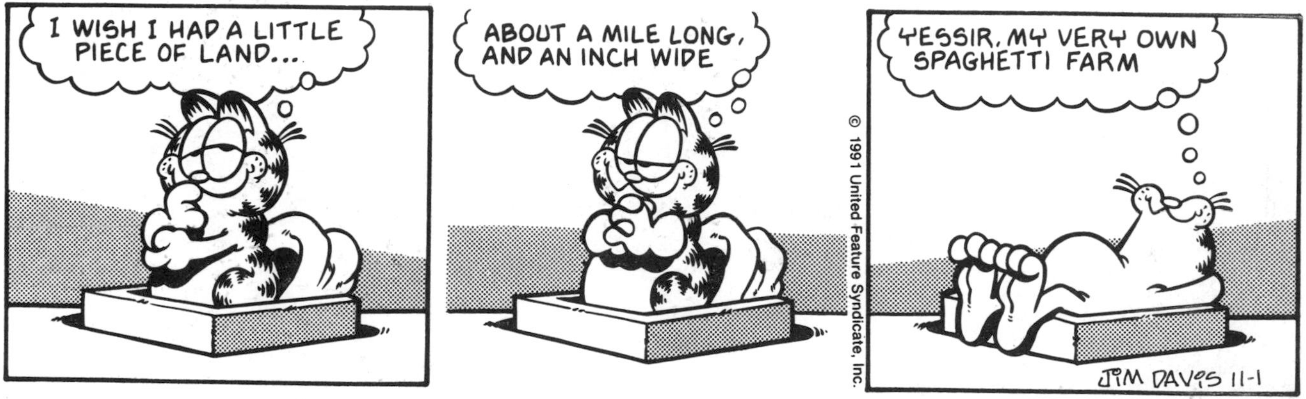
I WISH I HAD A LITTLE PIECE OF LAND...
ABOUT A MILE LONG, AND AN INCH WIDE
YESSIR, MY VERY OWN SPAGHETTI FARM
© 1991 United Feature Syndicate, Inc.
JIM DAVIS 11-1

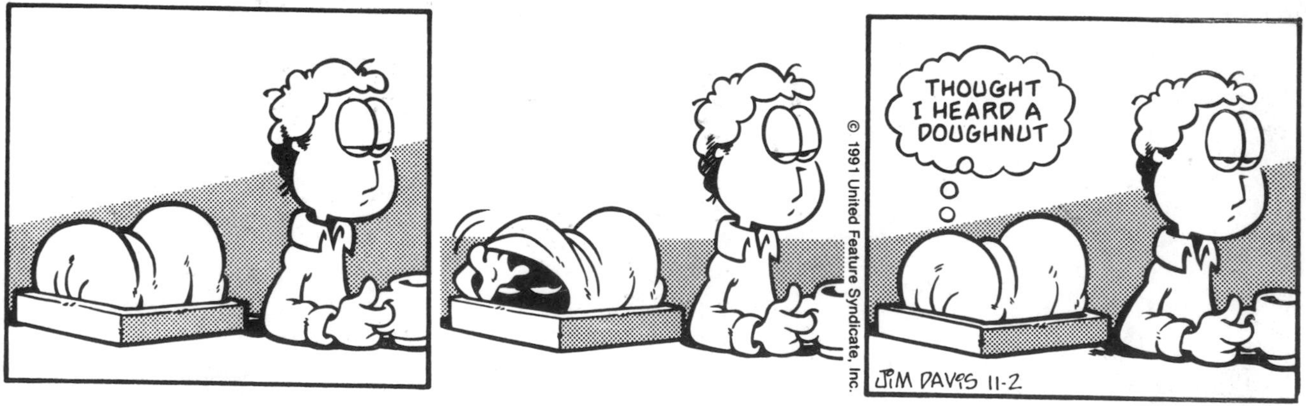
THOUGHT I HEARD A DOUGHNUT
© 1991 United Feature Syndicate, Inc.
JIM DAVIS 11-2

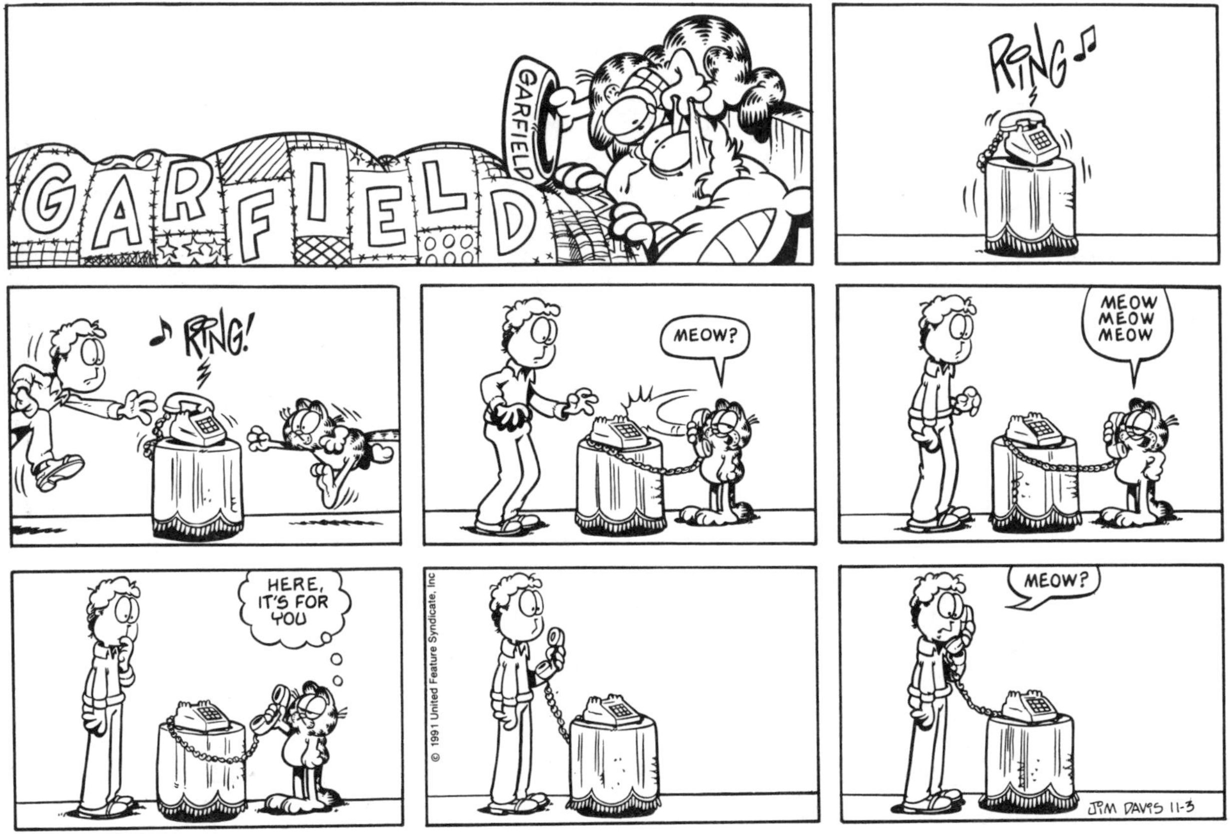
GARFIELD
GARFIELD
RING
RING!
MEOW?
MEOW MEOW MEOW
HERE, IT'S FOR YOU
© 1991 United Feature Syndicate, Inc
MEOW?
JIM DAVIS 11-3

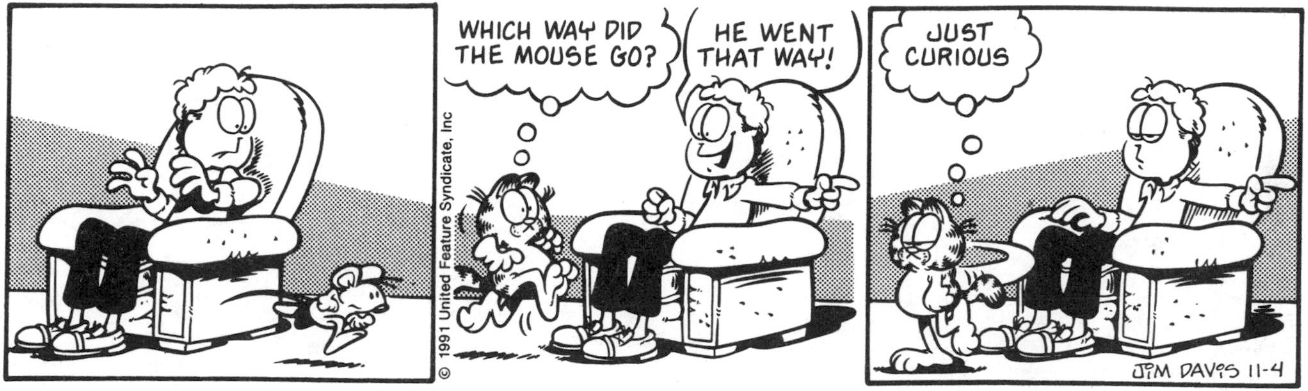
WHICH WAY DID THE MOUSE GO?
HE WENT THAT WAY!
JUST CURIOUS
© 1991 United Feature Syndicate, Inc
JIM DAVIS 11-4

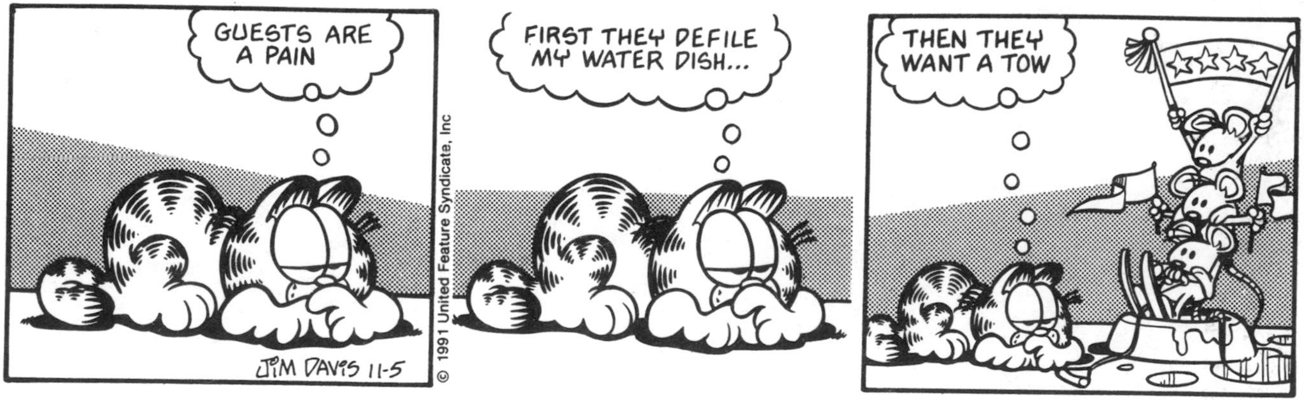
GUESTS ARE A PAIN
FIRST THEY DEFILE MY WATER DISH...
THEN THEY WANT A TOW
© 1991 United Feature Syndicate, Inc
JIM DAVIS 11-5

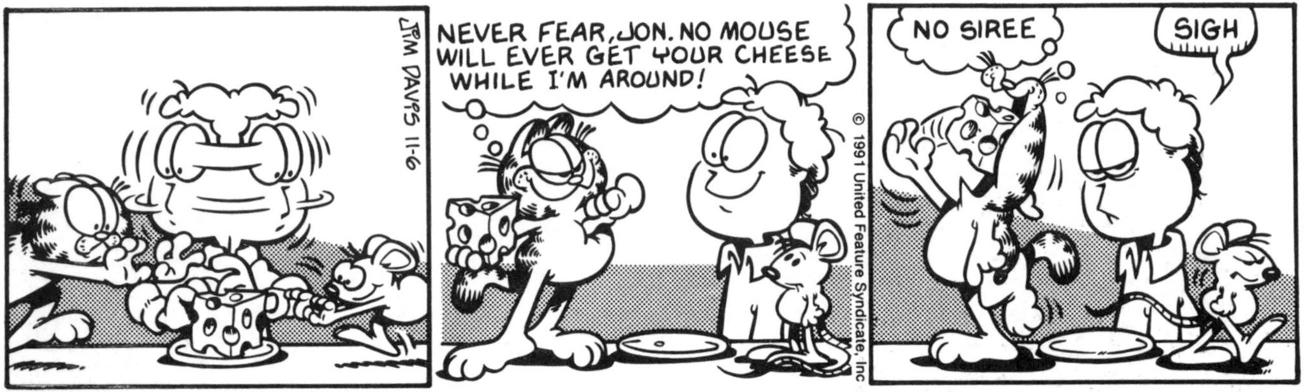
JIM DAVIS 11-6
NEVER FEAR, JON. NO MOUSE WILL EVER GET YOUR CHEESE WHILE I'M AROUND!
© 1991 United Feature Syndicate, Inc
NO SIREE
SIGH

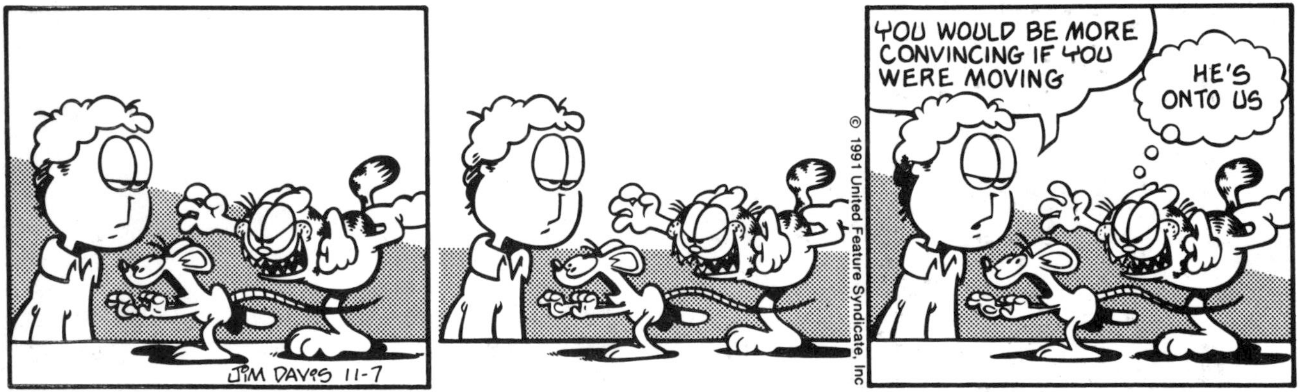
JIM DAVIS 11-7
© 1991 United Feature Syndicate, Inc
YOU WOULD BE MORE CONVINCING IF YOU WERE MOVING
HE'S ONTO US

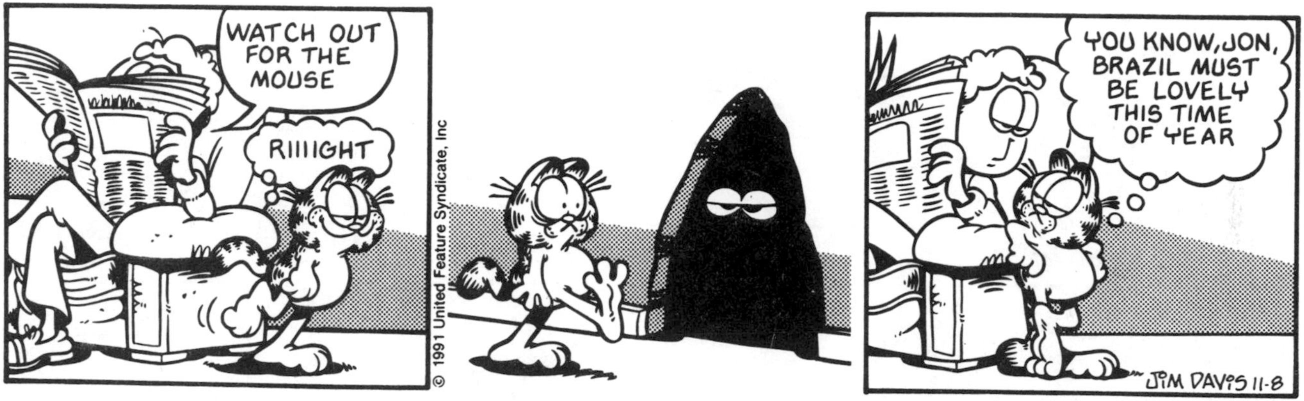
WATCH OUT FOR THE MOUSE
RIIIIGHT
© 1991 United Feature Syndicate, Inc
YOU KNOW, JON, BRAZIL MUST BE LOVELY THIS TIME OF YEAR
JIM DAVIS 11-8

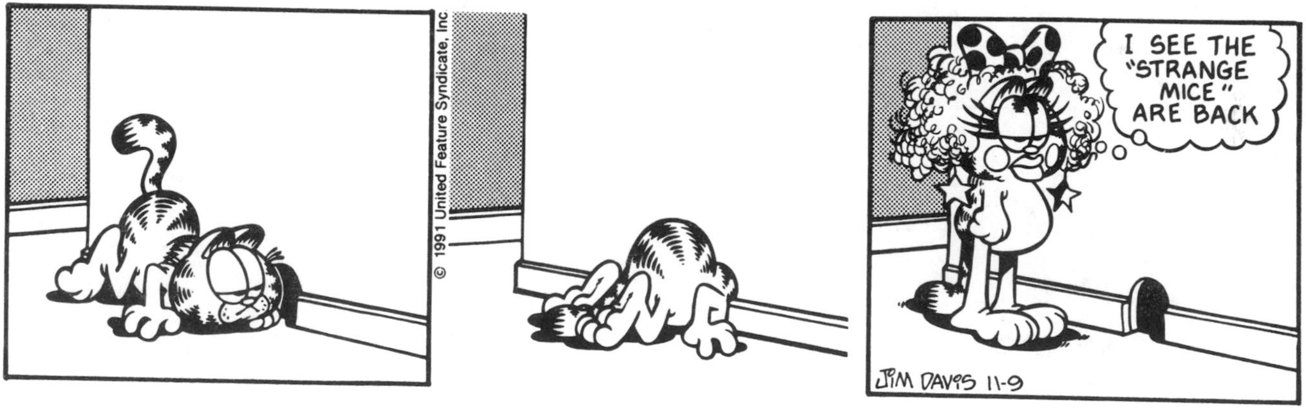
© 1991 United Feature Syndicate, Inc
I SEE THE "STRANGE MICE" ARE BACK
JIM DAVIS 11-9

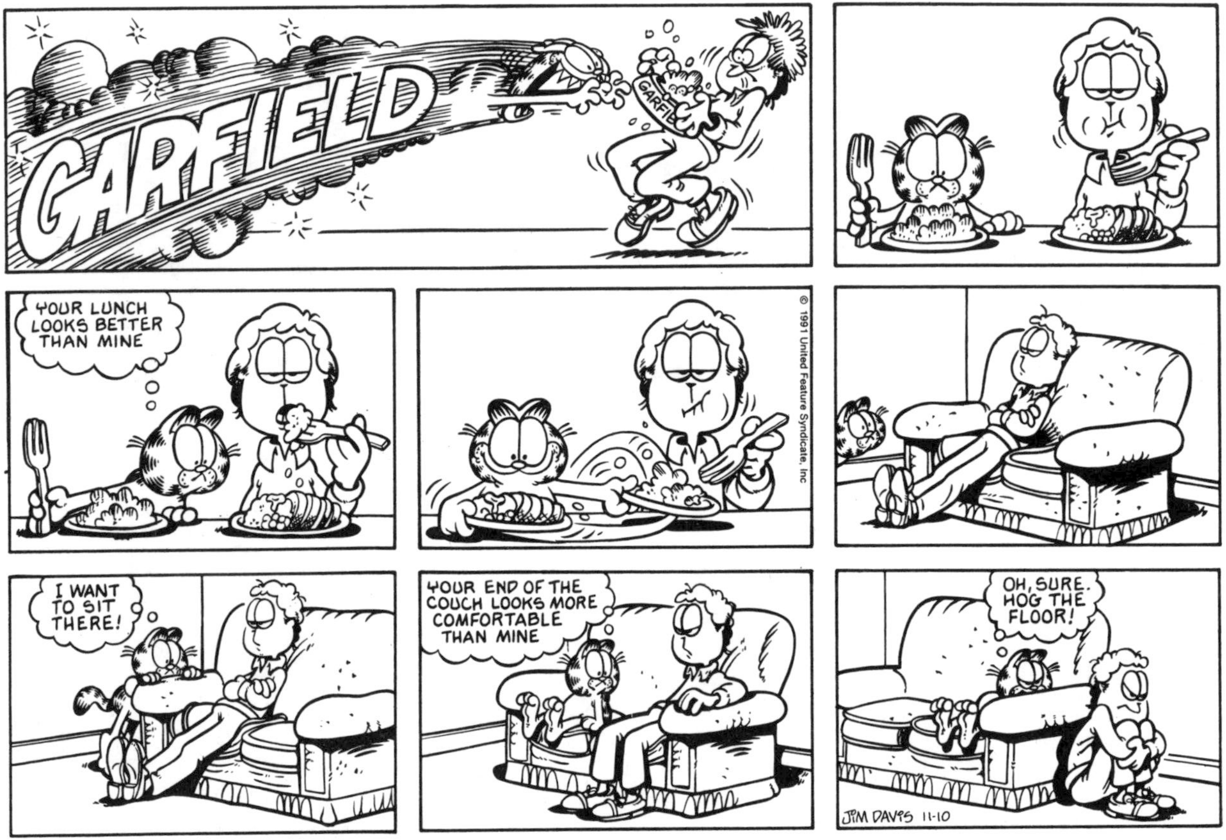
GARFIELD
YOUR LUNCH LOOKS BETTER THAN MINE
© 1991 United Feature Syndicate, Inc
I WANT TO SIT THERE!
YOUR END OF THE COUCH LOOKS MORE COMFORTABLE THAN MINE
OH, SURE. HOG THE FLOOR!
JIM DAVIS 11-10

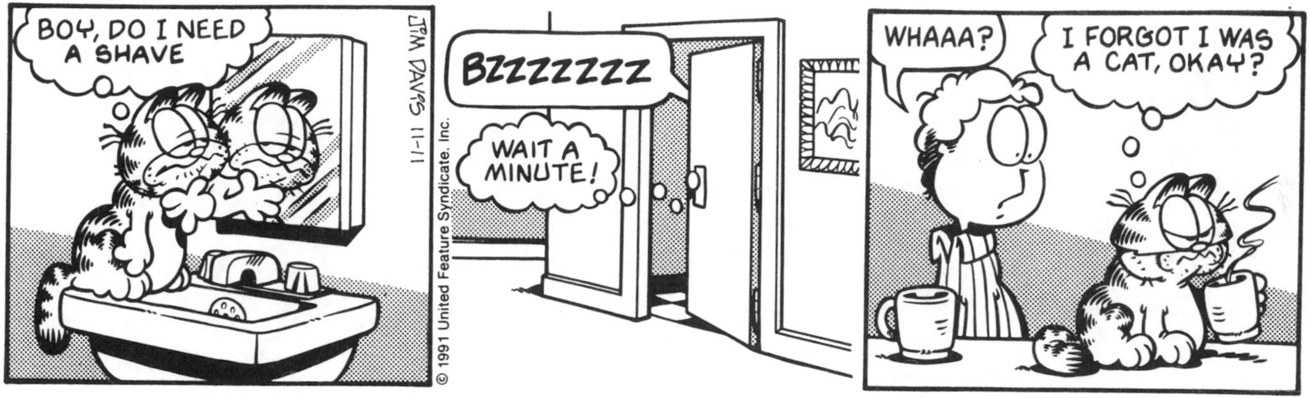
BOY, DO I NEED A SHAVE
JIM DAVIS 11-11
© 1991 United Feature Syndicate, Inc.
BZZZZZZZ
WAIT A MINUTE!
WHAAA?
I FORGOT I WAS A CAT, OKAY?

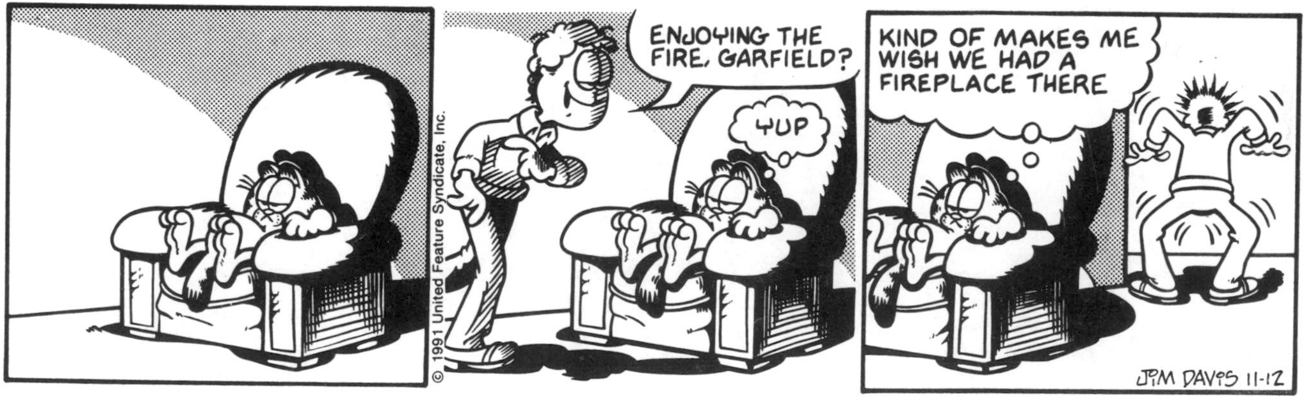
© 1991 United Feature Syndicate, Inc.
ENJOYING THE FIRE, GARFIELD?
YUP
KIND OF MAKES ME WISH WE HAD A FIREPLACE THERE
JIM DAVIS 11-12

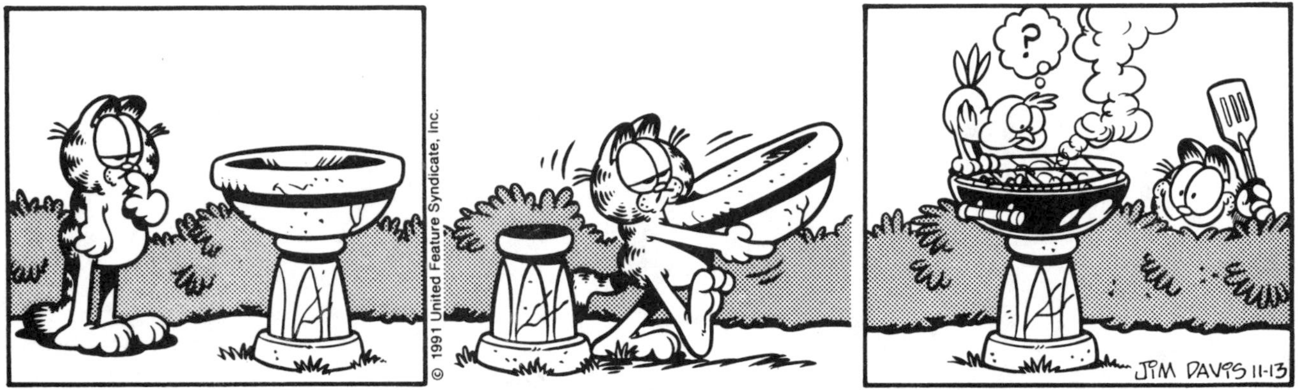
?
© 1991 United Feature Syndicate, Inc.
JIM DAVIS 11-13

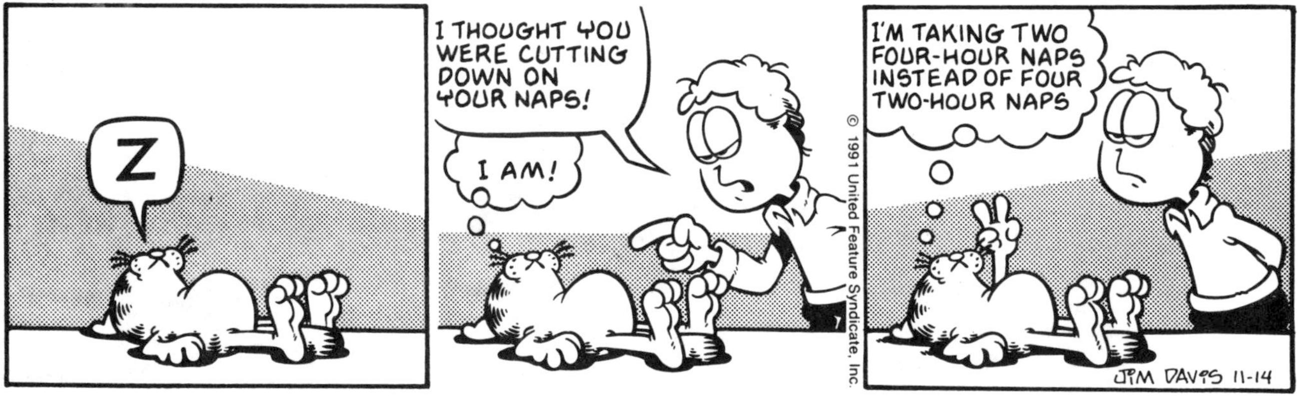
Z
I THOUGHT YOU WERE CUTTING DOWN ON YOUR NAPS!
I AM!
I'M TAKING TWO FOUR-HOUR NAPS INSTEAD OF FOUR TWO-HOUR NAPS
© 1991 United Feature Syndicate, Inc.
JIM DAVIS 11-14

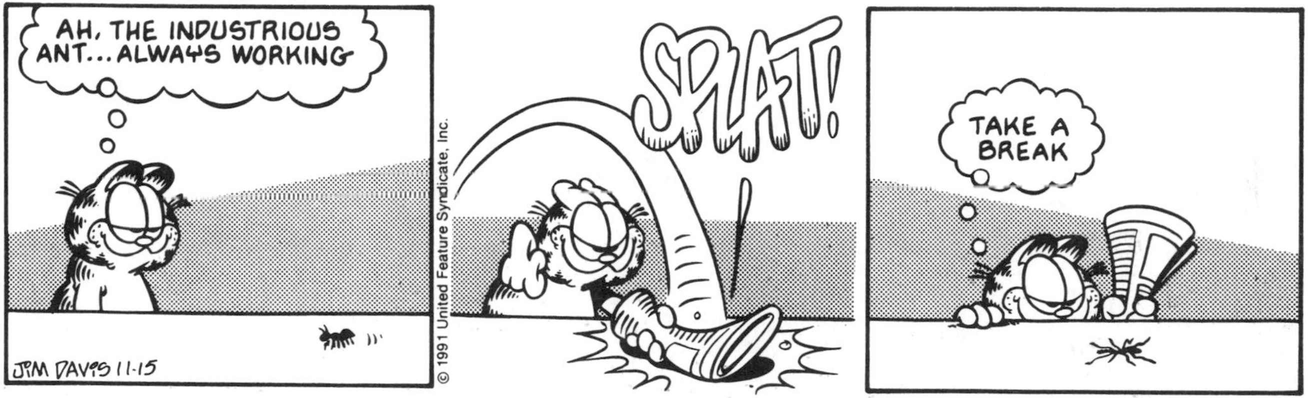
AH, THE INDUSTRIOUS ANT... ALWAYS WORKING
SPLAT!
TAKE A BREAK
JIM DAVIS 11-15
© 1991 United Feature Syndicate, Inc.

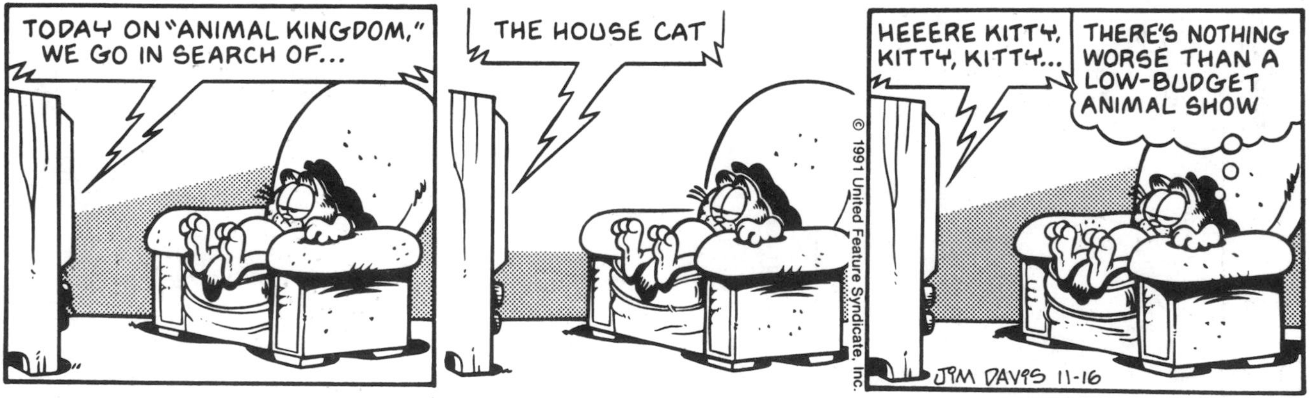
TODAY ON "ANIMAL KINGDOM," WE GO IN SEARCH OF...
THE HOUSE CAT
HEEERE KITTY, KITTY, KITTY...
THERE'S NOTHING WORSE THAN A LOW-BUDGET ANIMAL SHOW
JIM DAVIS 11-16
© 1991 United Feature Syndicate, Inc.

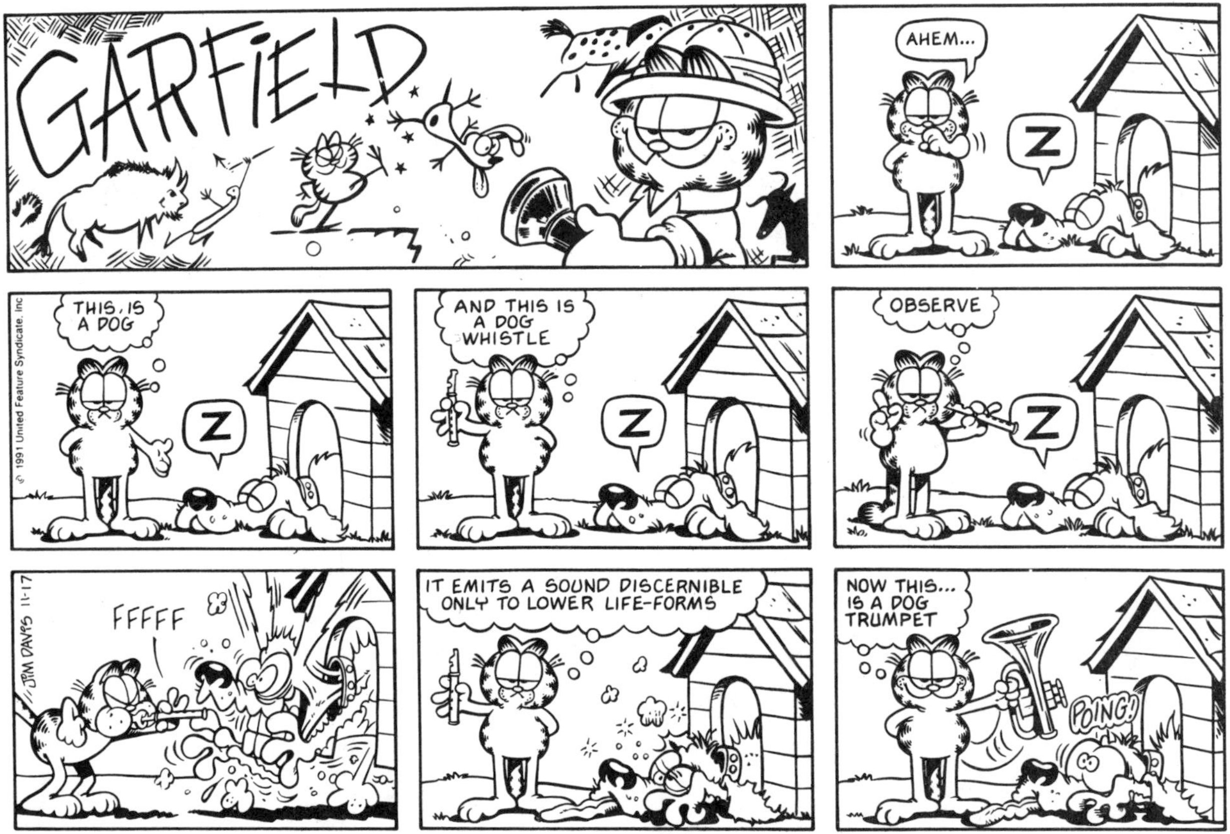
GARFIELD
AHEM...
Z
© 1991 United Feature Syndicate, Inc
THIS, IS A DOG
Z
AND THIS IS A DOG WHISTLE
Z
OBSERVE
Z
JIM DAVIS 11-17
FFFFF
IT EMITS A SOUND DISCERNIBLE ONLY TO LOWER LIFE-FORMS
NOW THIS... IS A DOG TRUMPET
POING!

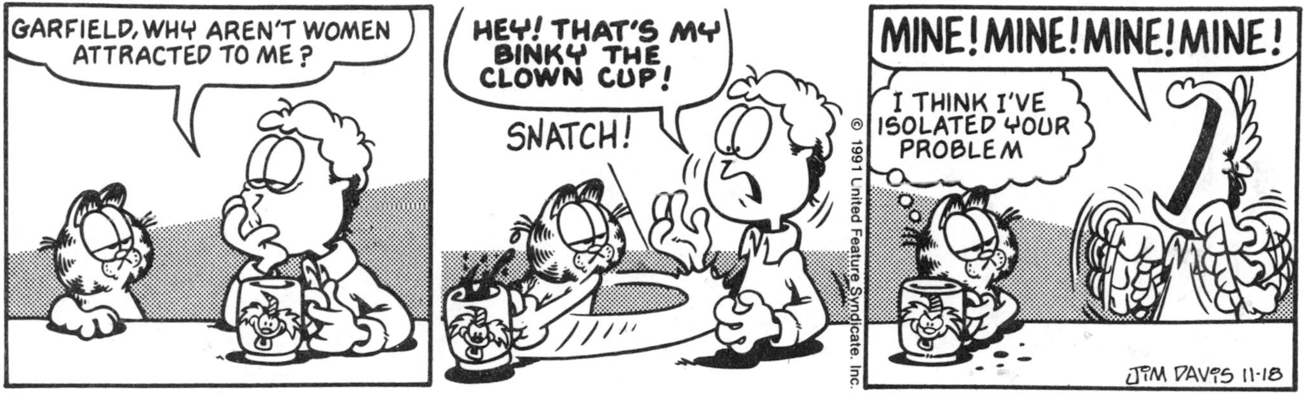
GARFIELD, WHY AREN'T WOMEN ATTRACTED TO ME?
HEY! THAT'S MY BINKY THE CLOWN CUP!
SNATCH!
MINE! MINE! MINE! MINE!
I THINK I'VE ISOLATED YOUR PROBLEM
JIM DAVIS 11-18
© 1991 United Feature Syndicate, Inc.

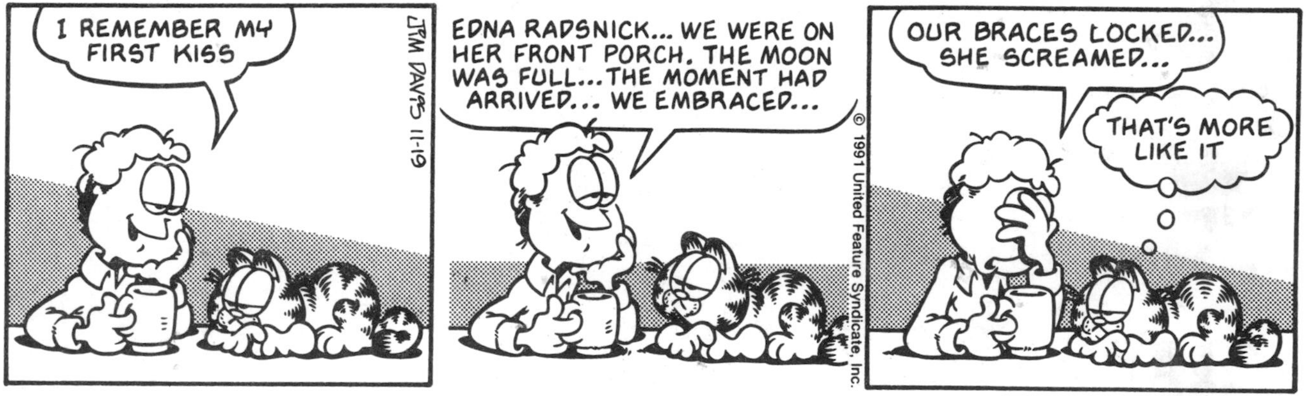
I REMEMBER MY FIRST KISS
JIM DAVIS 11-19
EDNA RADSNICK... WE WERE ON HER FRONT PORCH. THE MOON WAS FULL... THE MOMENT HAD ARRIVED... WE EMBRACED...
OUR BRACES LOCKED... SHE SCREAMED...
THAT'S MORE LIKE IT
© 1991 United Feature Syndicate, Inc.

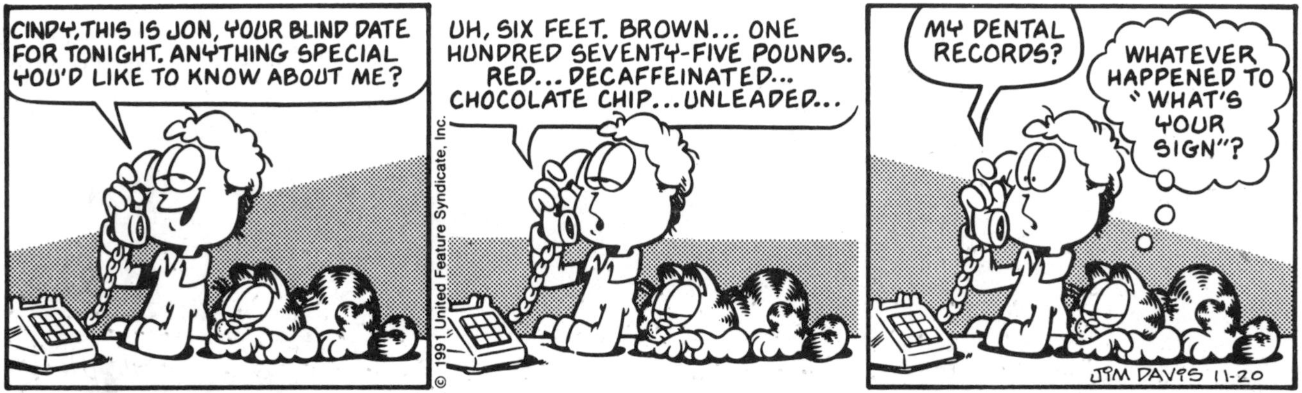
CINDY, THIS IS JON, YOUR BLIND DATE FOR TONIGHT. ANYTHING SPECIAL YOU'D LIKE TO KNOW ABOUT ME?
UH, SIX FEET. BROWN... ONE HUNDRED SEVENTY-FIVE POUNDS. RED... DECAFFEINATED... CHOCOLATE CHIP... UNLEADED...
MY DENTAL RECORDS?
WHATEVER HAPPENED TO "WHAT'S YOUR SIGN"?
JIM DAVIS 11-20
© 1991 United Feature Syndicate, Inc.

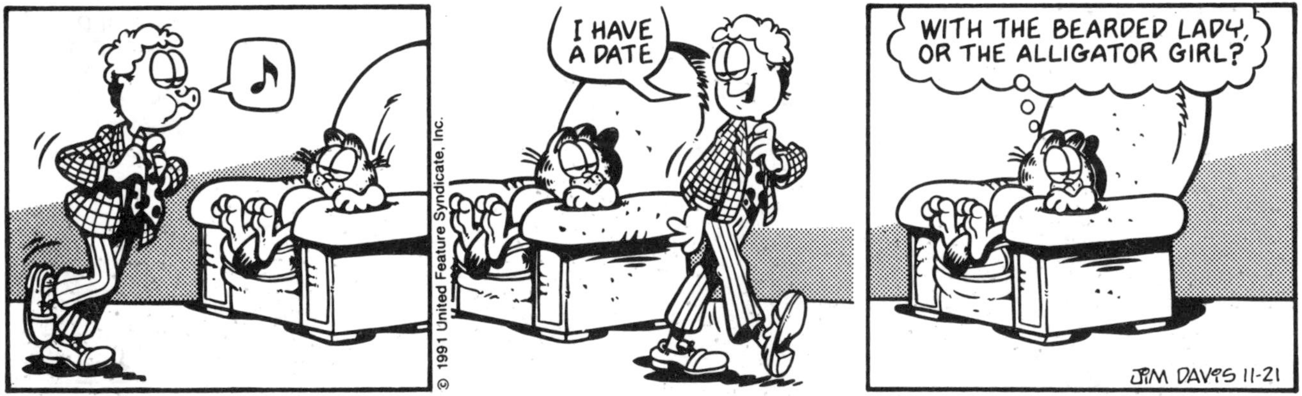
♪
I HAVE A DATE
WITH THE BEARDED LADY, OR THE ALLIGATOR GIRL?
JIM DAVIS 11-21
© 1991 United Feature Syndicate, Inc.

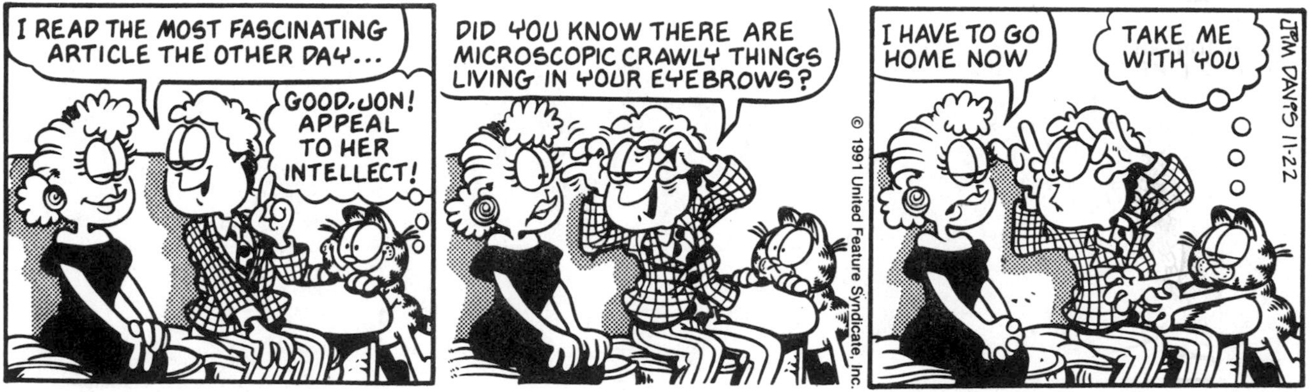
I READ THE MOST FASCINATING ARTICLE THE OTHER DAY...
GOOD, JON! APPEAL TO HER INTELLECT!
DID YOU KNOW THERE ARE MICROSCOPIC CRAWLY THINGS LIVING IN YOUR EYEBROWS?
© 1991 United Feature Syndicate, Inc.
I HAVE TO GO HOME NOW
TAKE ME WITH YOU
JIM DAVIS 11-22

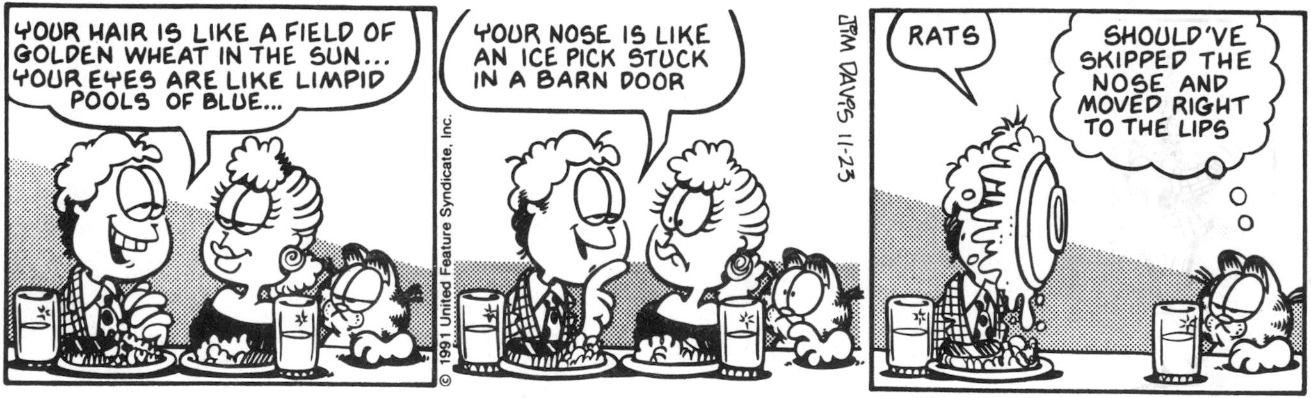
YOUR HAIR IS LIKE A FIELD OF GOLDEN WHEAT IN THE SUN... YOUR EYES ARE LIKE LIMPID POOLS OF BLUE...
© 1991 United Feature Syndicate, Inc.
YOUR NOSE IS LIKE AN ICE PICK STUCK IN A BARN DOOR
JIM DAVIS 11-23
RATS
SHOULD'VE SKIPPED THE NOSE AND MOVED RIGHT TO THE LIPS

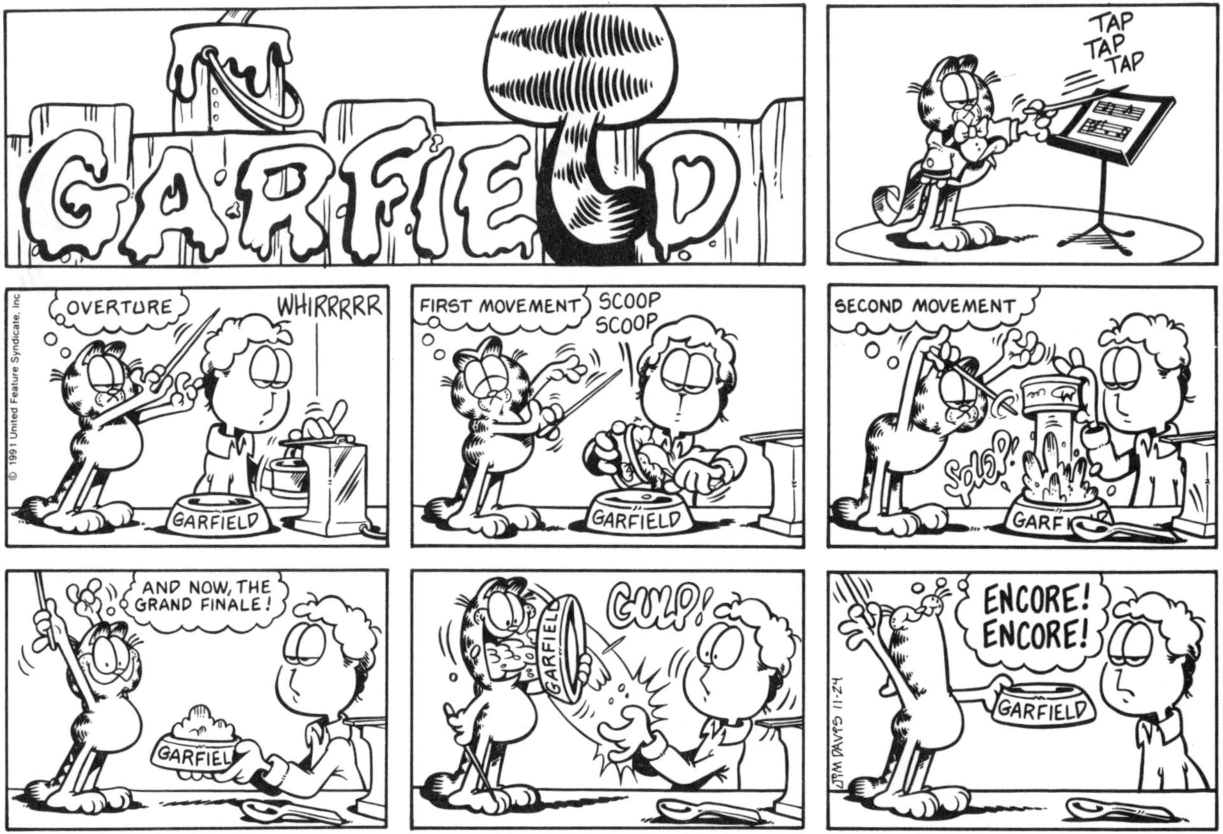
GARFIELD
TAP
TAP
TAP
© 1991 United Feature Syndicate, Inc
OVERTURE
WHIRRRRR
GARFIELD
FIRST MOVEMENT
SCOOP
SCOOP
GARFIELD
SECOND MOVEMENT
SPLOP!
AND NOW, THE GRAND FINALE!
GARFIEL
GULP!
GARFIELD
JPM DAVIS 11-24
ENCORE! ENCORE!
GARFIELD

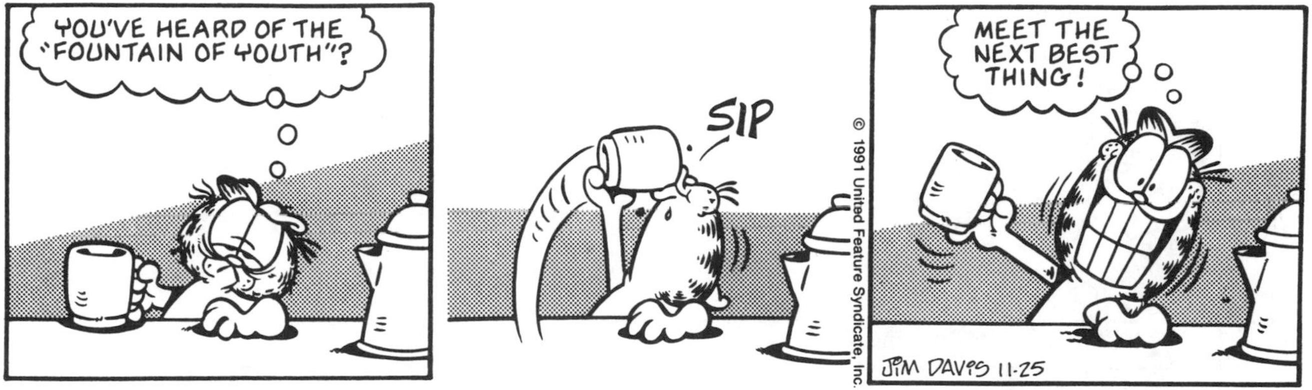
YOU'VE HEARD OF THE "FOUNTAIN OF YOUTH"?
SIP
MEET THE NEXT BEST THING!
© 1991 United Feature Syndicate, Inc.
JIM DAVIS 11-25

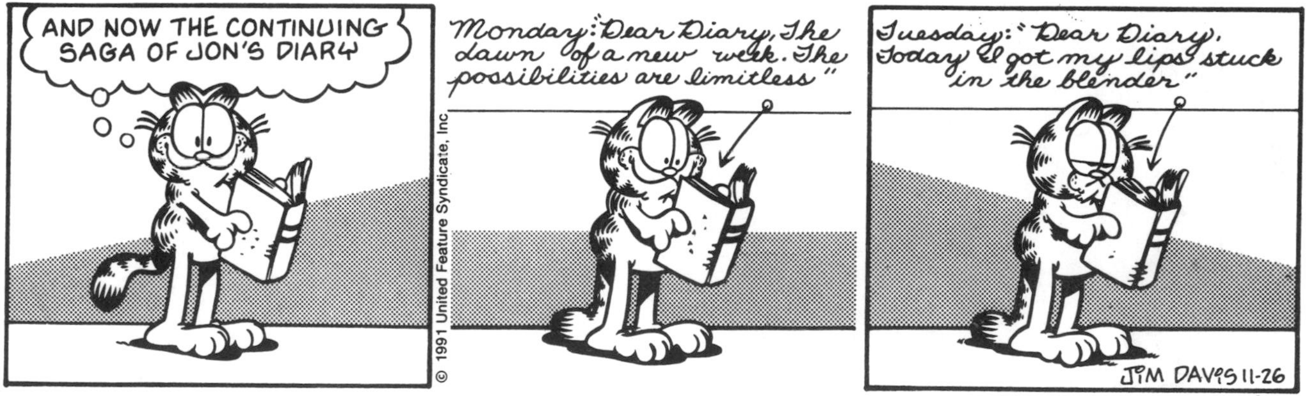
AND NOW THE CONTINUING SAGA OF JON'S DIARY
Monday: "Dear Diary, The dawn of a new week. The possibilities are limitless"
Tuesday: "Dear Diary, Today I got my lips stuck in the blender"
© 1991 United Feature Syndicate, Inc
JIM DAVIS 11-26

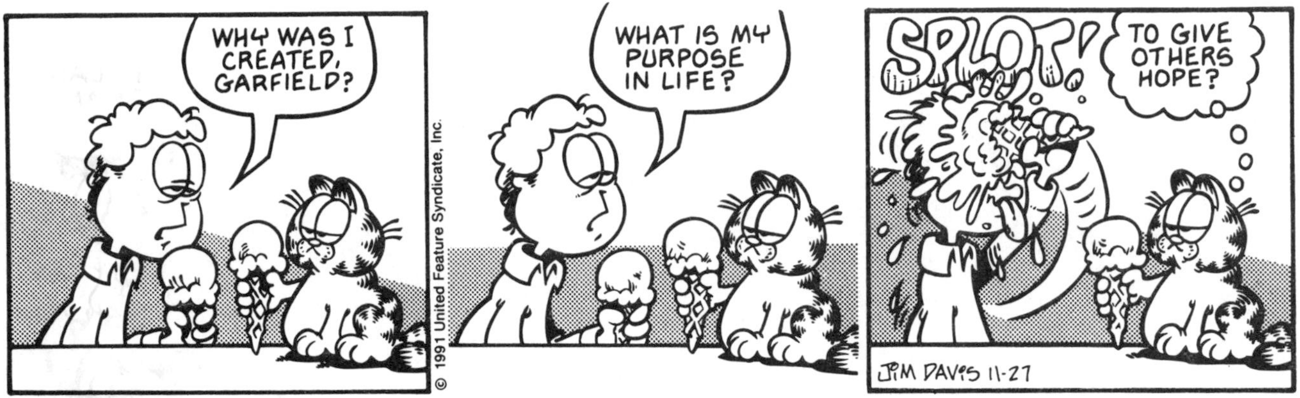
WHY WAS I CREATED, GARFIELD?
© 1991 United Feature Syndicate, Inc.
WHAT IS MY PURPOSE IN LIFE?
SPLOT!
TO GIVE OTHERS HOPE?
JIM DAVIS 11-27

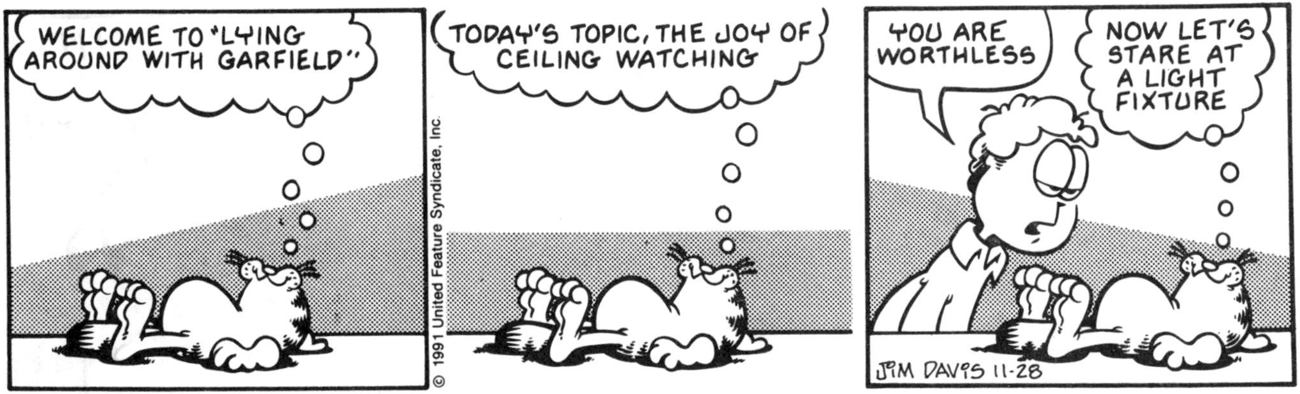
WELCOME TO "LYING AROUND WITH GARFIELD"
© 1991 United Feature Syndicate, Inc.
TODAY'S TOPIC, THE JOY OF CEILING WATCHING
YOU ARE WORTHLESS
NOW LET'S STARE AT A LIGHT FIXTURE
JIM DAVIS 11-28

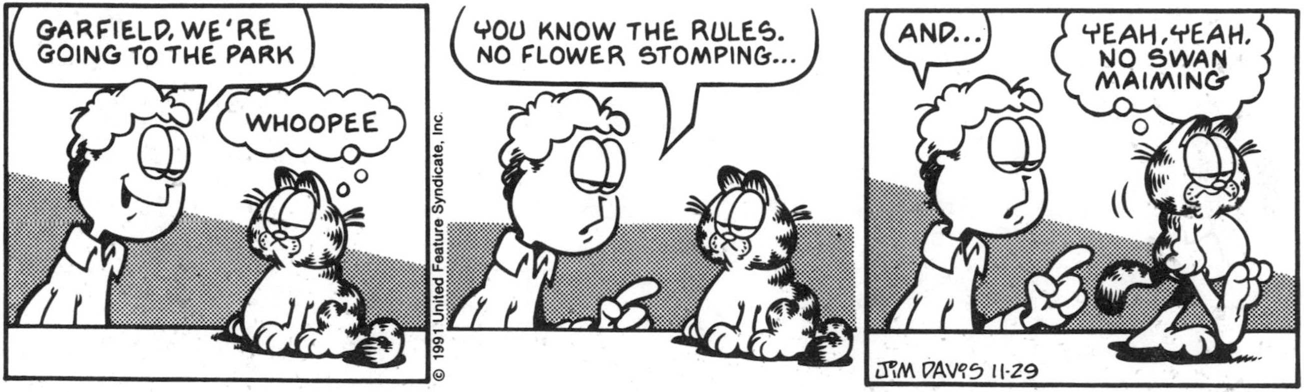
GARFIELD, WE'RE GOING TO THE PARK
WHOOPEE
YOU KNOW THE RULES. NO FLOWER STOMPING...
AND...
YEAH, YEAH. NO SWAN MAIMING
© 1991 United Feature Syndicate, Inc.
JIM DAVIS 11-29

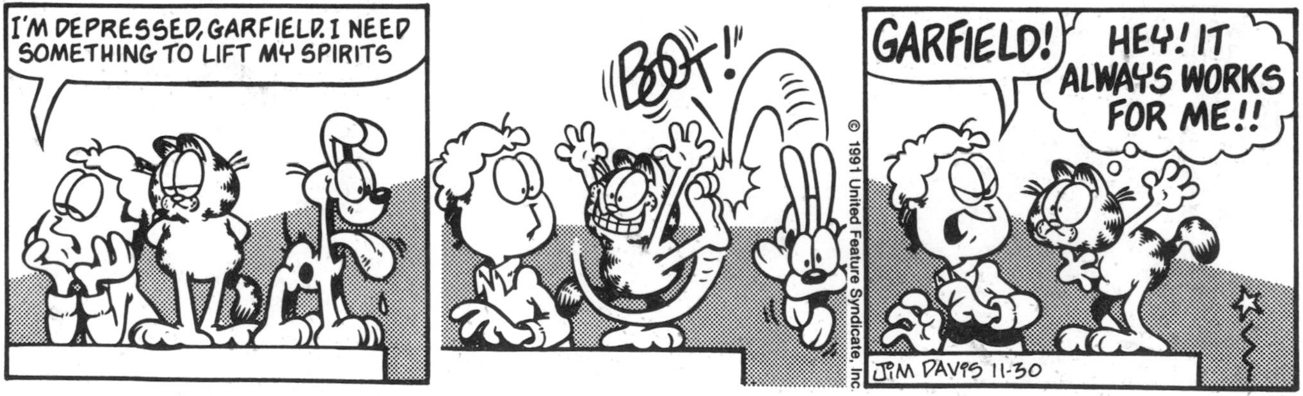
I'M DEPRESSED, GARFIELD. I NEED SOMETHING TO LIFT MY SPIRITS
BOOT!
GARFIELD!
HEY! IT ALWAYS WORKS FOR ME!!
© 1991 United Feature Syndicate, Inc.
JIM DAVIS 11-30

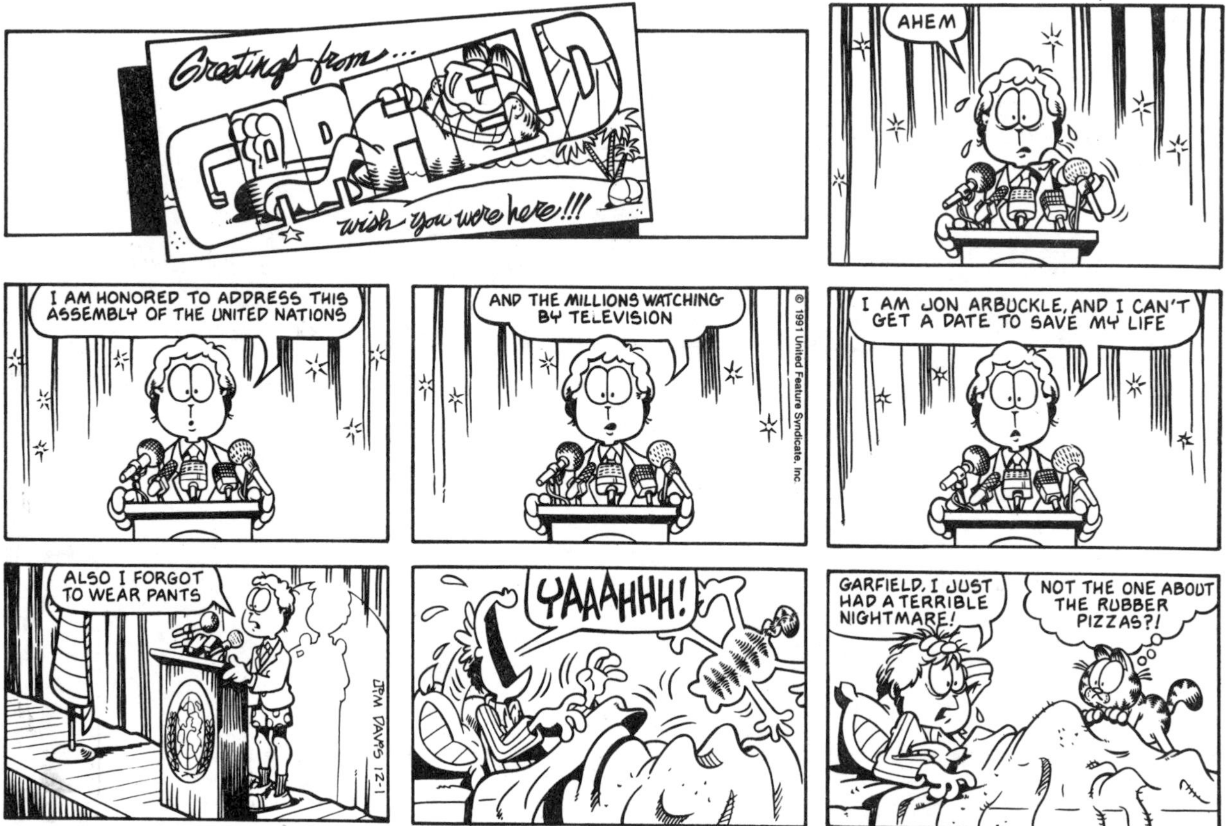
Greetings from...
GARFIELD
wish you were here!!!
AHEM
I AM HONORED TO ADDRESS THIS ASSEMBLY OF THE UNITED NATIONS
AND THE MILLIONS WATCHING BY TELEVISION
© 1991 United Feature Syndicate, Inc.
I AM JON ARBUCKLE, AND I CAN'T GET A DATE TO SAVE MY LIFE
ALSO I FORGOT TO WEAR PANTS
JIM DAVIS 12-1
YAAAHHH!
GARFIELD, I JUST HAD A TERRIBLE NIGHTMARE!
NOT THE ONE ABOUT THE RUBBER PIZZAS?!

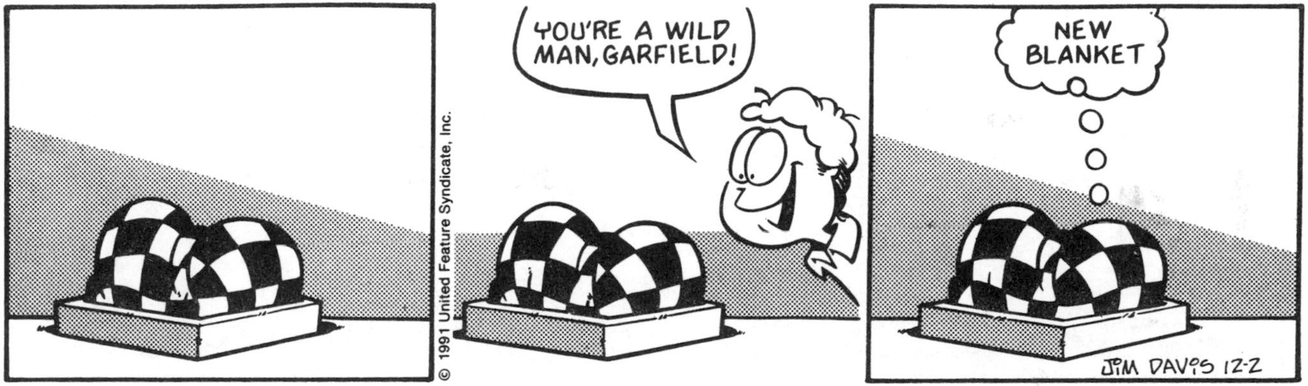

YOU'RE A WILD MAN, GARFIELD!
NEW BLANKET
© 1991 United Feature Syndicate, Inc.
JIM DAVIS 12-2

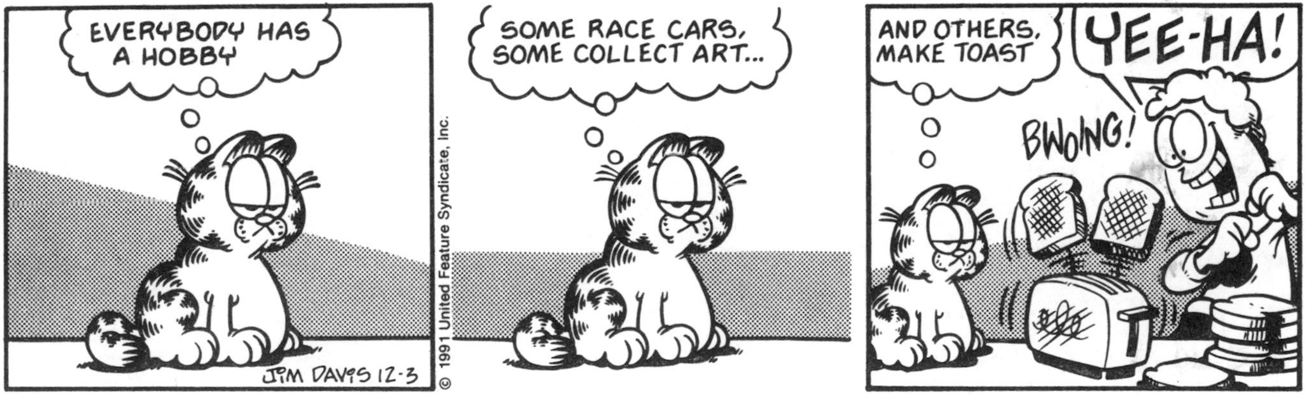

EVERYBODY HAS A HOBBY
SOME RACE CARS, SOME COLLECT ART...
AND OTHERS, MAKE TOAST
YEE-HA!
BWOING!
© 1991 United Feature Syndicate, Inc.
JIM DAVIS 12-3

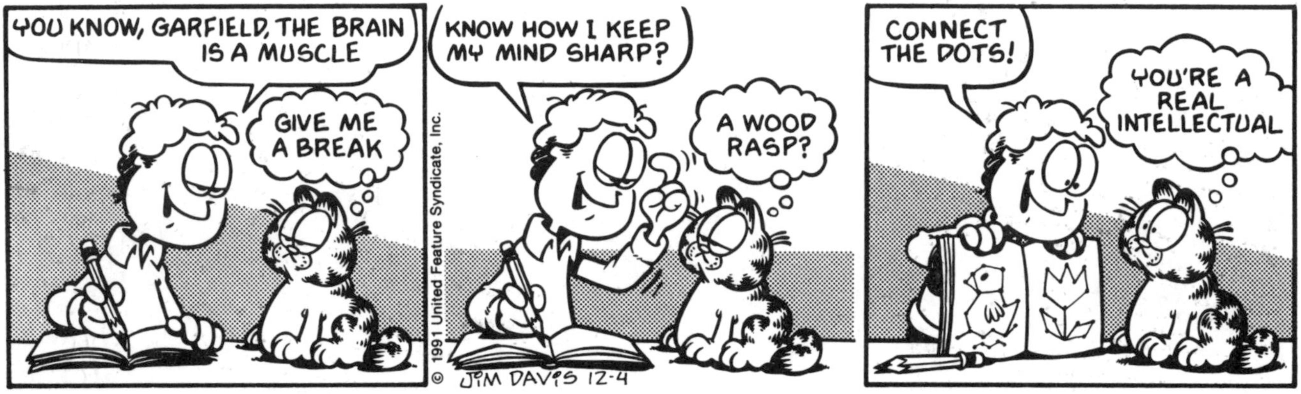
YOU KNOW, GARFIELD, THE BRAIN IS A MUSCLE
GIVE ME A BREAK
KNOW HOW I KEEP MY MIND SHARP?
A WOOD RASP?
CONNECT THE DOTS!
YOU'RE A REAL INTELLECTUAL
© 1991 United Feature Syndicate, Inc.
JIM DAVIS 12-4

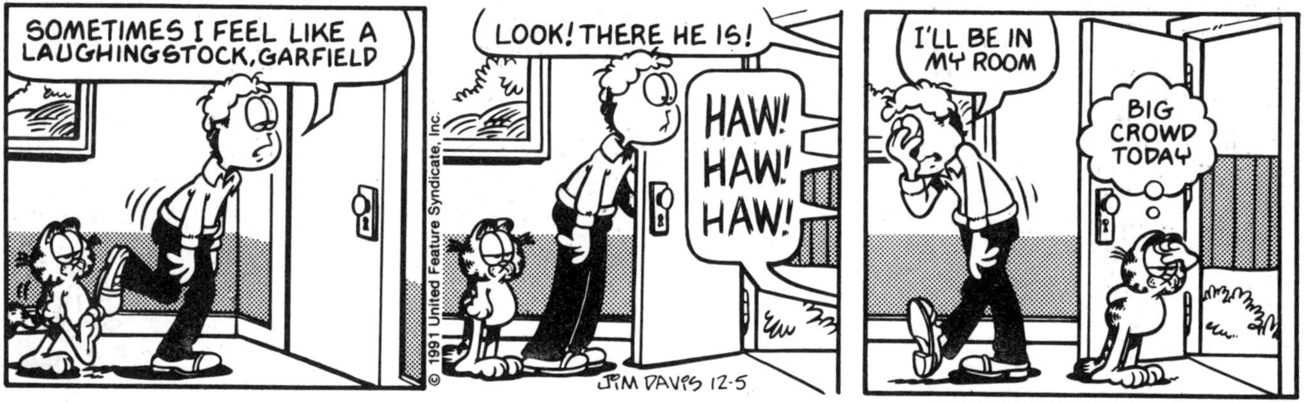
SOMETIMES I FEEL LIKE A LAUGHINGSTOCK, GARFIELD
LOOK! THERE HE IS!
HAW! HAW! HAW!
I'LL BE IN MY ROOM
BIG CROWD TODAY
© 1991 United Feature Syndicate, Inc.
JIM DAVIS 12-5

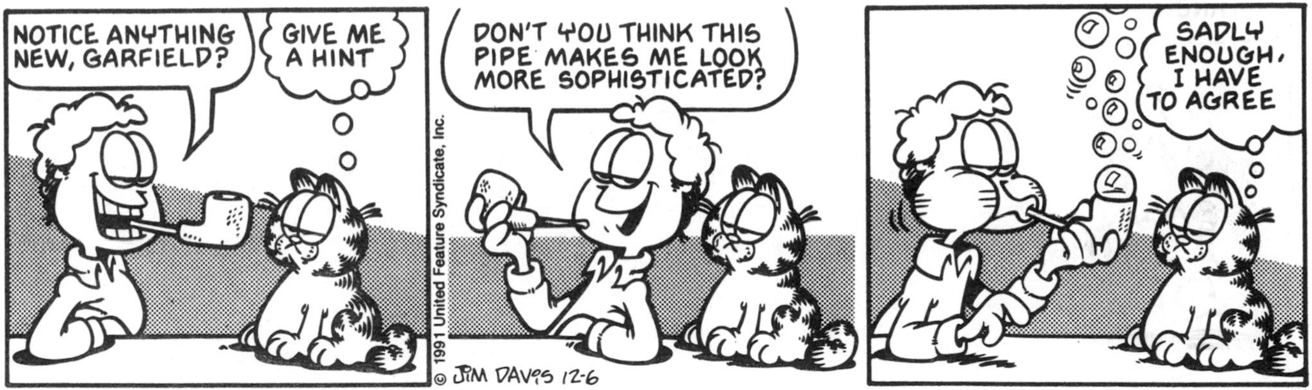
NOTICE ANYTHING NEW, GARFIELD?
GIVE ME A HINT
DON'T YOU THINK THIS PIPE MAKES ME LOOK MORE SOPHISTICATED?
SADLY ENOUGH, I HAVE TO AGREE
© 1991 United Feature Syndicate, Inc.
JIM DAVIS 12-6

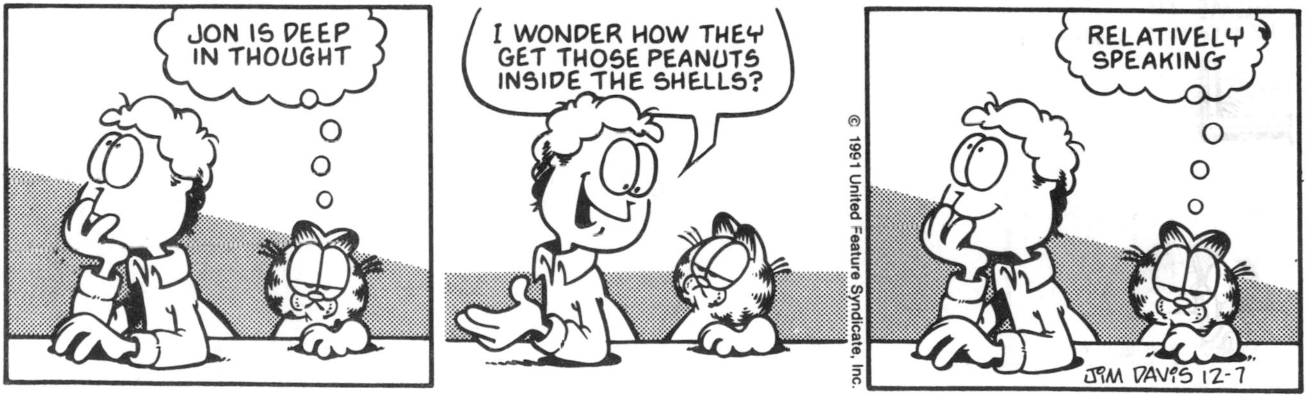
JON IS DEEP IN THOUGHT
I WONDER HOW THEY GET THOSE PEANUTS INSIDE THE SHELLS?
RELATIVELY SPEAKING
© 1991 United Feature Syndicate, Inc.
JIM DAVIS 12-7

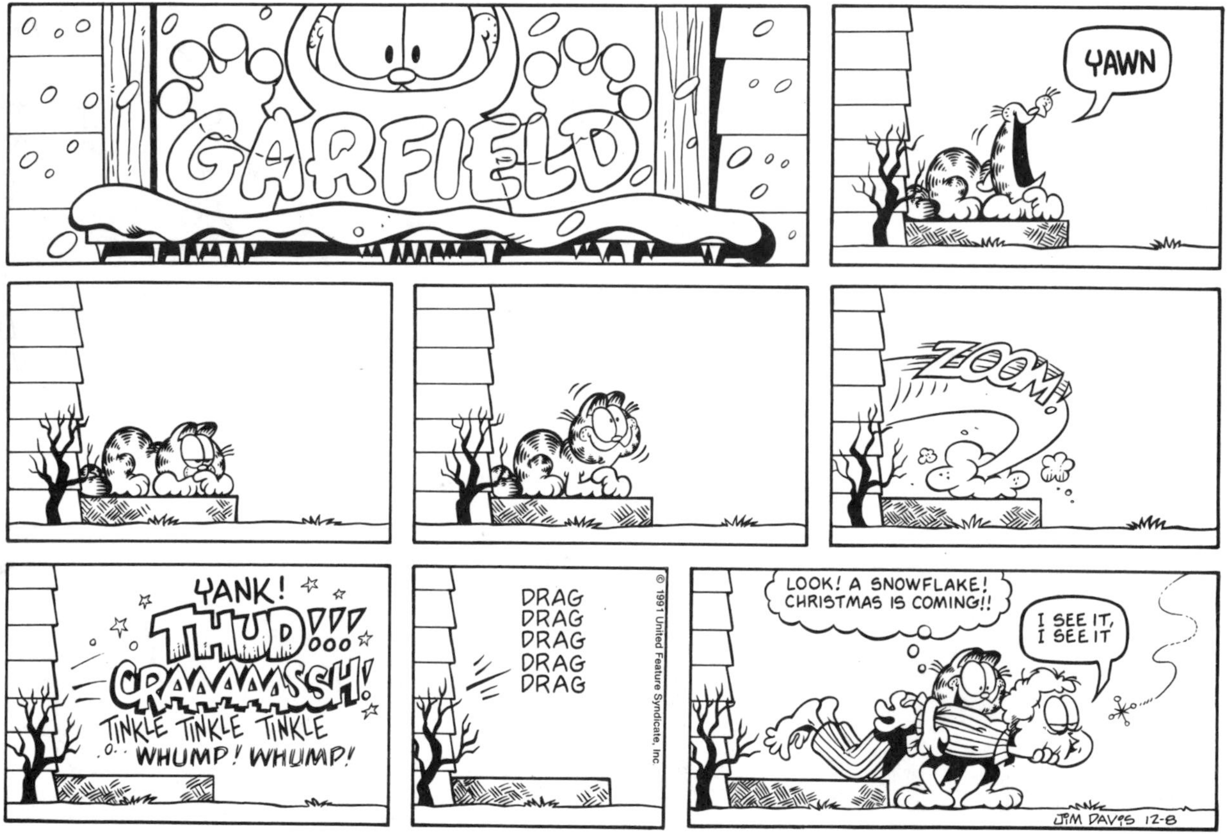
GARFIELD
YAWN
ZOOM
YANK! THUD!!! CRAAAAASSH! TINKLE TINKLE TINKLE WHUMP! WHUMP!
DRAG DRAG DRAG DRAG DRAG
© 1991 United Feature Syndicate, Inc.
LOOK! A SNOWFLAKE! CHRISTMAS IS COMING!!
I SEE IT, I SEE IT
JIM DAVIS 12-8

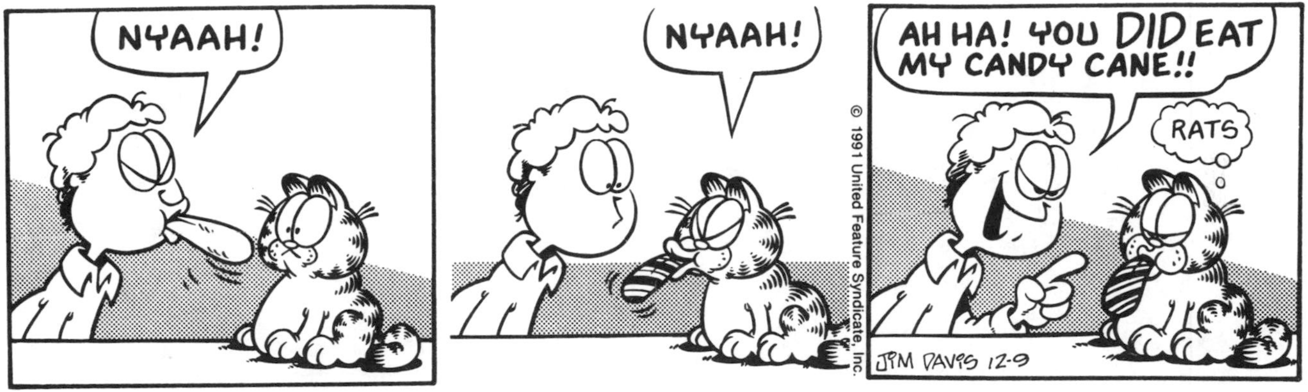
NYAAH!
NYAAH!
AH HA! YOU DID EAT MY CANDY CANE!!
RATS
© 1991 United Feature Syndicate, Inc.
JIM DAVIS 12-9

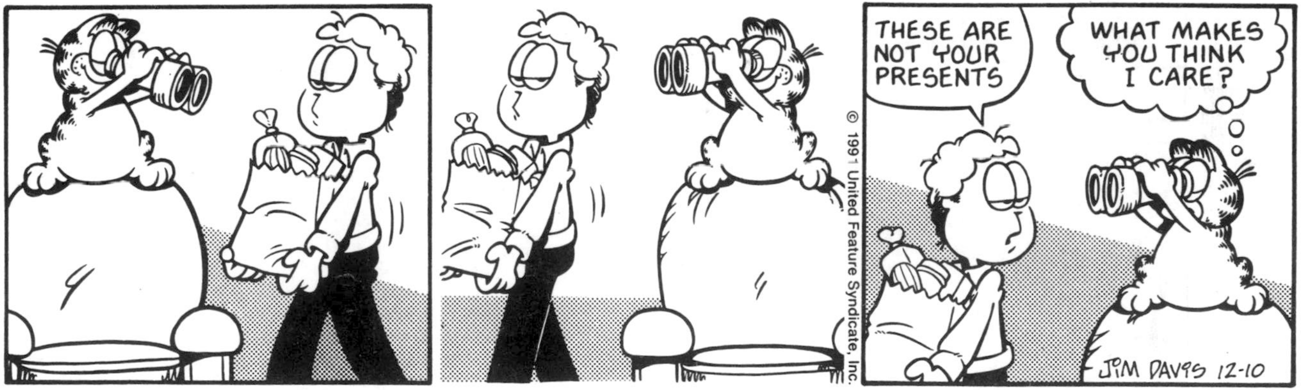
THESE ARE NOT YOUR PRESENTS
WHAT MAKES YOU THINK I CARE?
© 1991 United Feature Syndicate, Inc.
JIM DAVIS 12-10

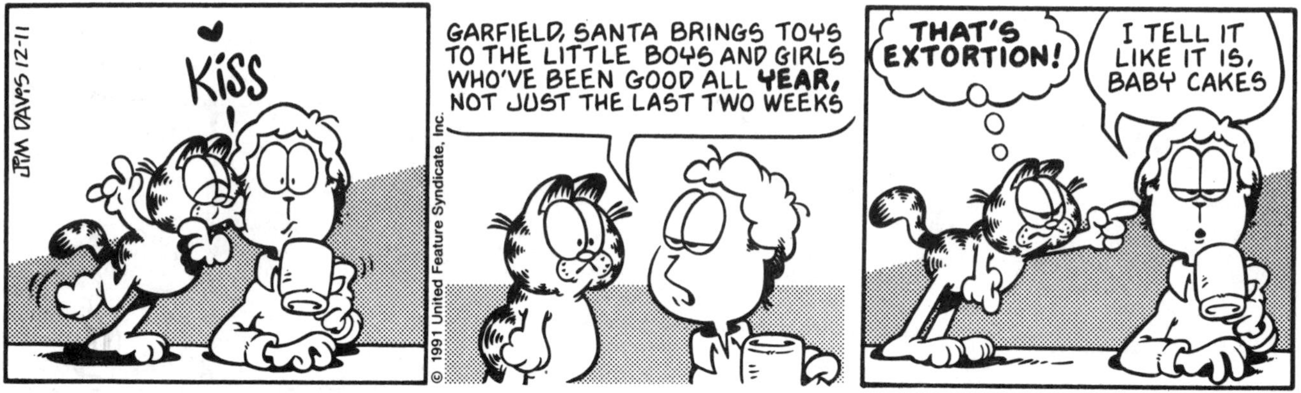
JIM DAVIS 12-11
KISS
© 1991 United Feature Syndicate, Inc.
GARFIELD, SANTA BRINGS TOYS TO THE LITTLE BOYS AND GIRLS WHO'VE BEEN GOOD ALL **YEAR,** NOT JUST THE LAST TWO WEEKS
THAT'S EXTORTION!
I TELL IT LIKE IT IS, BABY CAKES

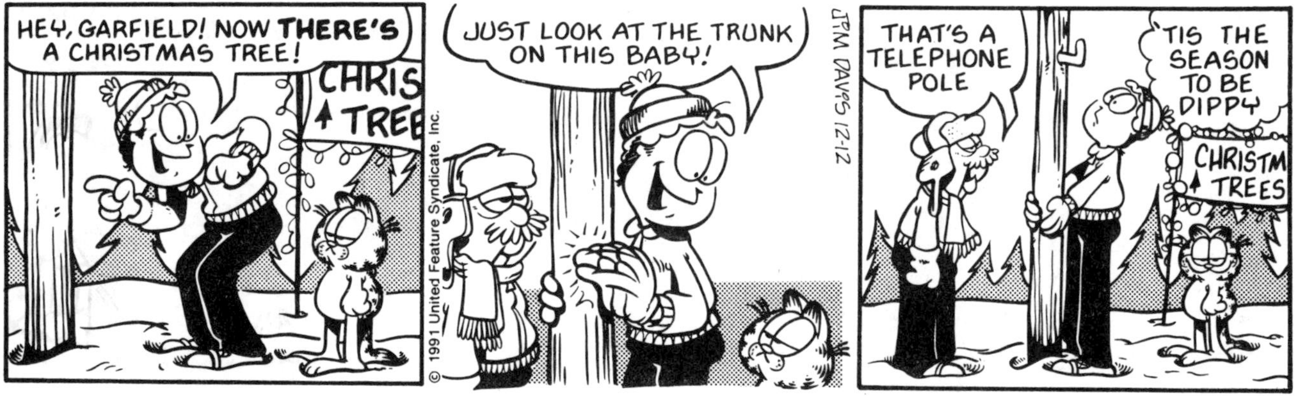
HEY, GARFIELD! NOW **THERE'S** A CHRISTMAS TREE!
CHRIS
TREE
© 1991 United Feature Syndicate, Inc.
JUST LOOK AT THE TRUNK ON THIS BABY!
JIM DAVIS 12-12
THAT'S A TELEPHONE POLE
'TIS THE SEASON TO BE DIPPY
CHRISTM
TREES

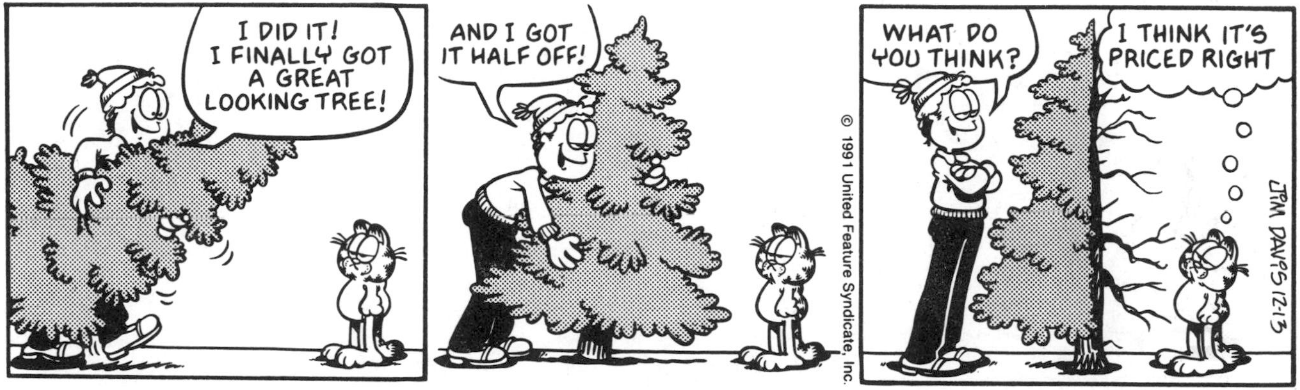
I DID IT! I FINALLY GOT A GREAT LOOKING TREE!
AND I GOT IT HALF OFF!
© 1991 United Feature Syndicate, Inc.
WHAT DO YOU THINK?
I THINK IT'S PRICED RIGHT
JIM DAVIS 12-13

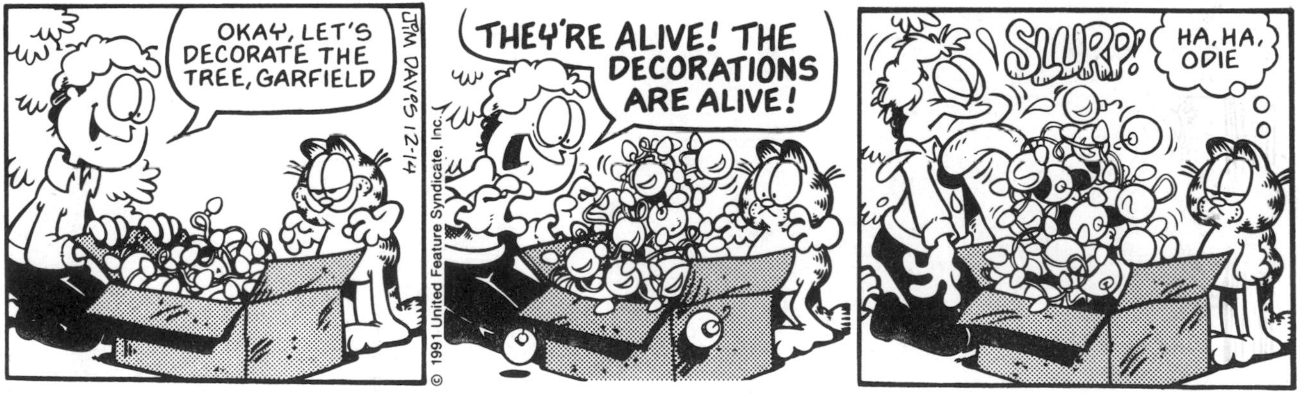
OKAY, LET'S DECORATE THE TREE, GARFIELD
JIM DAVIS 12-14
© 1991 United Feature Syndicate, Inc.
THEY'RE ALIVE! THE DECORATIONS ARE ALIVE!
SLURP!
HA, HA, ODIE

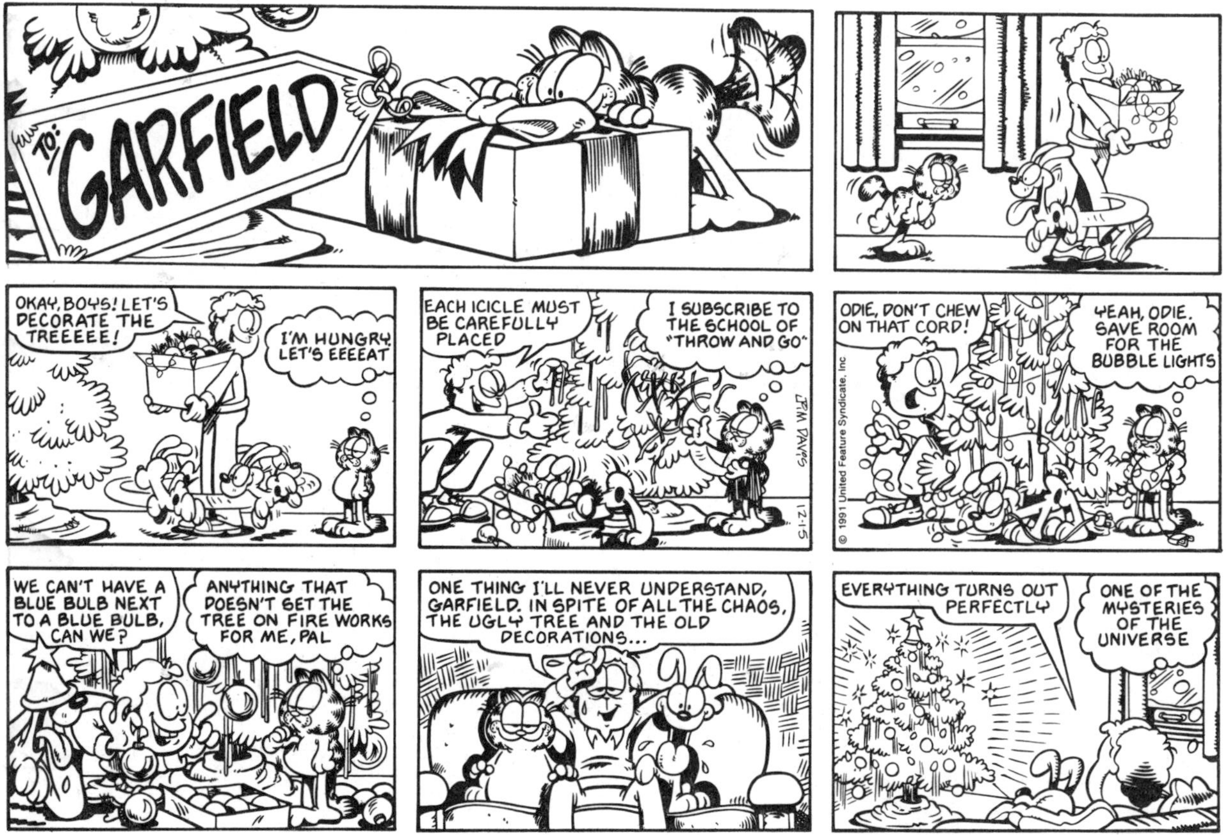

TO: GARFIELD
OKAY, BOYS! LET'S DECORATE THE TREEEEE!
I'M HUNGRY. LET'S EEEEAT
EACH ICICLE MUST BE CAREFULLY PLACED
I SUBSCRIBE TO THE SCHOOL OF "THROW AND GO"
JIM DAVIS
12-15
© 1991 United Feature Syndicate, Inc.
ODIE, DON'T CHEW ON THAT CORD!
YEAH, ODIE. SAVE ROOM FOR THE BUBBLE LIGHTS
WE CAN'T HAVE A BLUE BULB NEXT TO A BLUE BULB, CAN WE?
ANYTHING THAT DOESN'T SET THE TREE ON FIRE WORKS FOR ME, PAL
ONE THING I'LL NEVER UNDERSTAND, GARFIELD. IN SPITE OF ALL THE CHAOS, THE UGLY TREE AND THE OLD DECORATIONS...
EVERYTHING TURNS OUT PERFECTLY
ONE OF THE MYSTERIES OF THE UNIVERSE

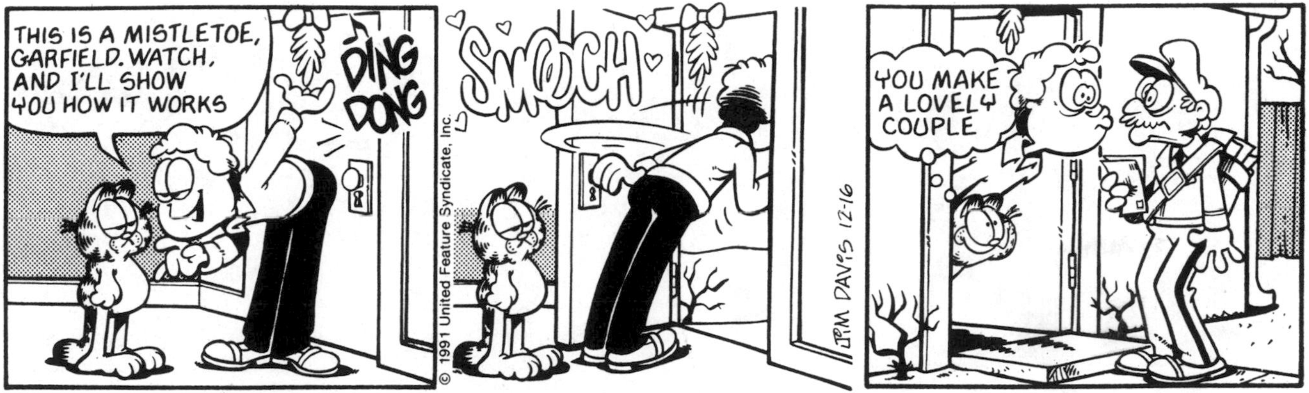
THIS IS A MISTLETOE, GARFIELD. WATCH, AND I'LL SHOW YOU HOW IT WORKS
DING DONG
SMOOCH
© 1991 United Feature Syndicate, Inc.
JIM DAVIS 12-16
YOU MAKE A LOVELY COUPLE

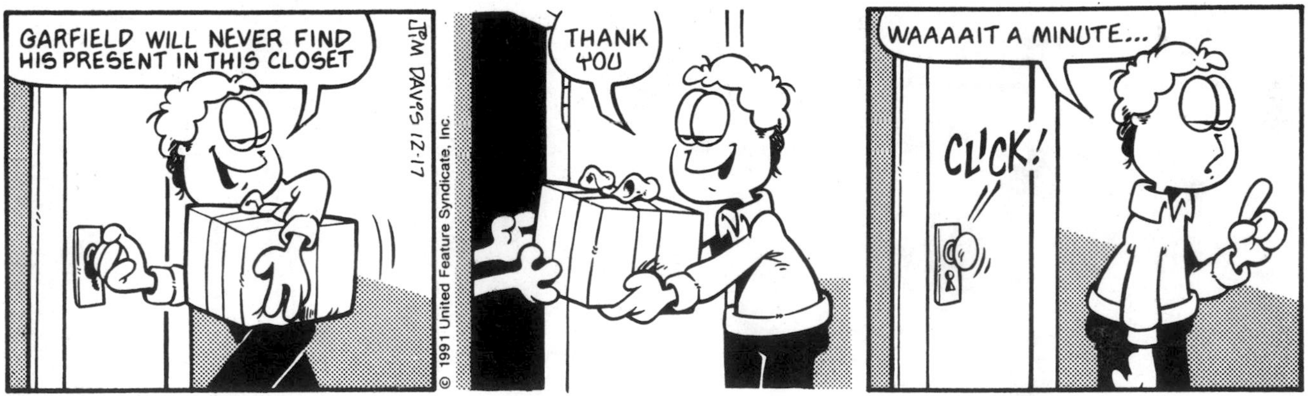
GARFIELD WILL NEVER FIND HIS PRESENT IN THIS CLOSET
JIM DAVIS 12-17
© 1991 United Feature Syndicate, Inc.
THANK YOU
WAAAAIT A MINUTE...
CLICK!

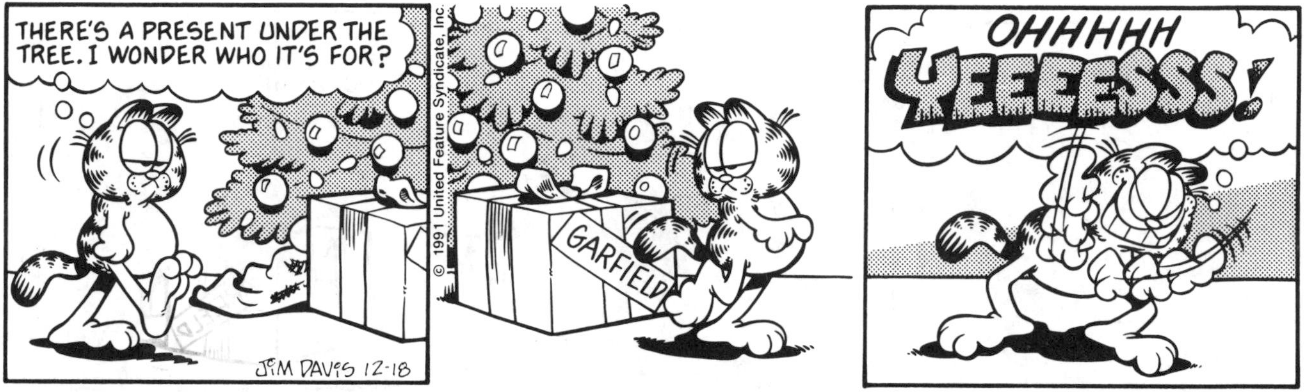
THERE'S A PRESENT UNDER THE TREE. I WONDER WHO IT'S FOR?
JIM DAVIS 12-18
© 1991 United Feature Syndicate, Inc.
GARFIELD
OHHHHH YEEEESSS!

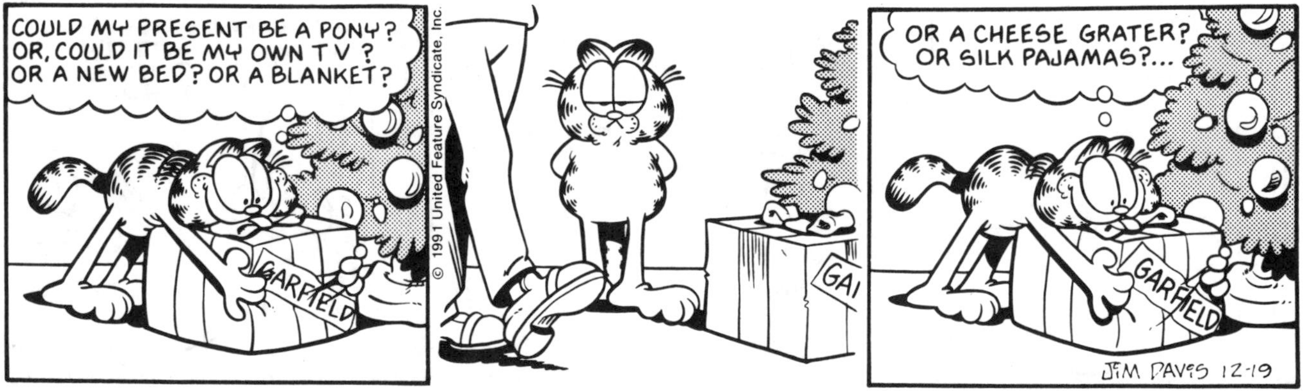
COULD MY PRESENT BE A PONY? OR, COULD IT BE MY OWN TV? OR A NEW BED? OR A BLANKET?
GARFIELD
© 1991 United Feature Syndicate, Inc.
GA
OR A CHEESE GRATER? OR SILK PAJAMAS?...
GARFIELD
JIM DAVIS 12-19

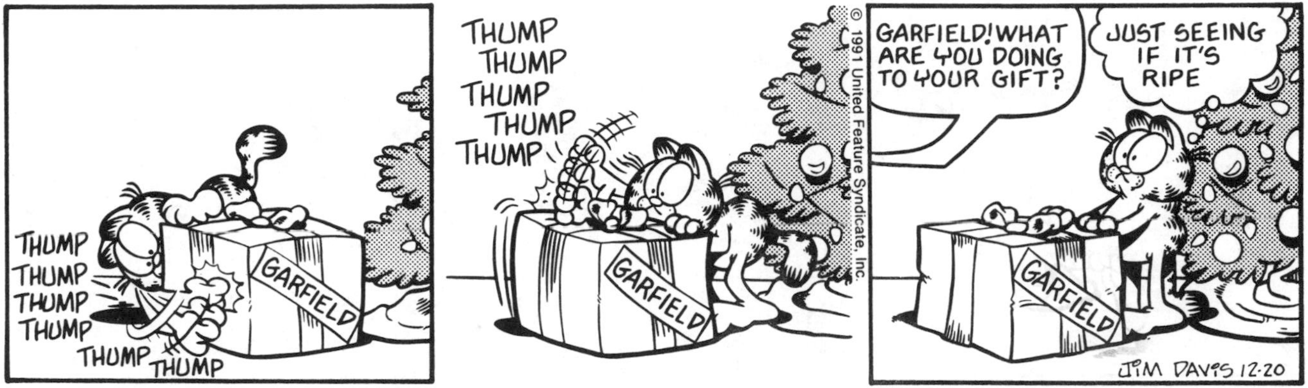
THUMP THUMP THUMP THUMP THUMP THUMP
THUMP THUMP THUMP THUMP THUMP
© 1991 United Feature Syndicate, Inc.
GARFIELD! WHAT ARE YOU DOING TO YOUR GIFT?
JUST SEEING IF IT'S RIPE
GARFIELD
JIM DAVIS 12-20

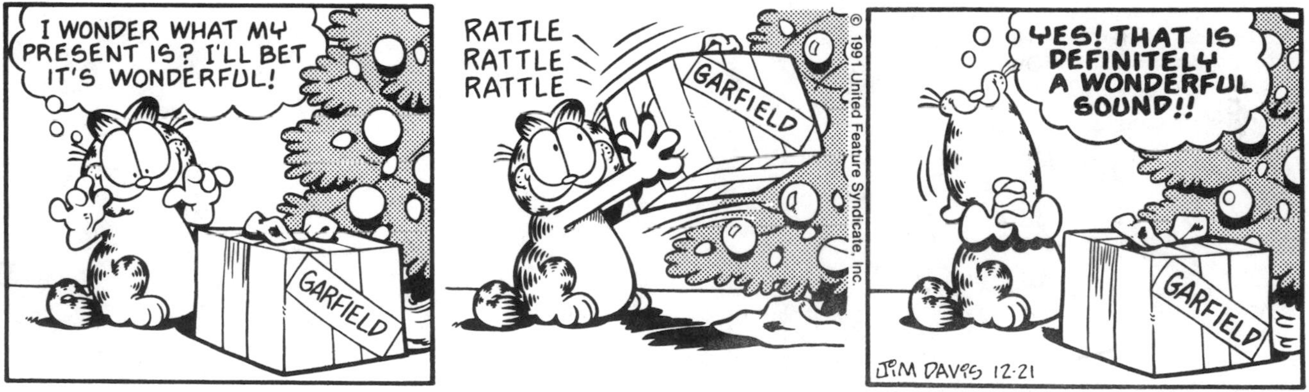
I WONDER WHAT MY PRESENT IS? I'LL BET IT'S WONDERFUL!
RATTLE RATTLE RATTLE
© 1991 United Feature Syndicate, Inc.
YES! THAT IS DEFINITELY A WONDERFUL SOUND!!
GARFIELD
JIM DAVIS 12-21

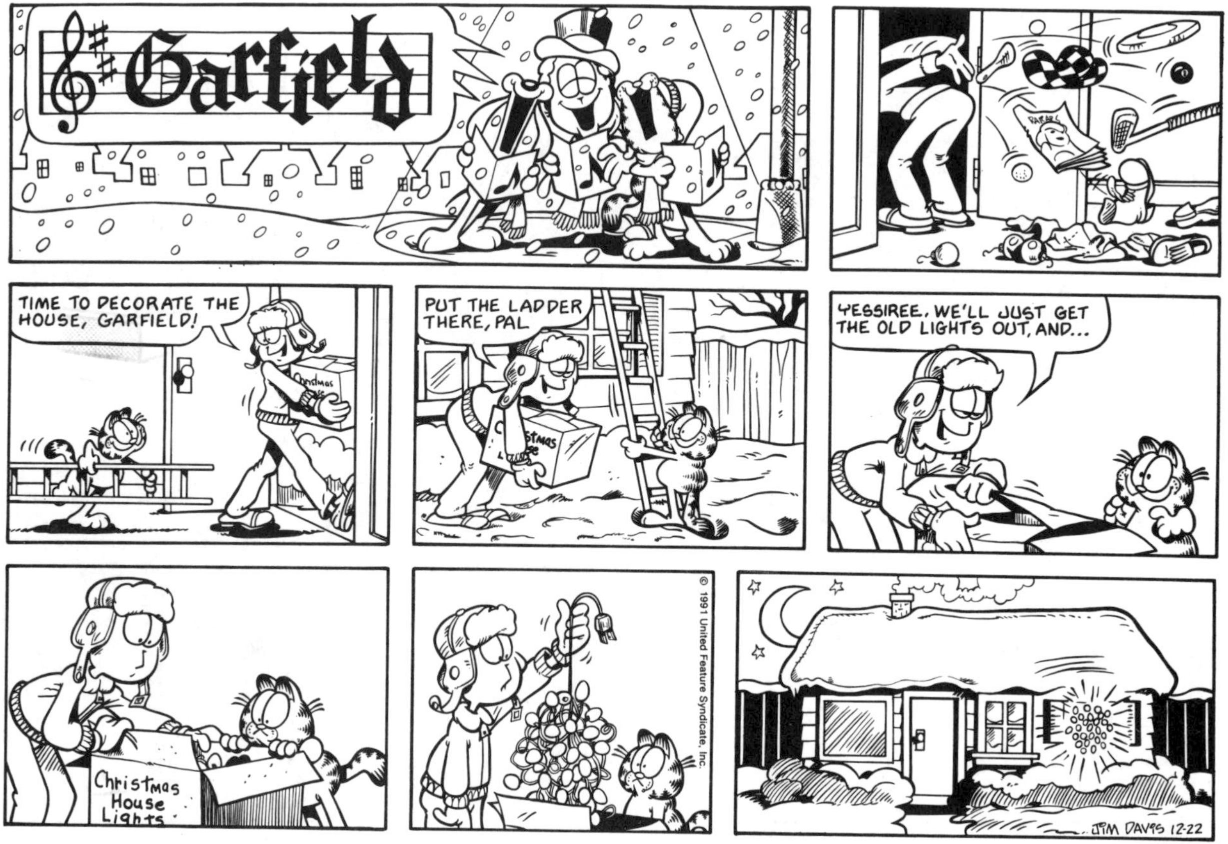
Garfield
TIME TO DECORATE THE HOUSE, GARFIELD!
Christmas
PUT THE LADDER THERE, PAL
YESSIREE, WE'LL JUST GET THE OLD LIGHTS OUT, AND...
Christmas House Lights
© 1991 United Feature Syndicate, Inc.
JIM DAVIS 12-22

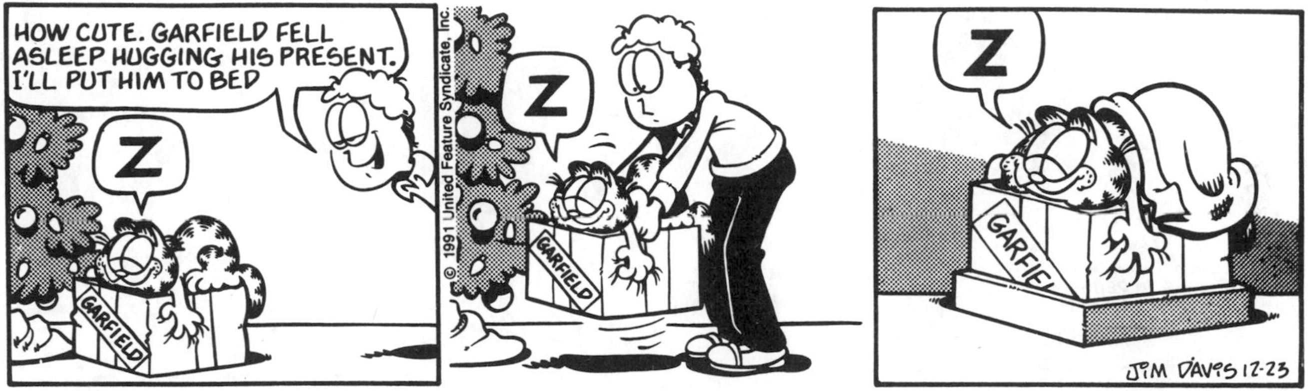
HOW CUTE. GARFIELD FELL ASLEEP HUGGING HIS PRESENT. I'LL PUT HIM TO BED
Z
GARFIELD
© 1991 United Feature Syndicate, Inc.
Z
GARFIELD
Z
GARFIEL
JIM DAVIS 12-23

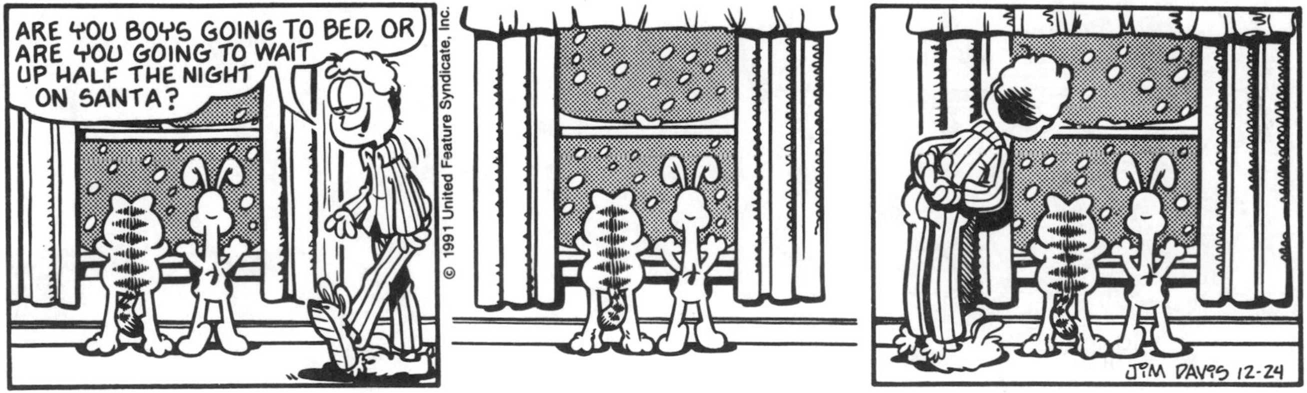
ARE YOU BOYS GOING TO BED, OR ARE YOU GOING TO WAIT UP HALF THE NIGHT ON SANTA?
© 1991 United Feature Syndicate, Inc.
JIM DAVIS 12-24

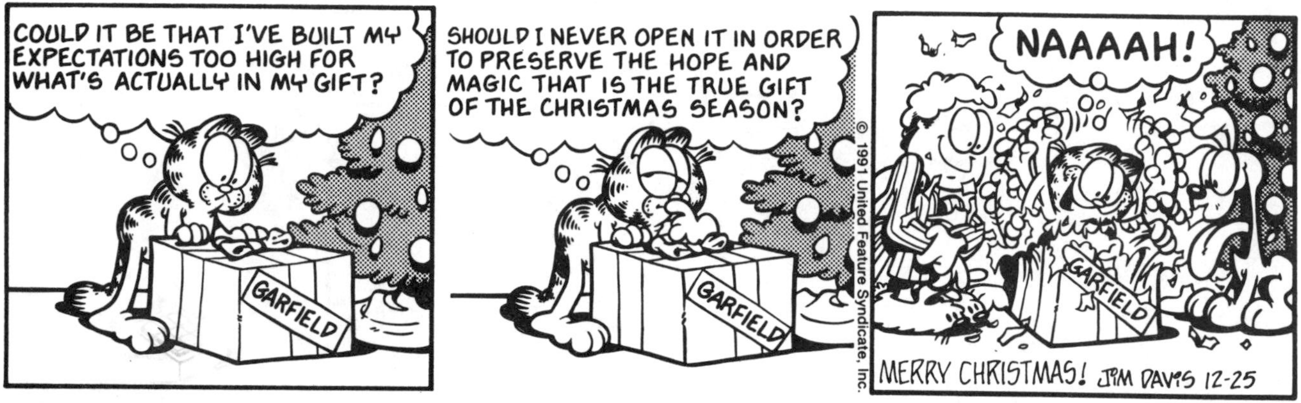
COULD IT BE THAT I'VE BUILT MY EXPECTATIONS TOO HIGH FOR WHAT'S ACTUALLY IN MY GIFT?
GARFIELD
SHOULD I NEVER OPEN IT IN ORDER TO PRESERVE THE HOPE AND MAGIC THAT IS THE TRUE GIFT OF THE CHRISTMAS SEASON?
GARFIELD
© 1991 United Feature Syndicate, Inc.
NAAAAH!
GARFIELD
MERRY CHRISTMAS! JIM DAVIS 12-25

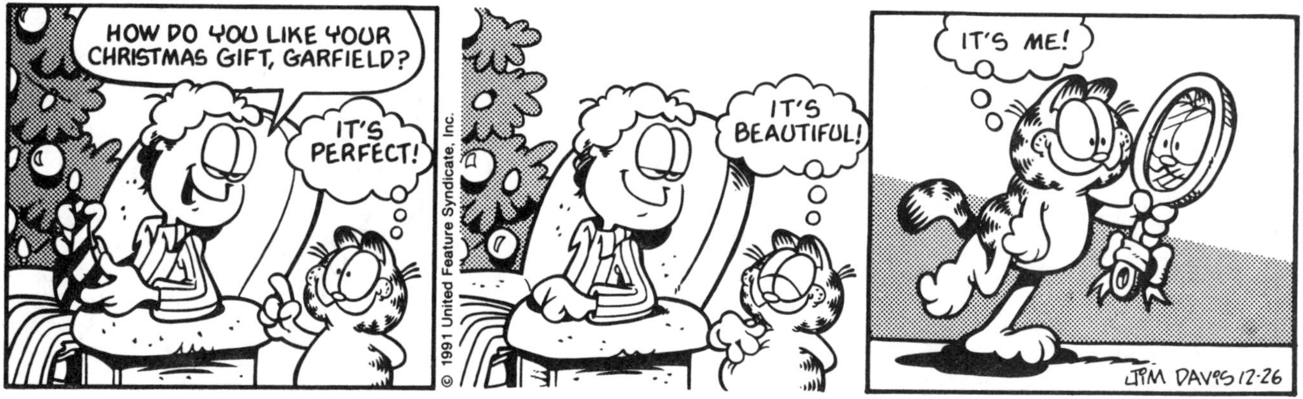
HOW DO YOU LIKE YOUR CHRISTMAS GIFT, GARFIELD?
IT'S PERFECT!
© 1991 United Feature Syndicate, Inc.
IT'S BEAUTIFUL!
IT'S ME!
JIM DAVIS 12-26

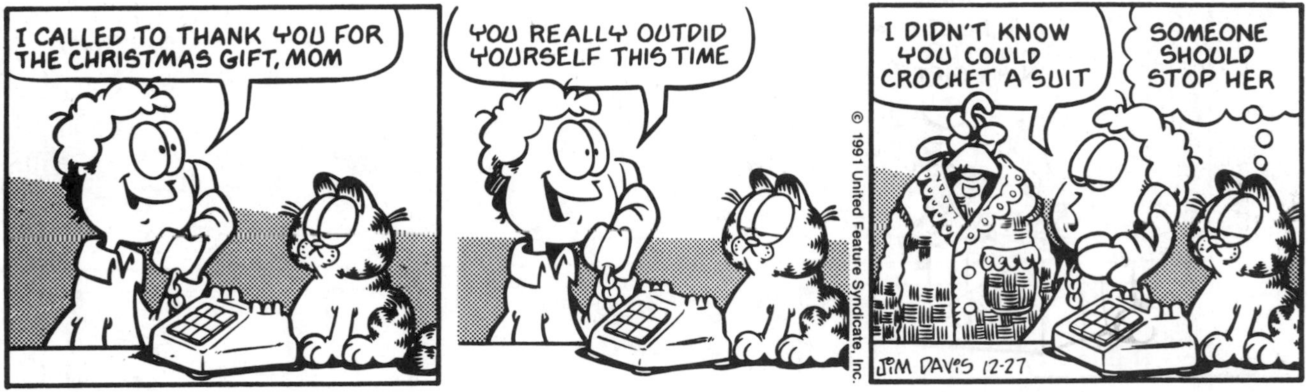
I CALLED TO THANK YOU FOR THE CHRISTMAS GIFT, MOM
YOU REALLY OUTDID YOURSELF THIS TIME
I DIDN'T KNOW YOU COULD CROCHET A SUIT
SOMEONE SHOULD STOP HER
JIM DAVIS 12-27
© 1991 United Feature Syndicate, Inc.

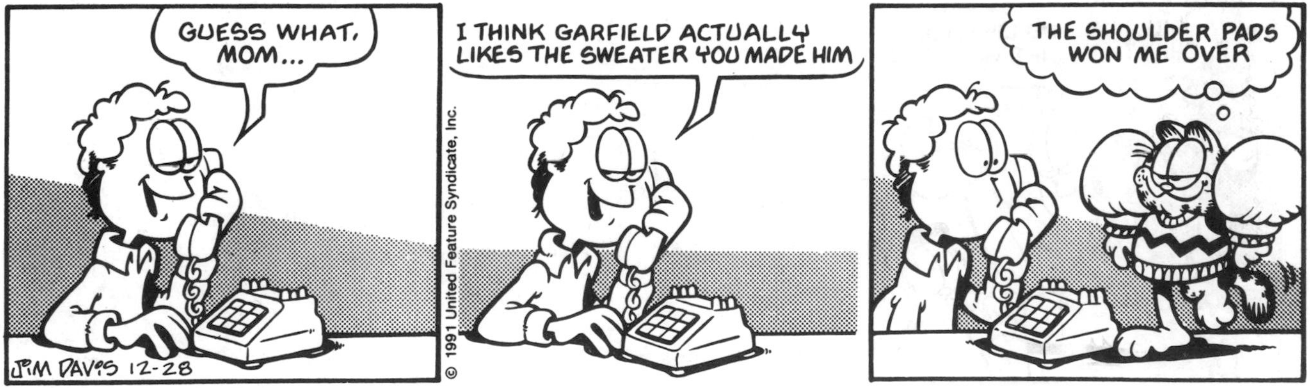
GUESS WHAT, MOM...
I THINK GARFIELD ACTUALLY LIKES THE SWEATER YOU MADE HIM
THE SHOULDER PADS WON ME OVER
JIM DAVIS 12-28
© 1991 United Feature Syndicate, Inc.

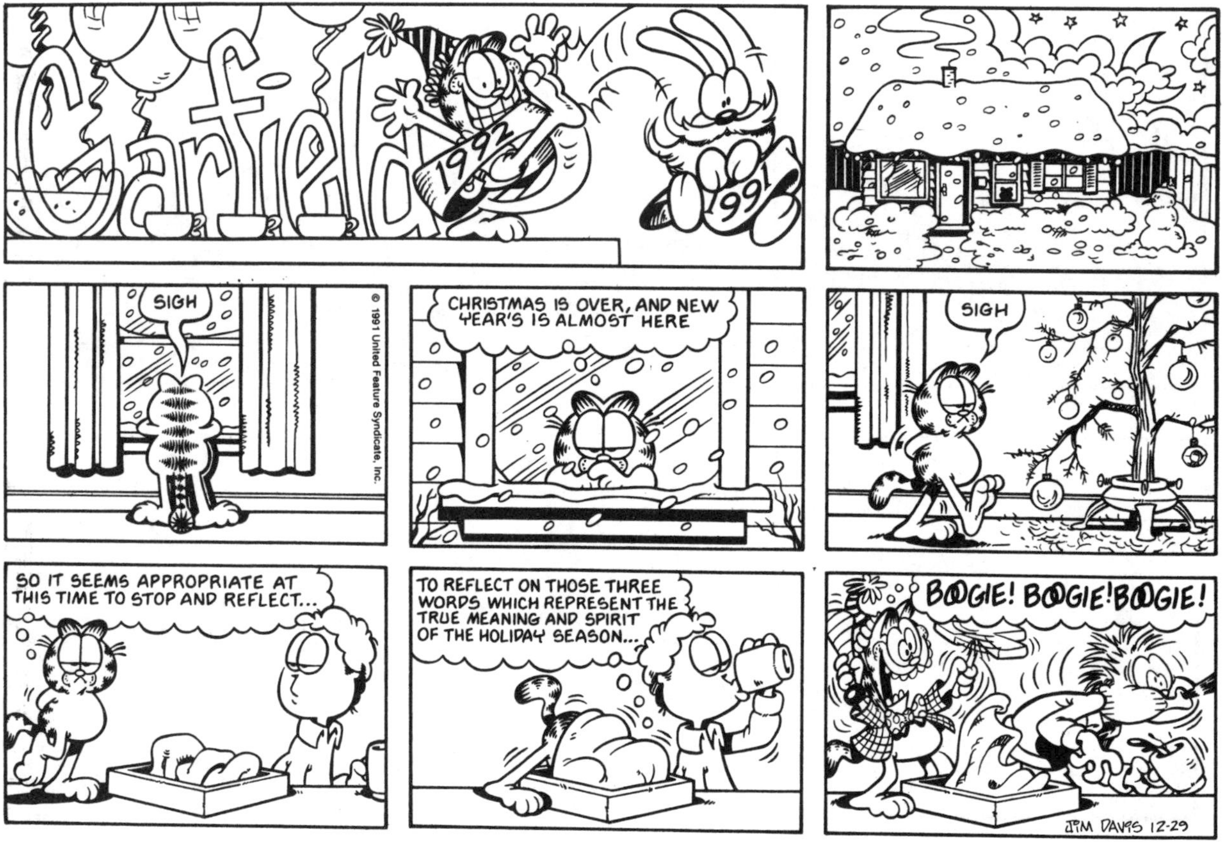

Garfield
1992
1991
SIGH
© 1991 United Feature Syndicate, Inc.
CHRISTMAS IS OVER, AND NEW YEAR'S IS ALMOST HERE
SIGH
SO IT SEEMS APPROPRIATE AT THIS TIME TO STOP AND REFLECT...
TO REFLECT ON THOSE THREE WORDS WHICH REPRESENT THE TRUE MEANING AND SPIRIT OF THE HOLIDAY SEASON...
BOOGIE! BOOGIE! BOOGIE!
JIM DAVIS 12-29

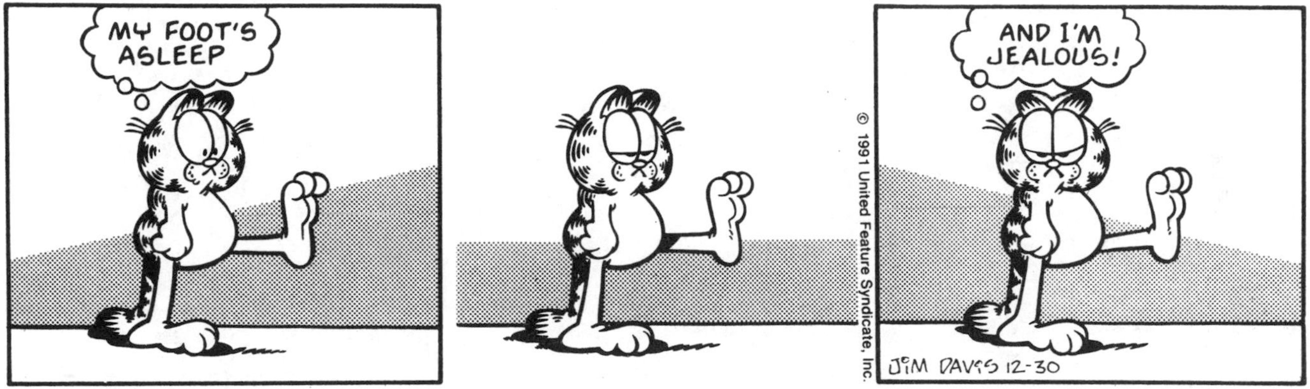
MY FOOT'S ASLEEP
AND I'M JEALOUS!
JIM DAVIS 12-30

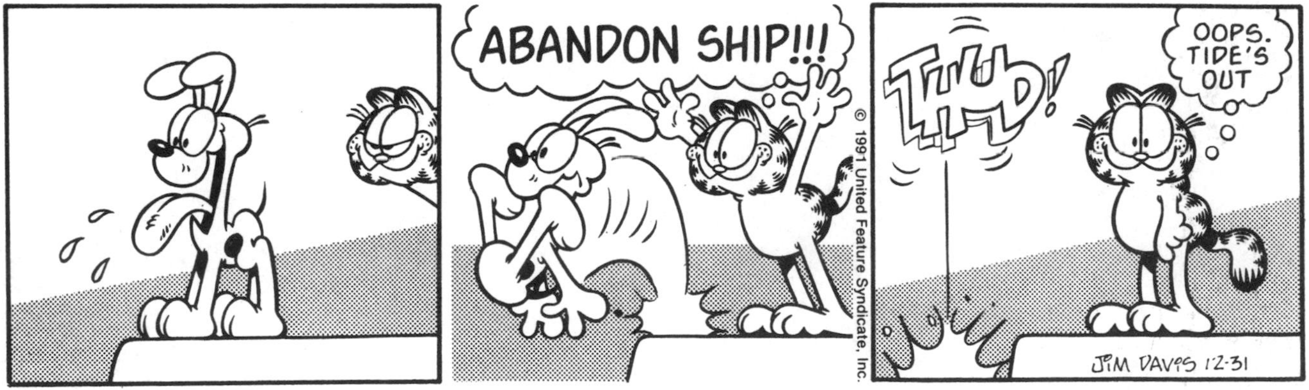
ABANDON SHIP!!!
THUD!
OOPS. TIDE'S OUT
JIM DAVIS 12-31

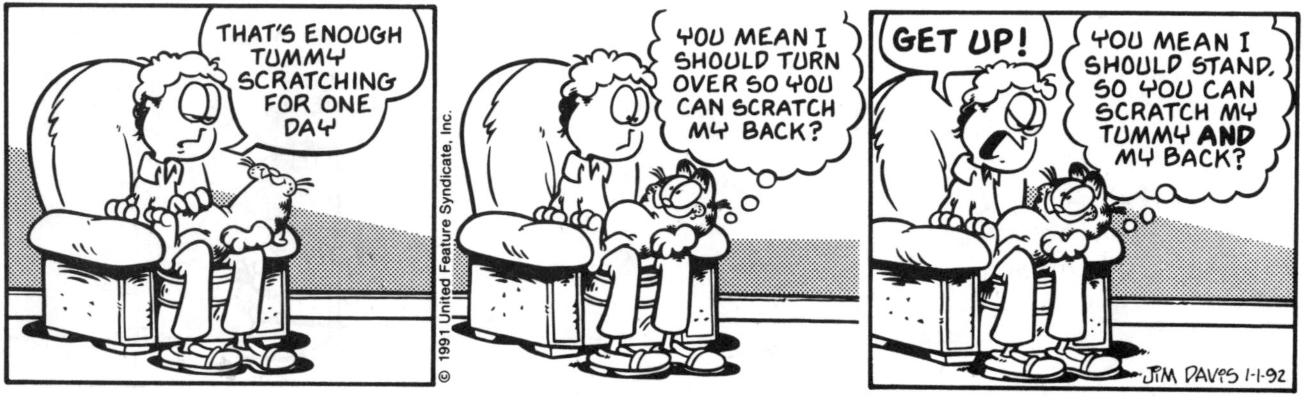
THAT'S ENOUGH TUMMY SCRATCHING FOR ONE DAY
YOU MEAN I SHOULD TURN OVER SO YOU CAN SCRATCH MY BACK?
GET UP!
YOU MEAN I SHOULD STAND, SO YOU CAN SCRATCH MY TUMMY **AND** MY BACK?
JIM DAVIS 1-1-92

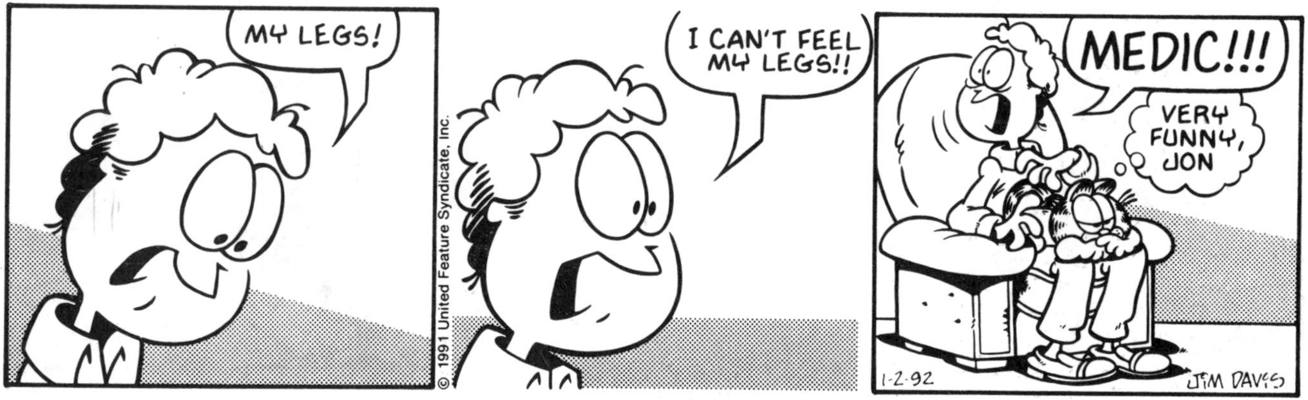
MY LEGS!
I CAN'T FEEL MY LEGS!!
MEDIC!!!
VERY FUNNY, JON
1-2-92
JIM DAVIS

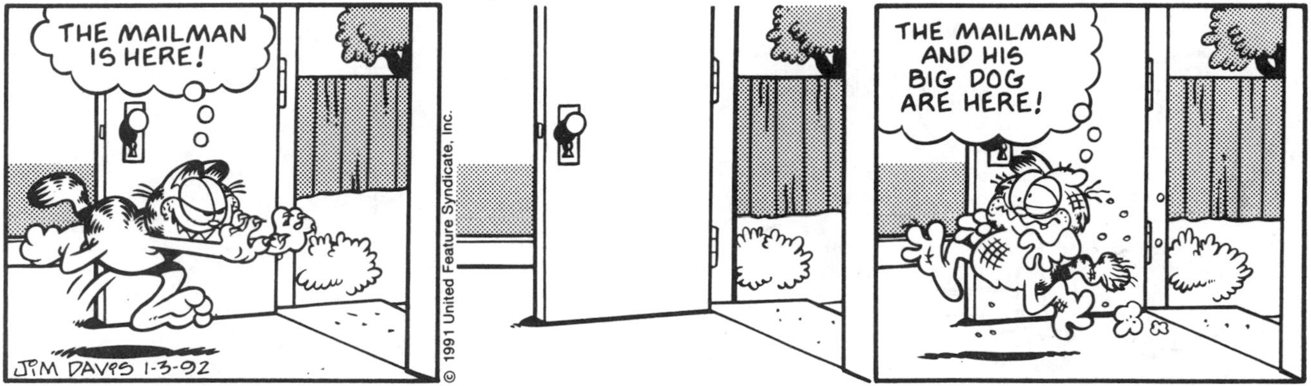
THE MAILMAN IS HERE!
JIM DAVIS 1-3-92
© 1991 United Feature Syndicate, Inc.
THE MAILMAN AND HIS BIG DOG ARE HERE!

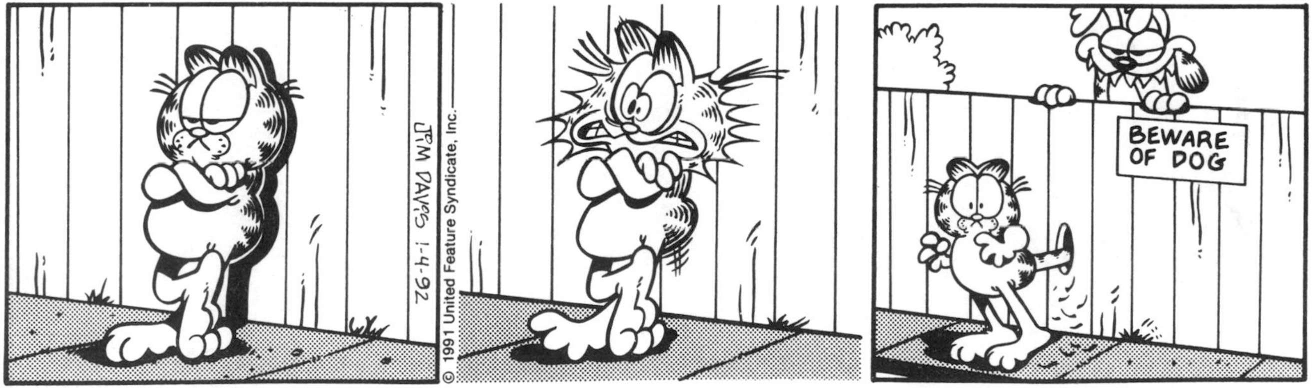
JIM DAVIS 1-4-92
© 1991 United Feature Syndicate, Inc.
BEWARE OF DOG

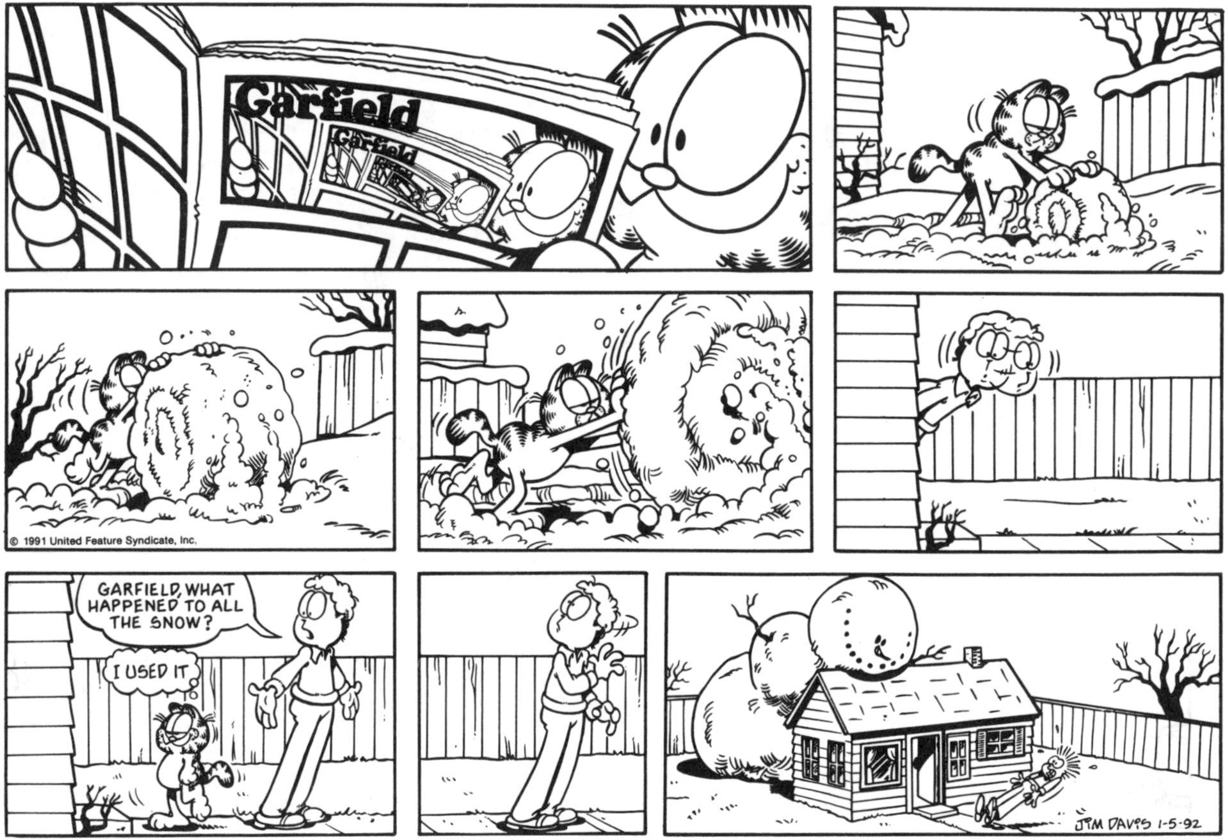
Garfield
Garfield
© 1991 United Feature Syndicate, Inc.
GARFIELD, WHAT HAPPENED TO ALL THE SNOW?
I USED IT
JIM DAVIS 1-5-92

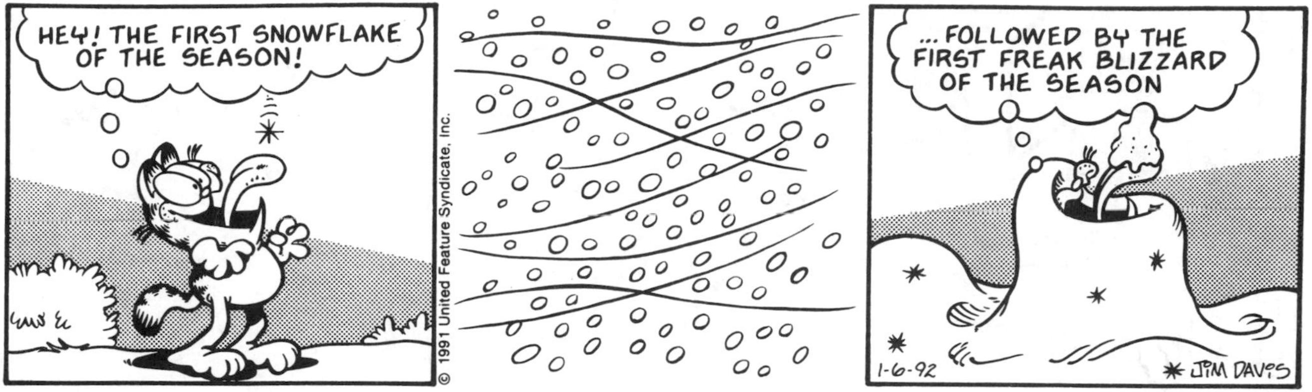
HEY! THE FIRST SNOWFLAKE OF THE SEASON!
© 1991 United Feature Syndicate, Inc.
...FOLLOWED BY THE FIRST FREAK BLIZZARD OF THE SEASON
1-6-92
JIM DAVIS

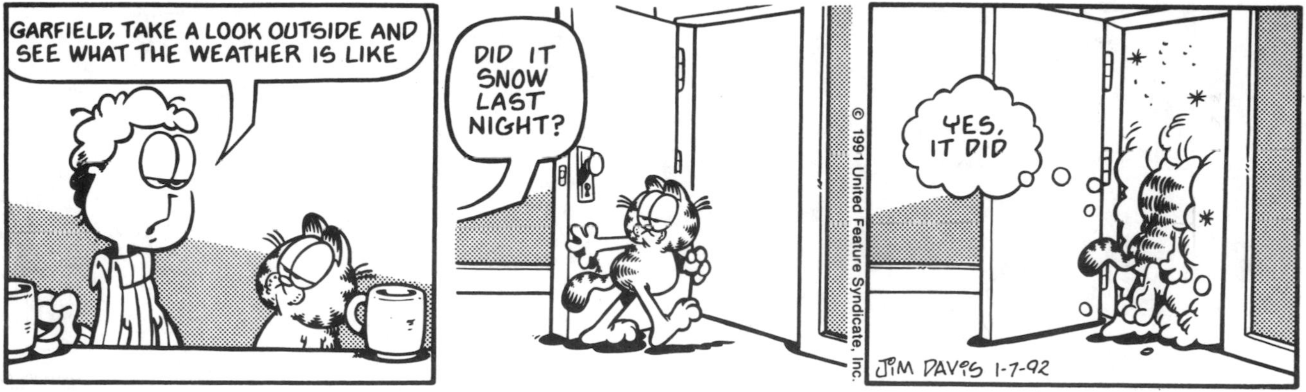
GARFIELD, TAKE A LOOK OUTSIDE AND SEE WHAT THE WEATHER IS LIKE
DID IT SNOW LAST NIGHT?
© 1991 United Feature Syndicate, Inc.
YES, IT DID
JIM DAVIS 1-7-92

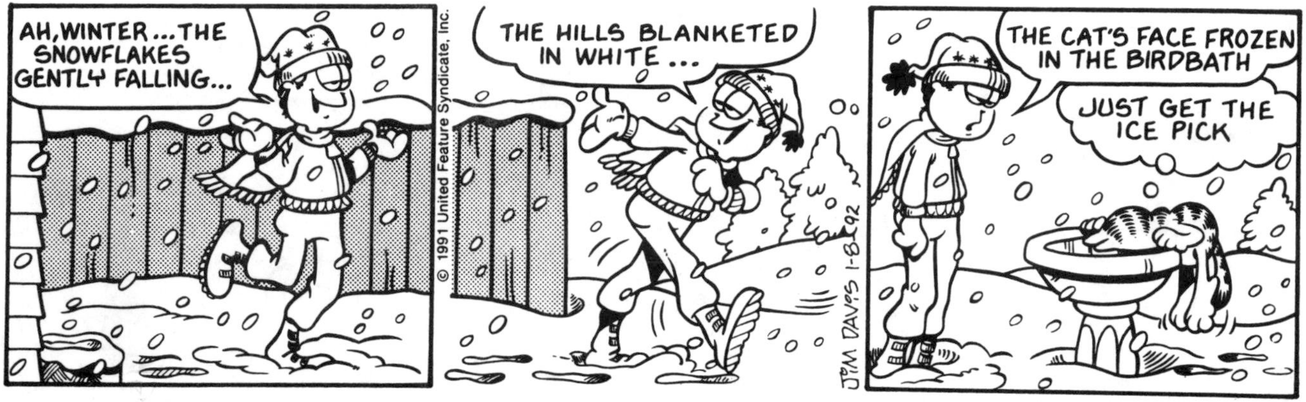
AH, WINTER... THE SNOWFLAKES GENTLY FALLING...
© 1991 United Feature Syndicate, Inc.
THE HILLS BLANKETED IN WHITE...
JIM DAVIS 1-8-92
THE CAT'S FACE FROZEN IN THE BIRDBATH
JUST GET THE ICE PICK

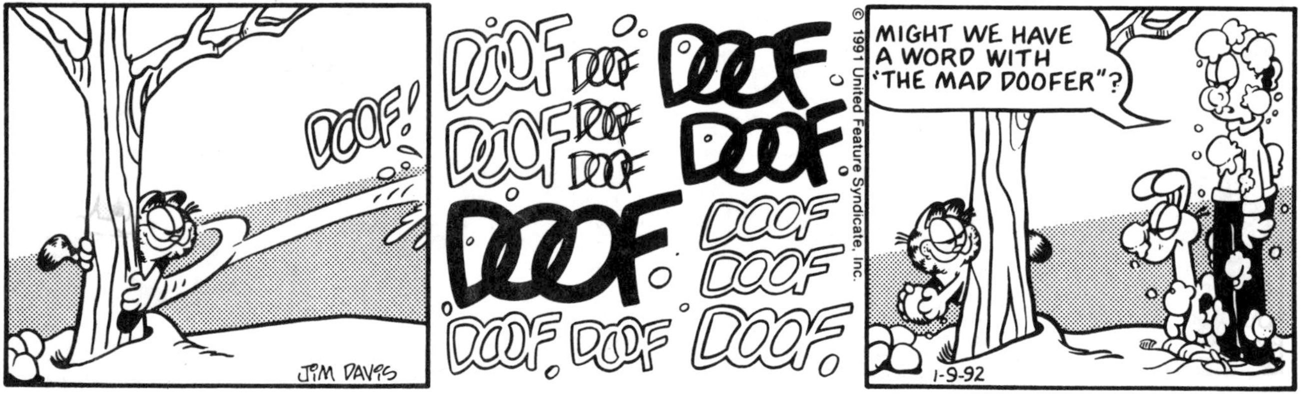
DOOF!
JIM DAVIS
DOOF DOOF DOOF
DOOF DOOF DOOF
DOOF
DOOF
DOOF DOOF DOOF
DOOF DOOF DOOF
© 1991 United Feature Syndicate, Inc.
MIGHT WE HAVE A WORD WITH "THE MAD DOOFER"?
1-9-92

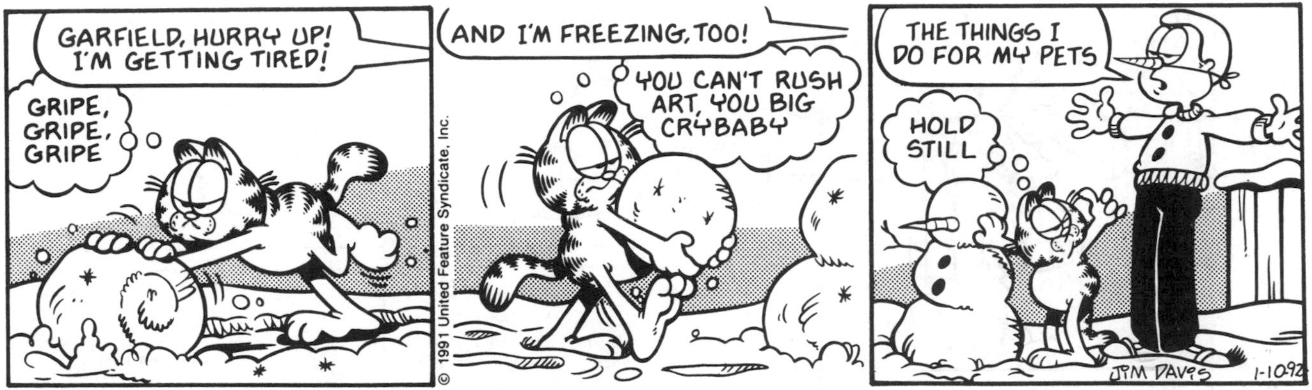
GARFIELD, HURRY UP! I'M GETTING TIRED!
GRIPE, GRIPE, GRIPE
© 1991 United Feature Syndicate, Inc.
AND I'M FREEZING, TOO!
YOU CAN'T RUSH ART, YOU BIG CRYBABY
THE THINGS I DO FOR MY PETS
HOLD STILL
JIM DAVIS 1-10-92

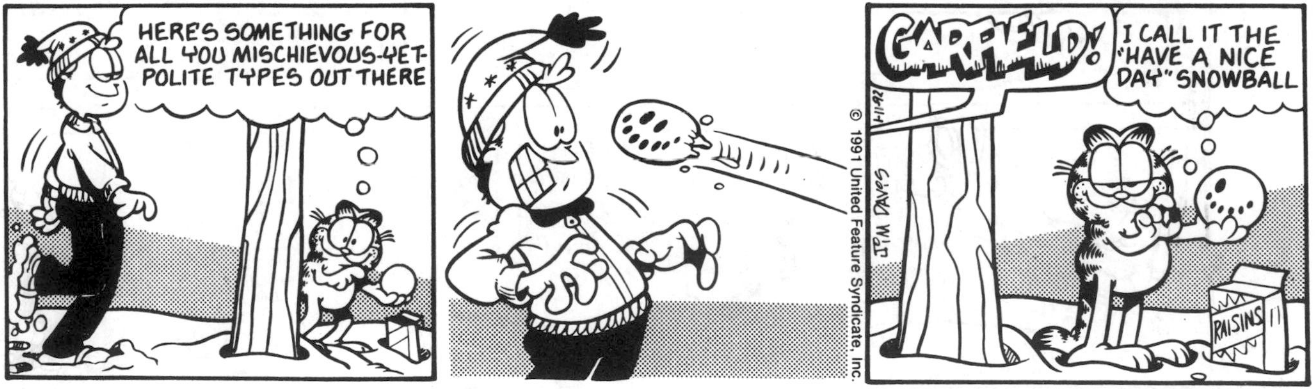
HERE'S SOMETHING FOR ALL YOU MISCHIEVOUS-YET-POLITE TYPES OUT THERE
© 1991 United Feature Syndicate, Inc.
JIM DAVIS 1-11-92
GARFIELD!
I CALL IT THE "HAVE A NICE DAY" SNOWBALL
RAISINS

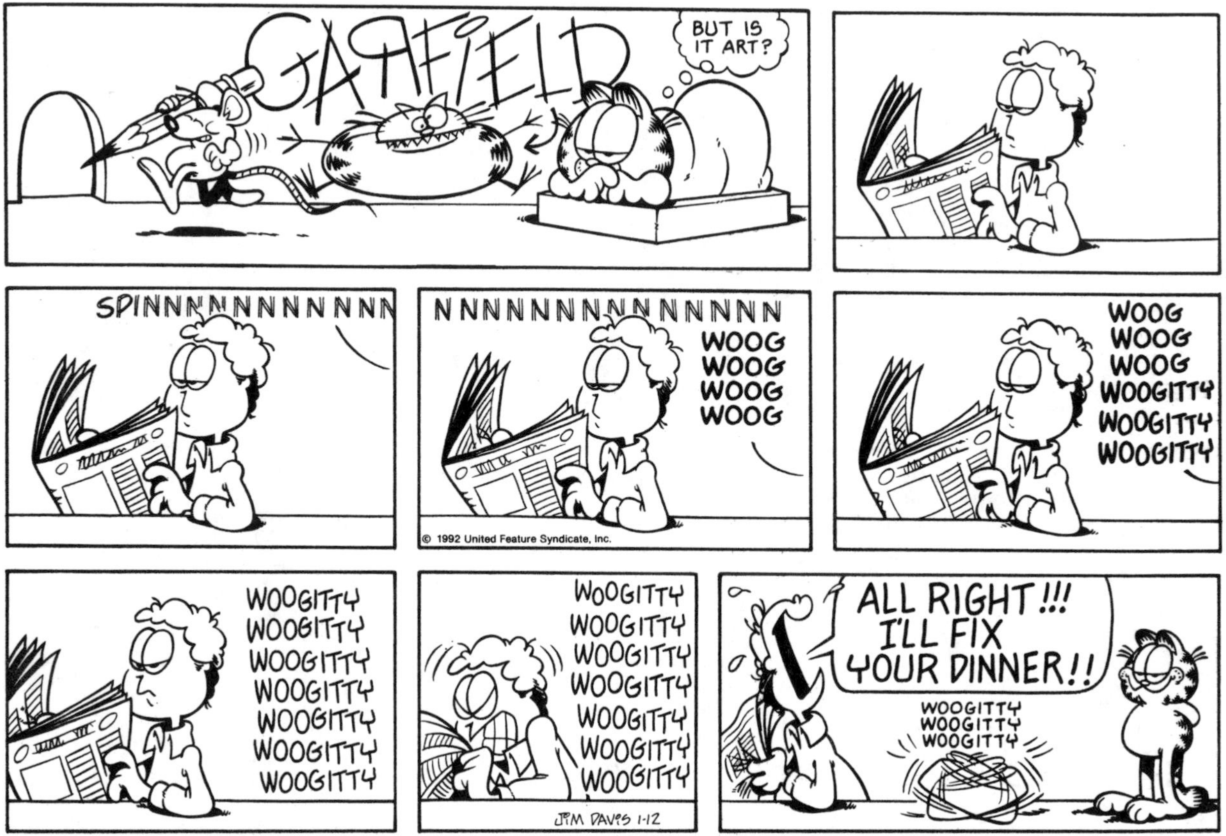
GARFIELD
BUT IS IT ART?
SPINNNNNNNNNNNN
NNNNNNNNNNNNNNNN
WOOG WOOG WOOG WOOG
© 1992 United Feature Syndicate, Inc.
WOOG WOOG WOOG WOOGITTY WOOGITTY WOOGITTY
WOOGITTY WOOGITTY WOOGITTY WOOGITTY WOOGITTY WOOGITTY WOOGITTY
WOOGITTY WOOGITTY WOOGITTY WOOGITTY WOOGITTY WOOGITTY WOOGITTY WOOGITTY
JIM DAVIS 1-12
ALL RIGHT!!! I'LL FIX YOUR DINNER!!
WOOGITTY WOOGITTY WOOGITTY

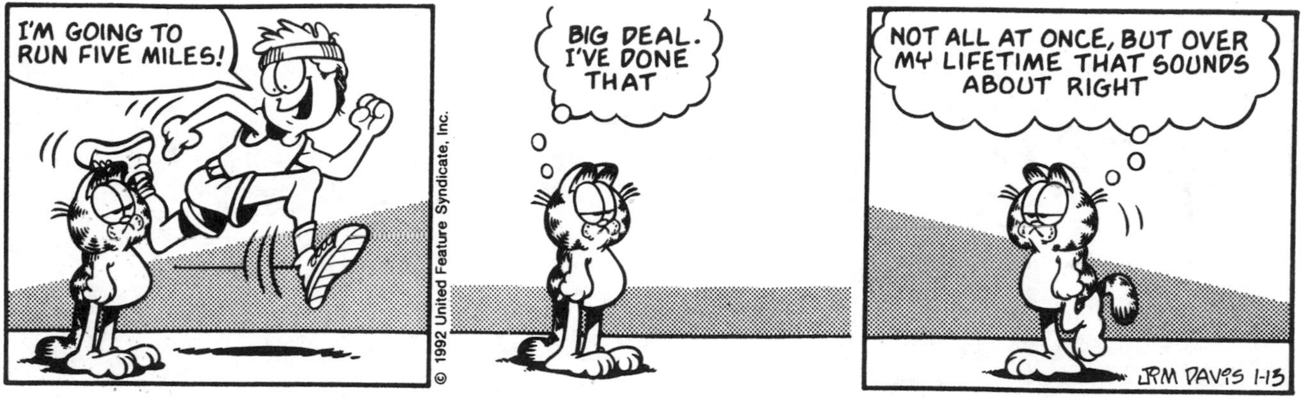
I'M GOING TO RUN FIVE MILES!
© 1992 United Feature Syndicate, Inc.
BIG DEAL. I'VE DONE THAT
NOT ALL AT ONCE, BUT OVER MY LIFETIME THAT SOUNDS ABOUT RIGHT
JIM DAVIS 1-13

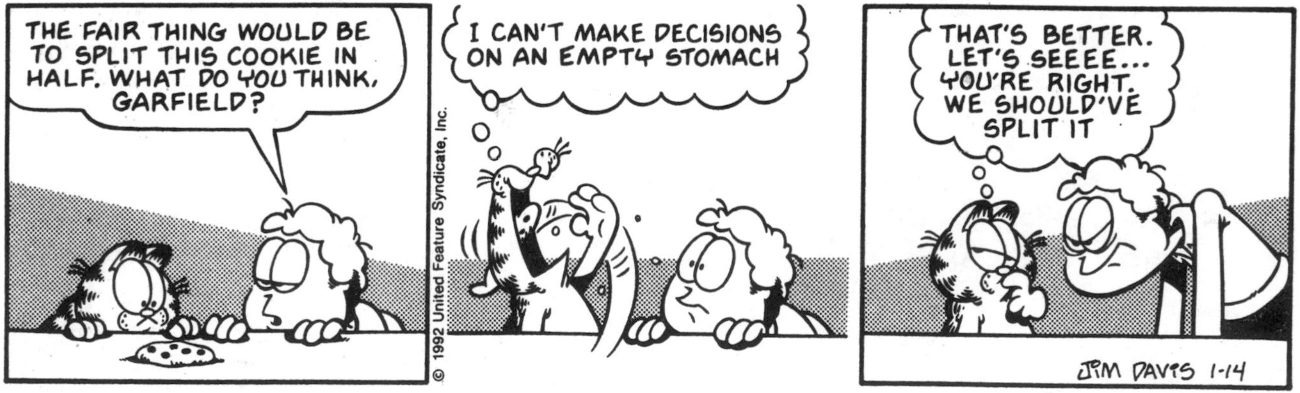
THE FAIR THING WOULD BE TO SPLIT THIS COOKIE IN HALF. WHAT DO YOU THINK, GARFIELD?
© 1992 United Feature Syndicate, Inc.
I CAN'T MAKE DECISIONS ON AN EMPTY STOMACH
THAT'S BETTER. LET'S SEEEE... YOU'RE RIGHT. WE SHOULD'VE SPLIT IT
JIM DAVIS 1-14

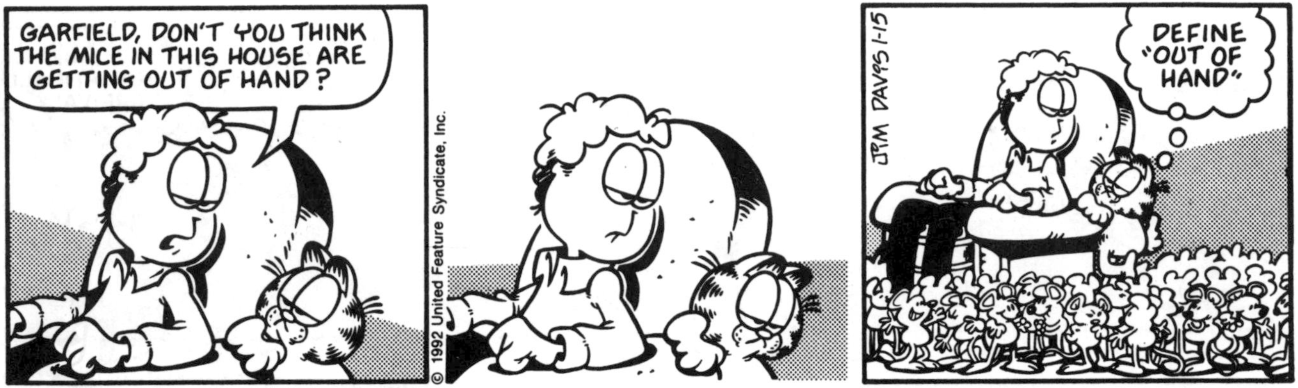
GARFIELD, DON'T YOU THINK THE MICE IN THIS HOUSE ARE GETTING OUT OF HAND?
© 1992 United Feature Syndicate, Inc.
JIM DAVIS 1-15
DEFINE "OUT OF HAND"

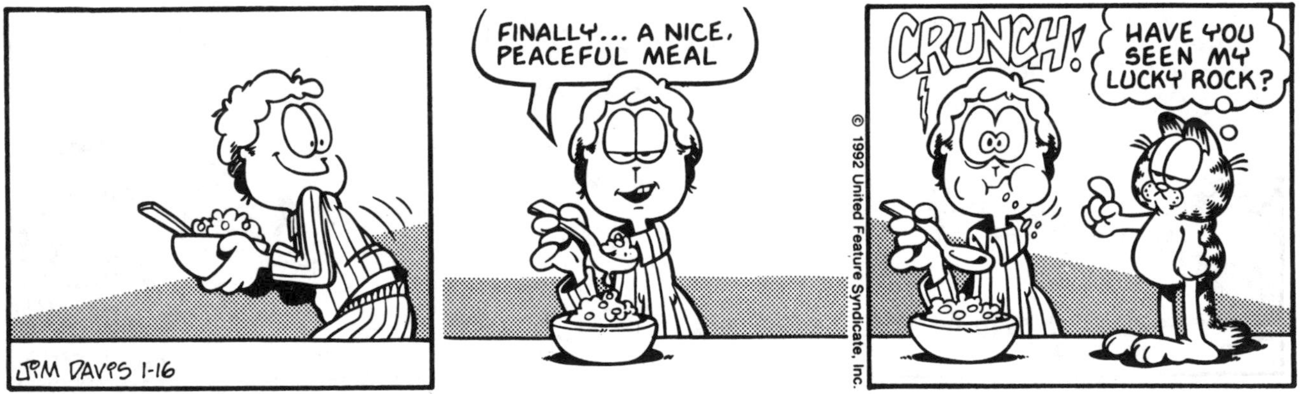
JIM DAVIS 1-16
FINALLY... A NICE, PEACEFUL MEAL
© 1992 United Feature Syndicate, Inc.
CRUNCH!
HAVE YOU SEEN MY LUCKY ROCK?

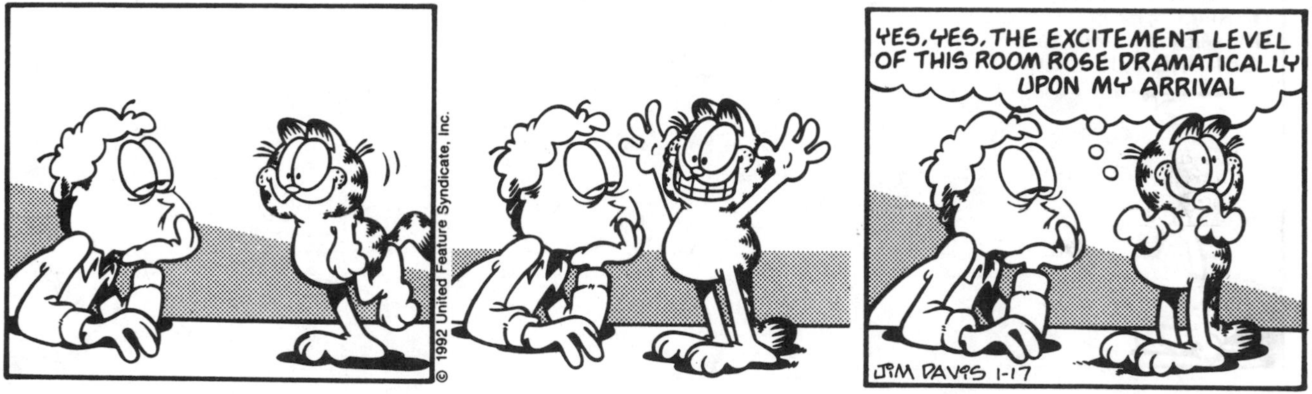
© 1992 United Feature Syndicate, Inc.
YES, YES, THE EXCITEMENT LEVEL OF THIS ROOM ROSE DRAMATICALLY UPON MY ARRIVAL
JIM DAVIS 1-17

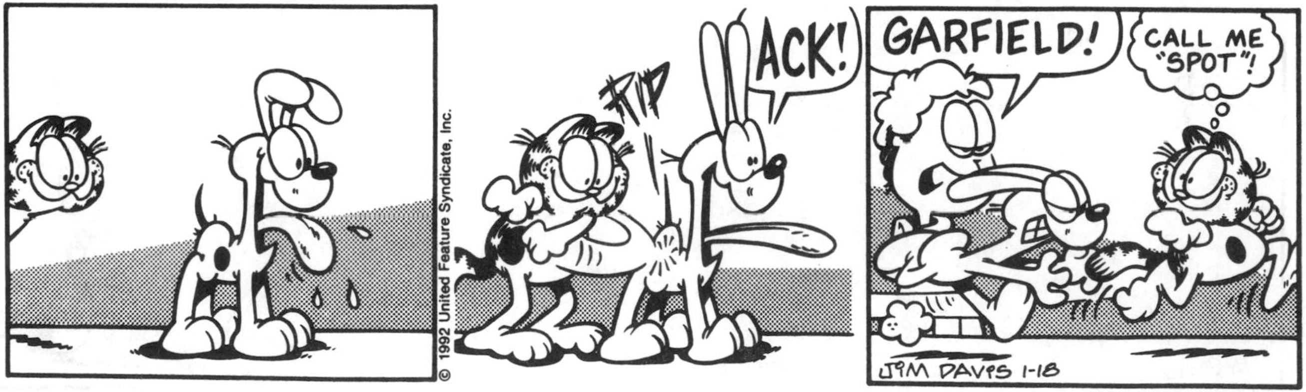
© 1992 United Feature Syndicate, Inc.
RIP
ACK!
GARFIELD!
CALL ME "SPOT"!
JIM DAVIS 1-18

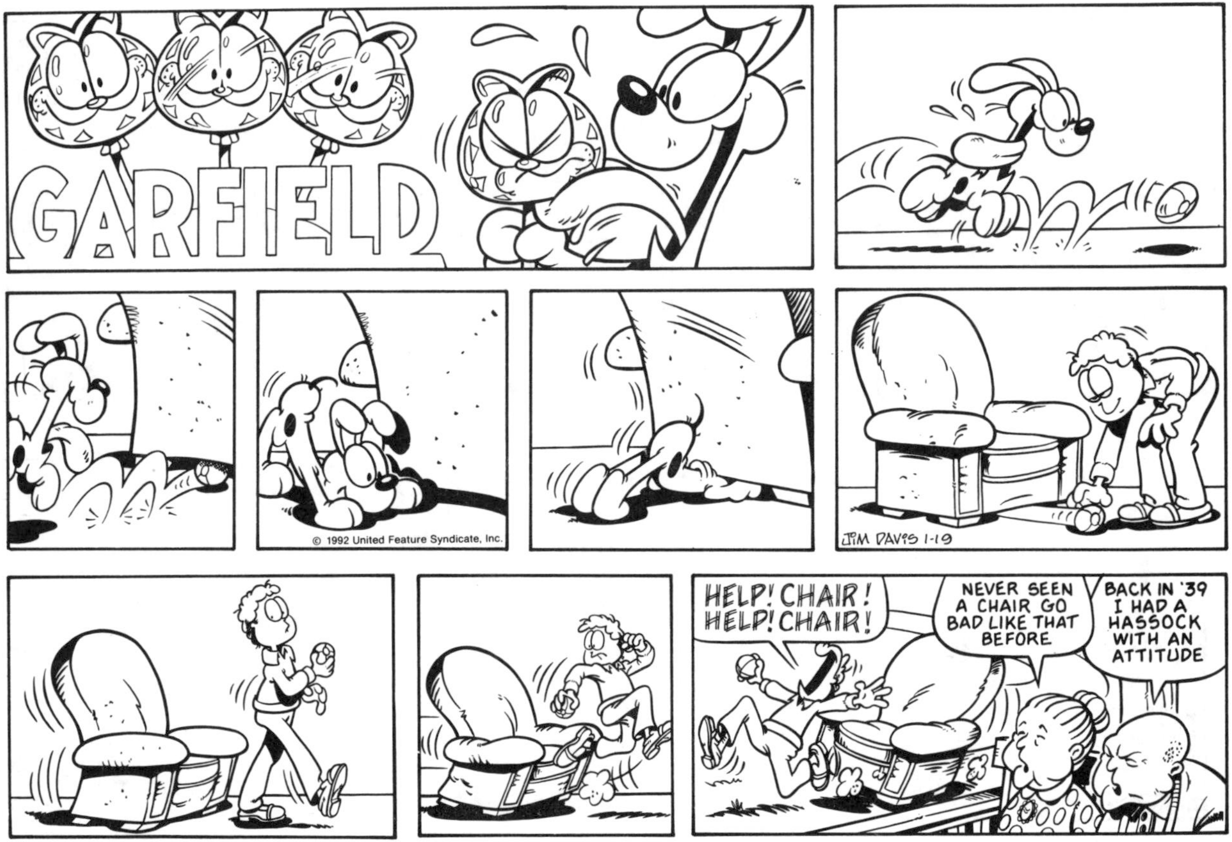
GARFIELD
© 1992 United Feature Syndicate, Inc.
JIM DAVIS 1-19
HELP! CHAIR! HELP! CHAIR!
NEVER SEEN A CHAIR GO BAD LIKE THAT BEFORE
BACK IN '39 I HAD A HASSOCK WITH AN ATTITUDE

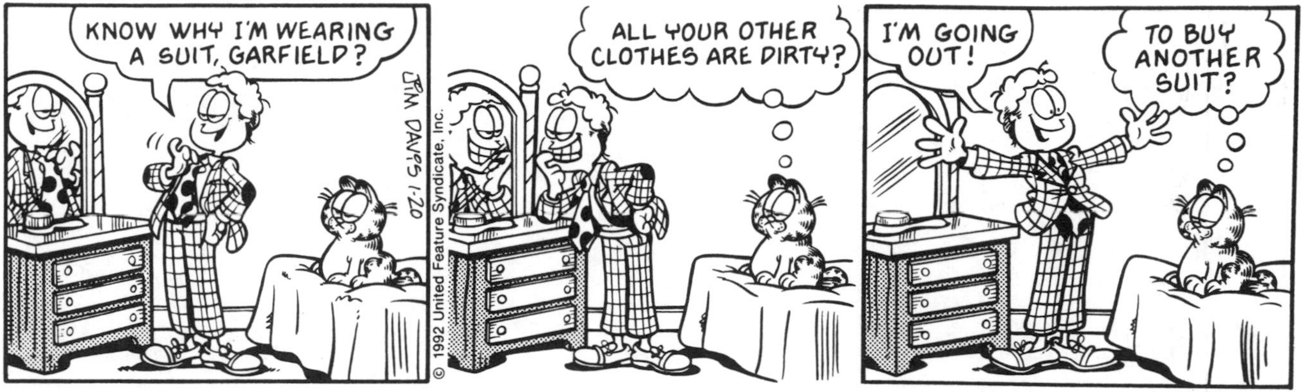
KNOW WHY I'M WEARING A SUIT, GARFIELD?
JIM DAVIS 1·20
© 1992 United Feature Syndicate, Inc.
ALL YOUR OTHER CLOTHES ARE DIRTY?
I'M GOING OUT!
TO BUY ANOTHER SUIT?

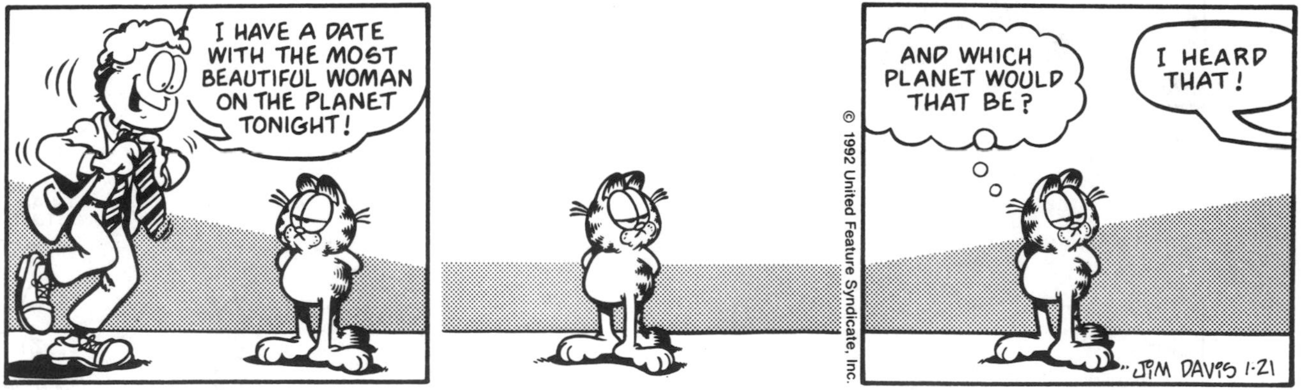
I HAVE A DATE WITH THE MOST BEAUTIFUL WOMAN ON THE PLANET TONIGHT!
© 1992 United Feature Syndicate, Inc.
AND WHICH PLANET WOULD THAT BE?
I HEARD THAT!
JIM DAVIS 1·21

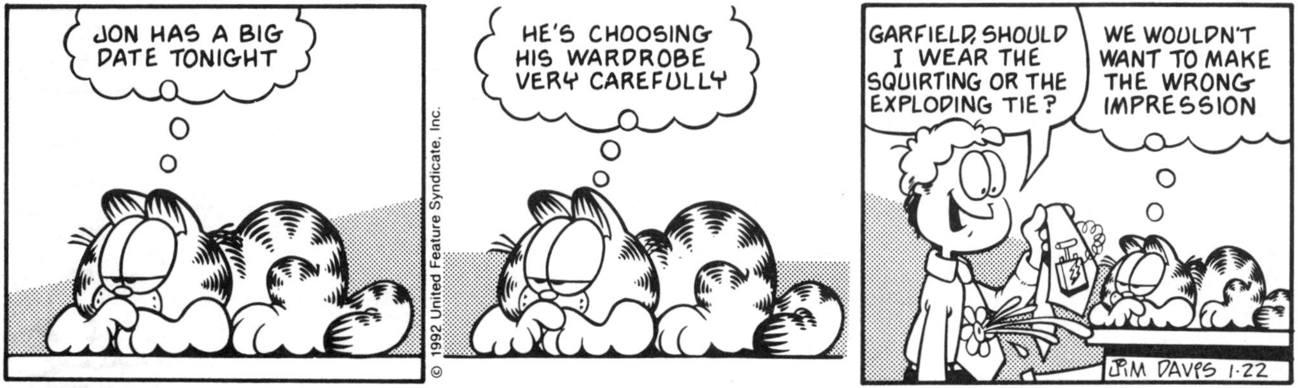
JON HAS A BIG DATE TONIGHT
HE'S CHOOSING HIS WARDROBE VERY CAREFULLY
GARFIELD, SHOULD I WEAR THE SQUIRTING OR THE EXPLODING TIE?
WE WOULDN'T WANT TO MAKE THE WRONG IMPRESSION
JIM DAVIS 1-22
© 1992 United Feature Syndicate, Inc.

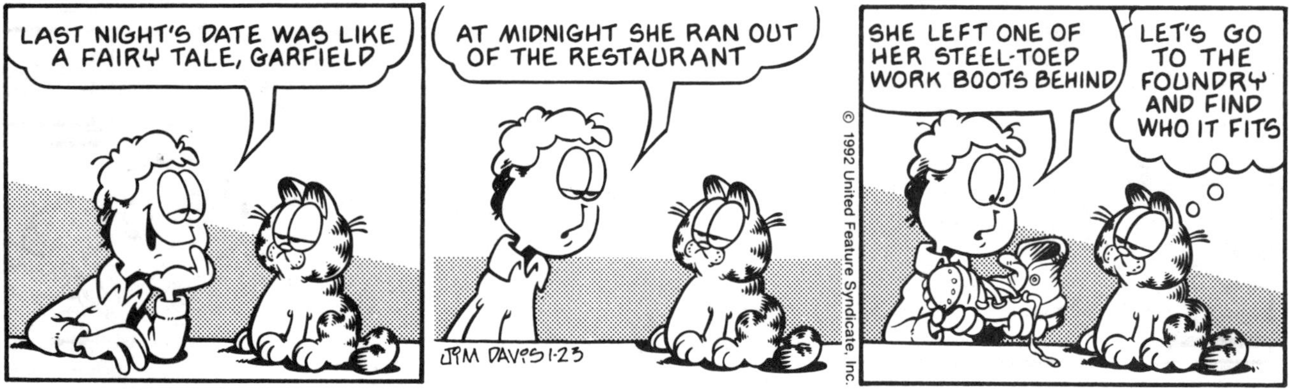
LAST NIGHT'S DATE WAS LIKE A FAIRY TALE, GARFIELD
AT MIDNIGHT SHE RAN OUT OF THE RESTAURANT
JIM DAVIS 1-23
SHE LEFT ONE OF HER STEEL-TOED WORK BOOTS BEHIND
LET'S GO TO THE FOUNDRY AND FIND WHO IT FITS
© 1992 United Feature Syndicate, Inc.

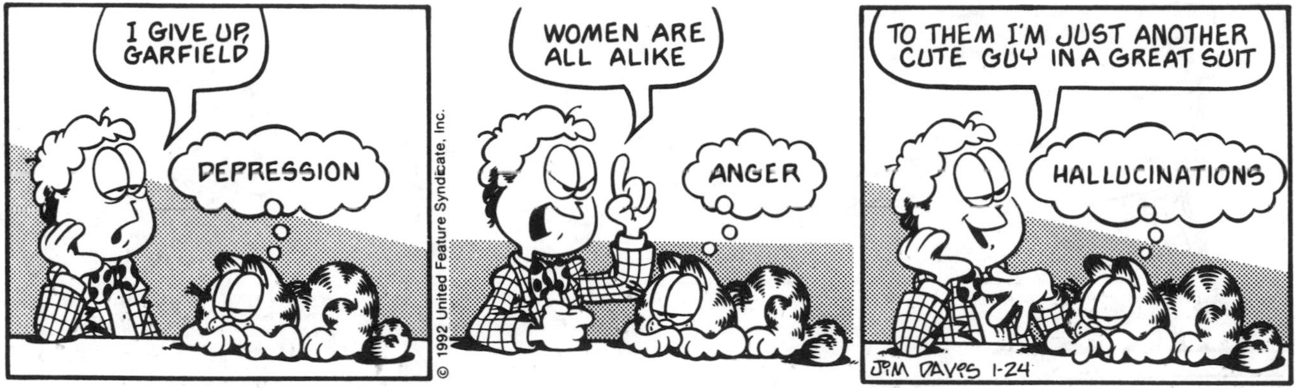
I GIVE UP, GARFIELD
DEPRESSION
© 1992 United Feature Syndicate, Inc.
WOMEN ARE ALL ALIKE
ANGER
TO THEM I'M JUST ANOTHER CUTE GUY IN A GREAT SUIT
HALLUCINATIONS
JIM DAVIS 1-24

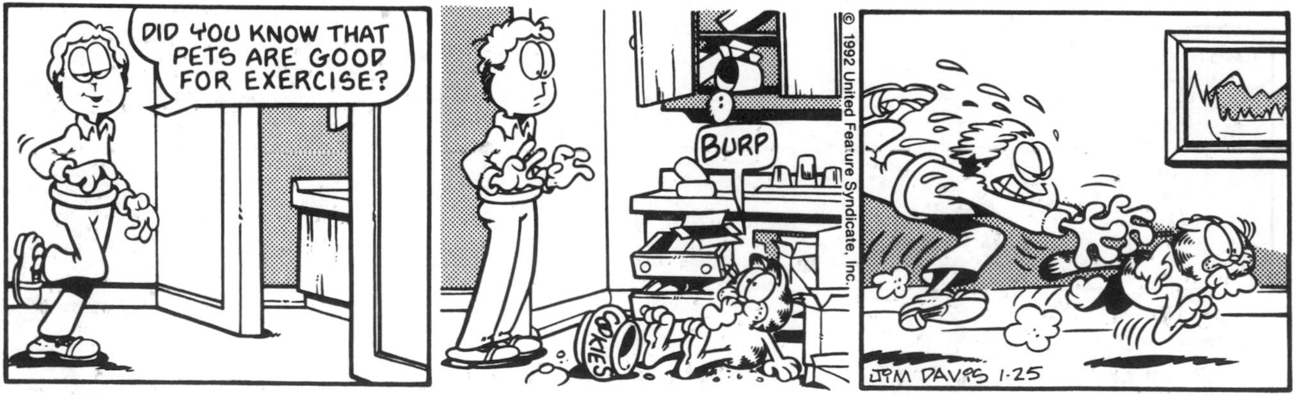
DID YOU KNOW THAT PETS ARE GOOD FOR EXERCISE?
BURP
COOKIES
© 1992 United Feature Syndicate, Inc.
JIM DAVIS 1-25

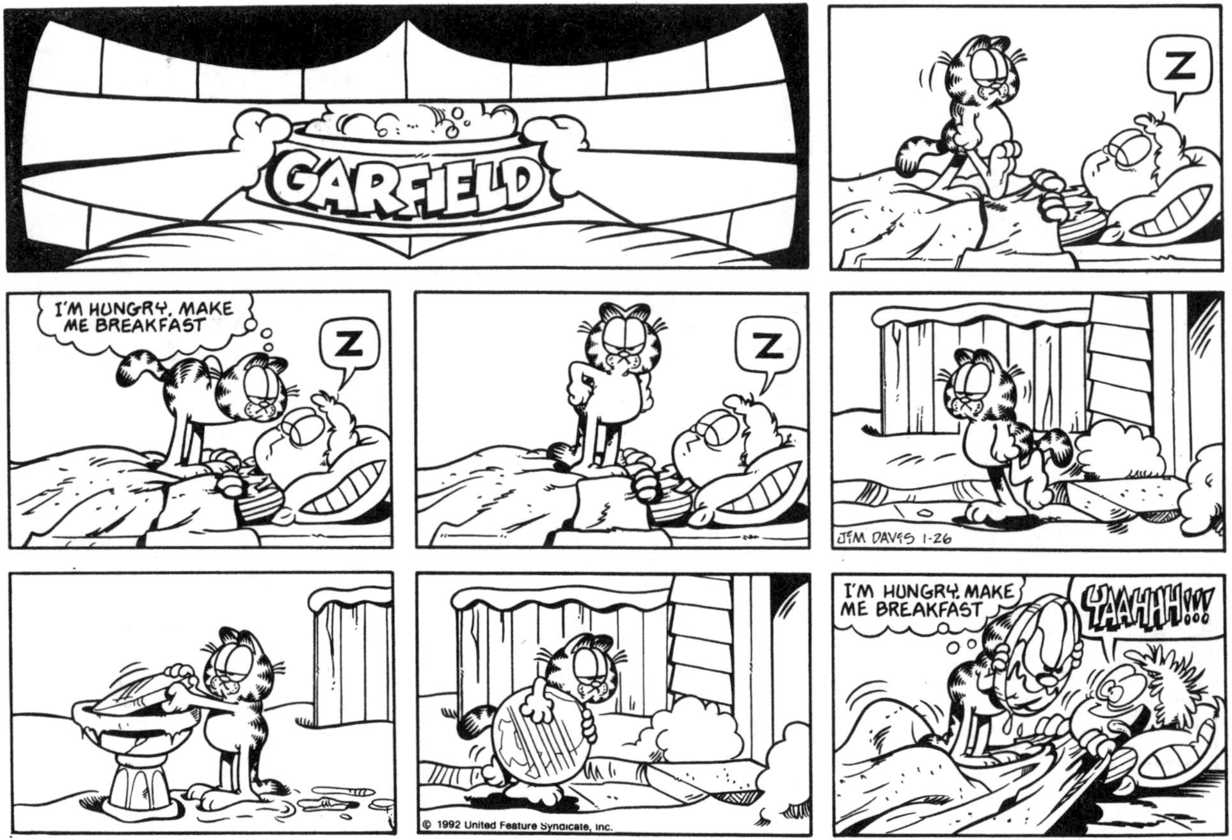
GARFIELD
Z
I'M HUNGRY. MAKE ME BREAKFAST
Z
Z
JIM DAVIS 1-26
© 1992 United Feature Syndicate, Inc.
I'M HUNGRY. MAKE ME BREAKFAST
YAAHHH!!!

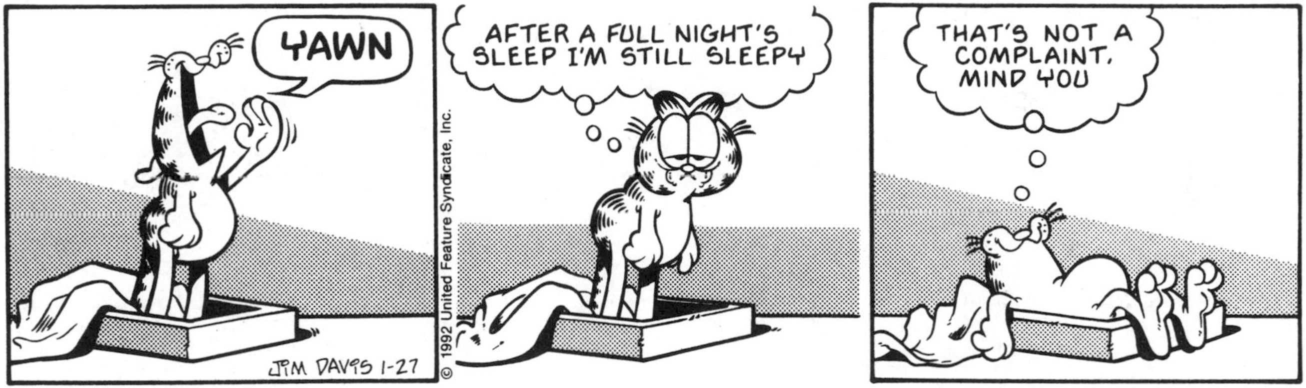
YAWN
JIM DAVIS 1-27
© 1992 United Feature Syndicate, Inc.
AFTER A FULL NIGHT'S SLEEP I'M STILL SLEEPY
THAT'S NOT A COMPLAINT, MIND YOU

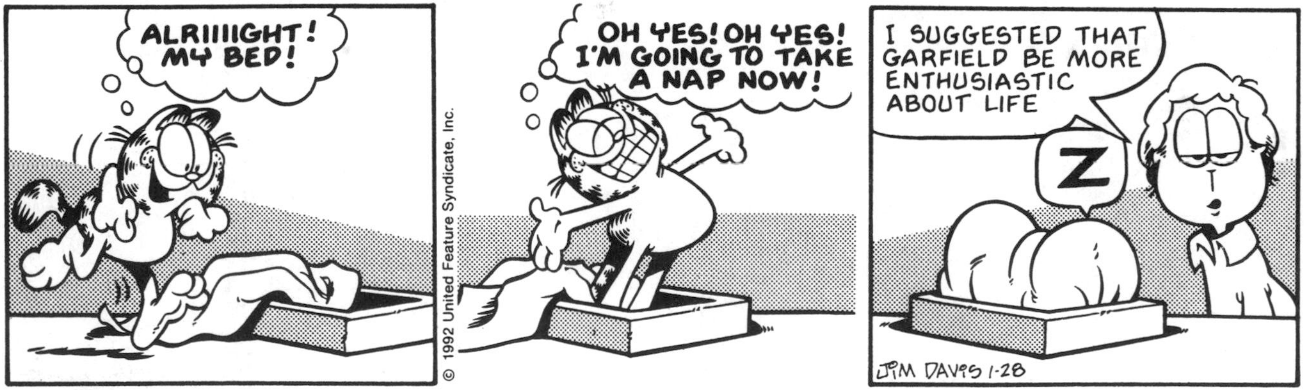
ALRIIIIGHT! MY BED!
© 1992 United Feature Syndicate, Inc.
OH YES! OH YES! I'M GOING TO TAKE A NAP NOW!
I SUGGESTED THAT GARFIELD BE MORE ENTHUSIASTIC ABOUT LIFE
Z
JIM DAVIS 1-28

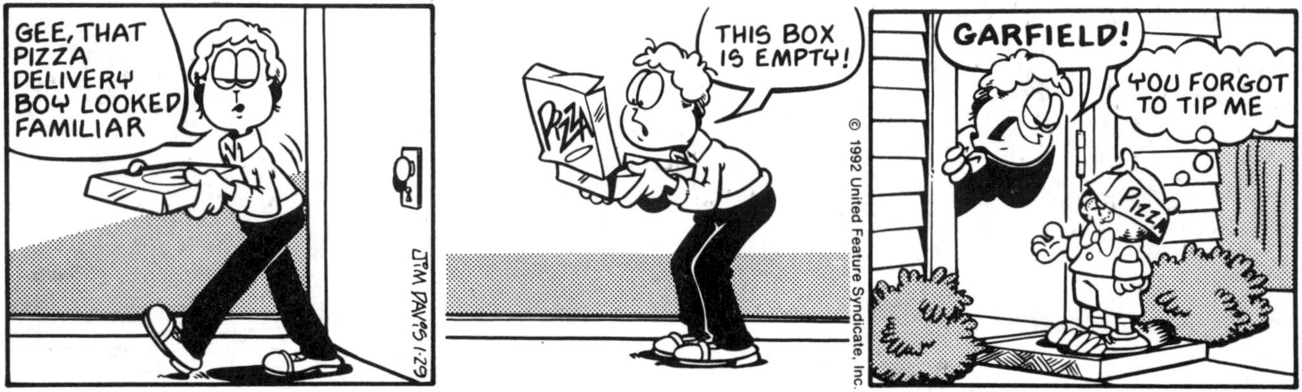
GEE, THAT PIZZA DELIVERY BOY LOOKED FAMILIAR
JIM DAVIS 1-29
THIS BOX IS EMPTY!
PIZZA
© 1992 United Feature Syndicate, Inc.
GARFIELD!
YOU FORGOT TO TIP ME
PIZZA

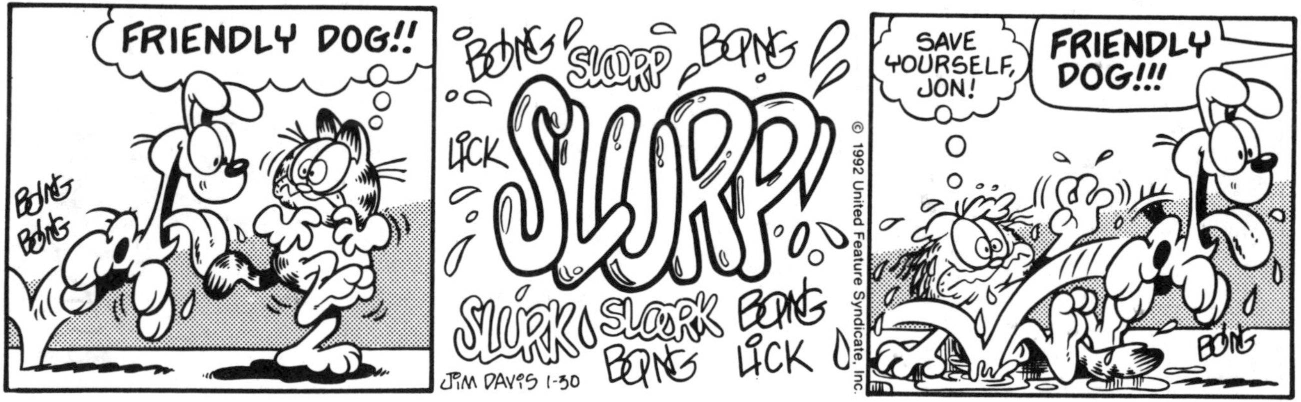
FRIENDLY DOG!!
BOING BOING
BOING SLOORP BOING
LICK
SLURP
SLURK SLOORK BOING BOING LICK
JIM DAVIS 1-30
© 1992 United Feature Syndicate, Inc.
SAVE YOURSELF, JON!
FRIENDLY DOG!!!
BOING

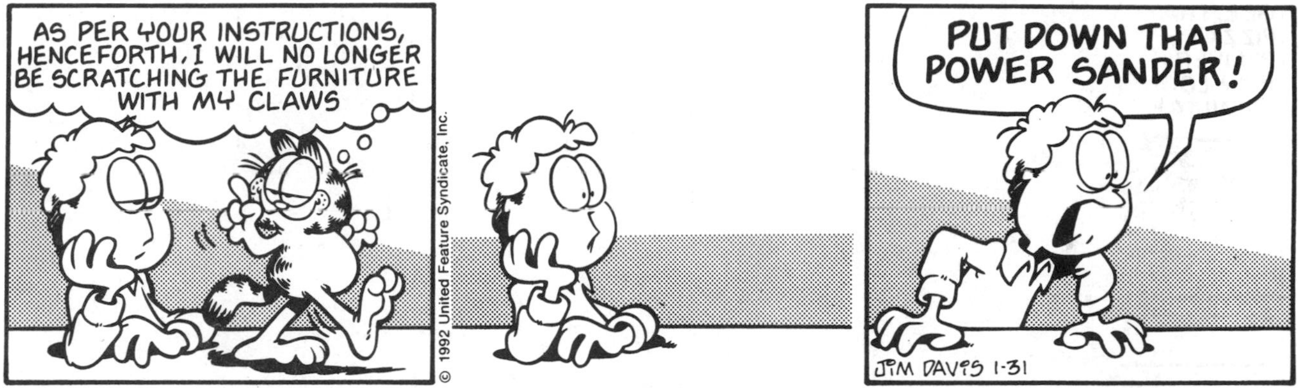
AS PER YOUR INSTRUCTIONS, HENCEFORTH, I WILL NO LONGER BE SCRATCHING THE FURNITURE WITH MY CLAWS
PUT DOWN THAT POWER SANDER!
© 1992 United Feature Syndicate, Inc.
JIM DAVIS 1-31

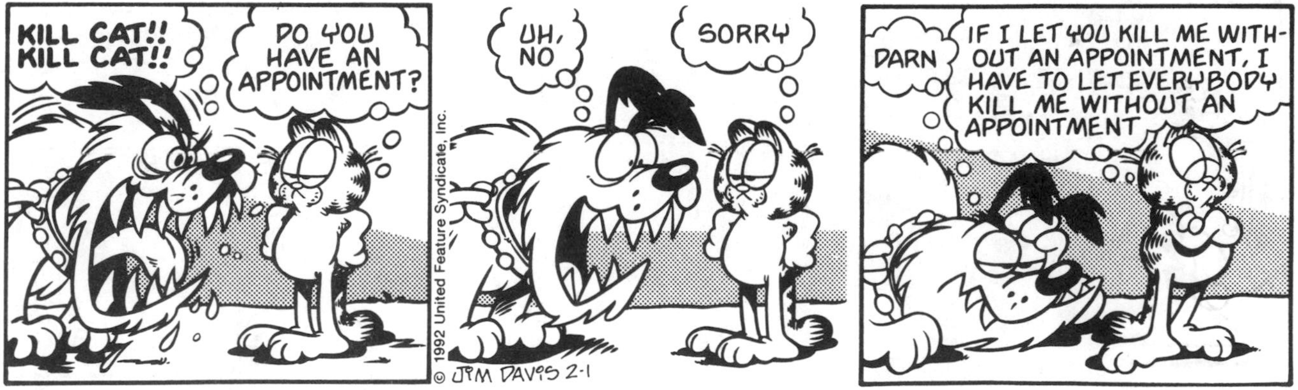
KILL CAT!! KILL CAT!!
DO YOU HAVE AN APPOINTMENT?
UH, NO
SORRY
DARN
IF I LET YOU KILL ME WITHOUT AN APPOINTMENT, I HAVE TO LET EVERYBODY KILL ME WITHOUT AN APPOINTMENT
© 1992 United Feature Syndicate, Inc.
© JIM DAVIS 2-1

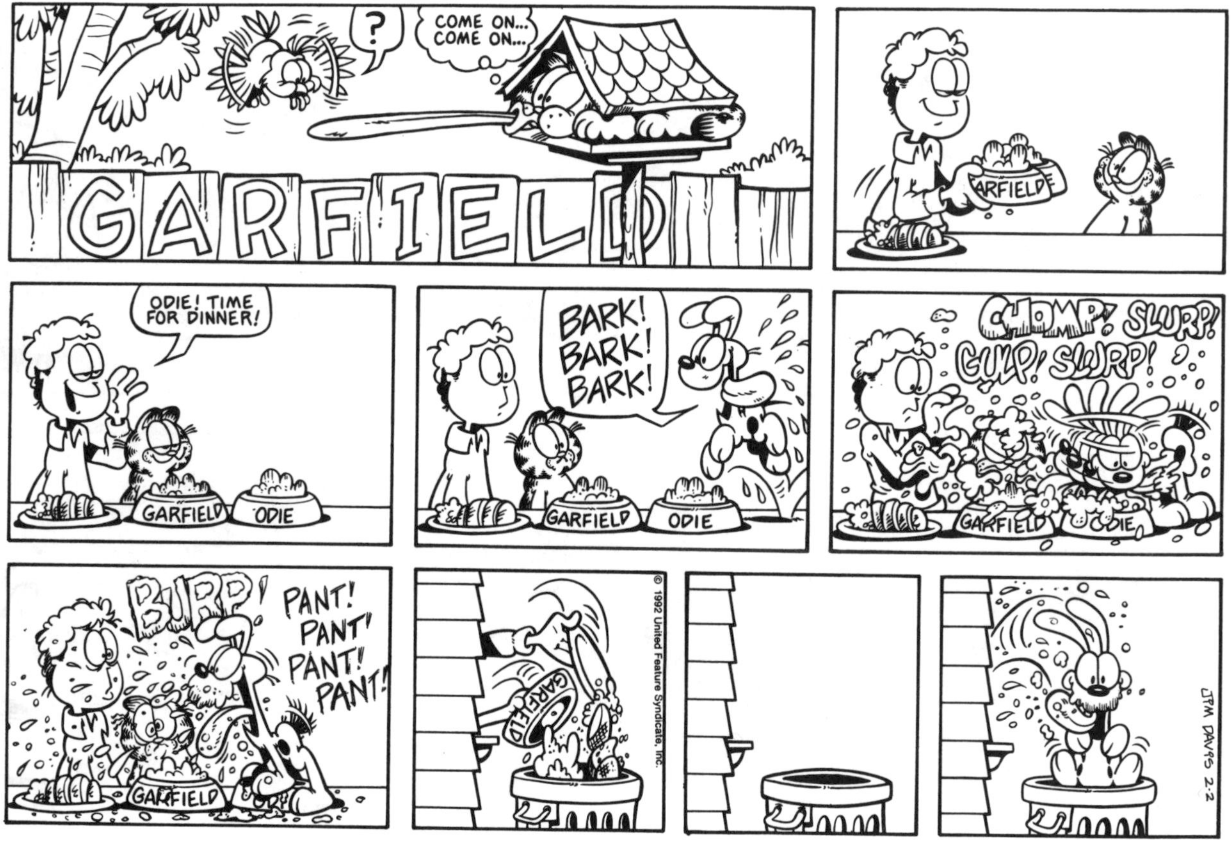
?
COME ON... COME ON...
GARFIELD
GARFIELD
ODIE! TIME FOR DINNER!
GARFIELD
ODIE
BARK! BARK! BARK!
GARFIELD
ODIE
CHOMP! SLURP!
GULP! SLURP!
GARFIELD
ODIE
BURP!
PANT! PANT! PANT! PANT!
GARFIELD
© 1992 United Feature Syndicate, Inc.
GARFIELD
JPM DAVIS 2-2

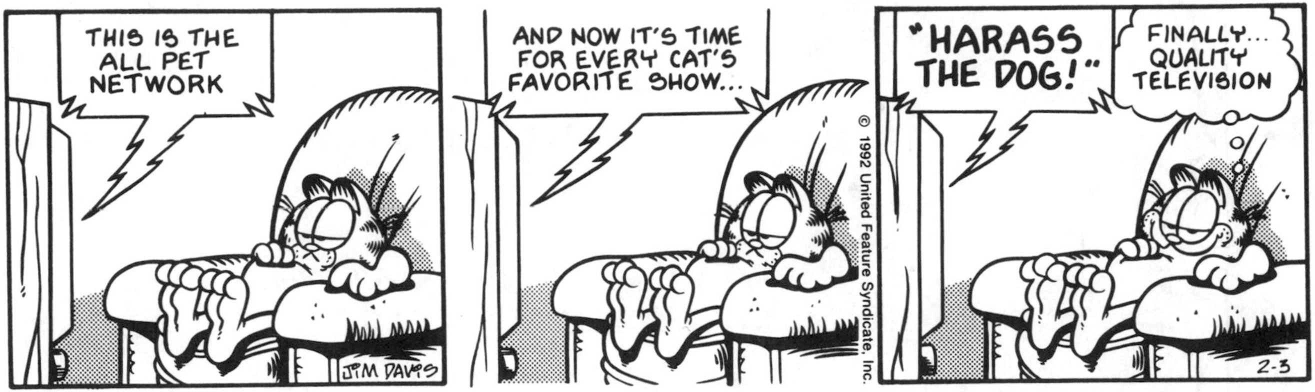
THIS IS THE ALL PET NETWORK
AND NOW IT'S TIME FOR EVERY CAT'S FAVORITE SHOW...
"HARASS THE DOG!"
FINALLY... QUALITY TELEVISION
JIM DAVIS
2-3
© 1992 United Feature Syndicate, Inc.

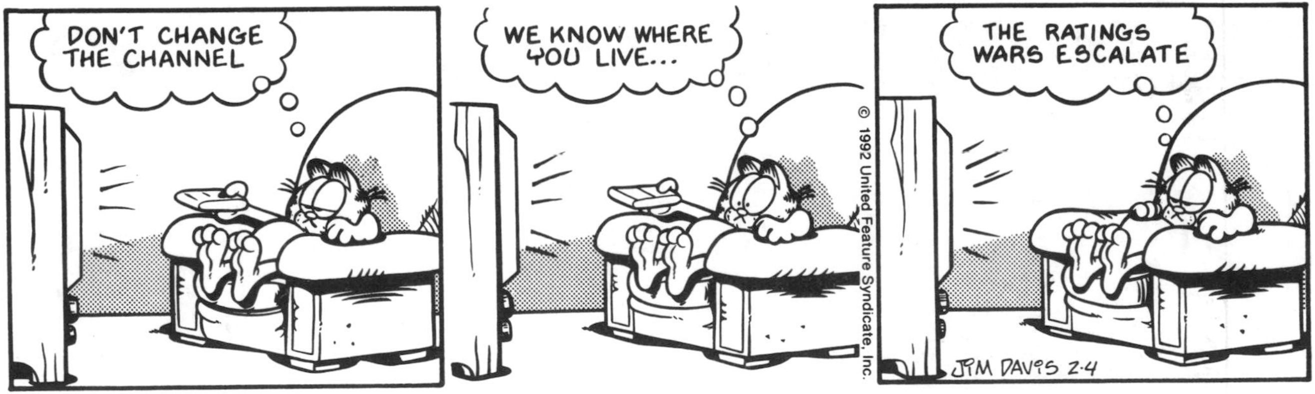
DON'T CHANGE THE CHANNEL
WE KNOW WHERE YOU LIVE...
THE RATINGS WARS ESCALATE
JIM DAVIS 2-4
© 1992 United Feature Syndicate, Inc.

'TOON TATTLER

"100% FACT FREE"

MIRACLE LASAGNA CURES COMMON DIET!!

THOUSANDS SAVED FROM LIFETIME OF THINNESS

WOMAN SURVIVES DATE WITH DWEEB

VICTIM BORED BEYOND RECOGNITION!

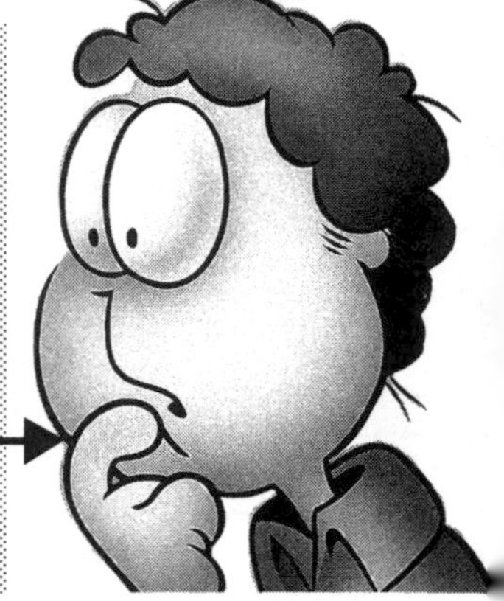

CATNAP KING KIDNAPPED BY ALIENS!

GARFIELD RETURNED UNHARMED... AND REFRESHED!

"Nothing like napping for a light-year!"

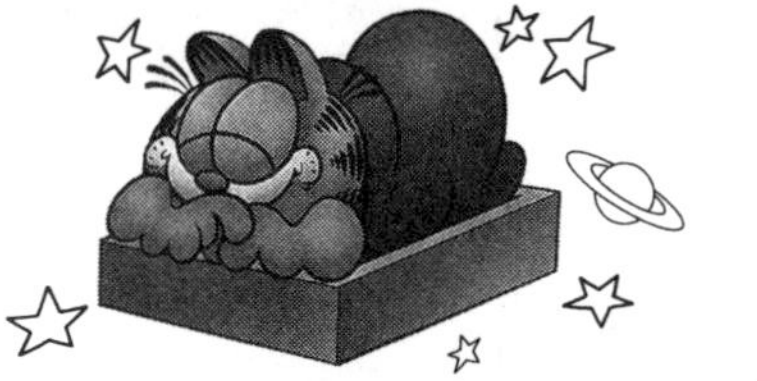

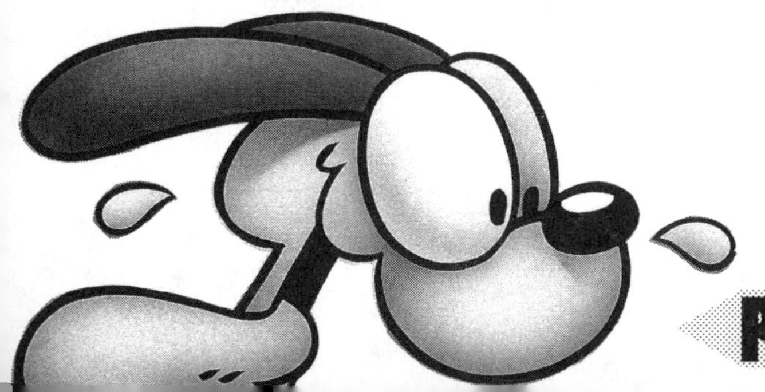

PLUS PICS OF BIZARRE SPACE CREATURE!

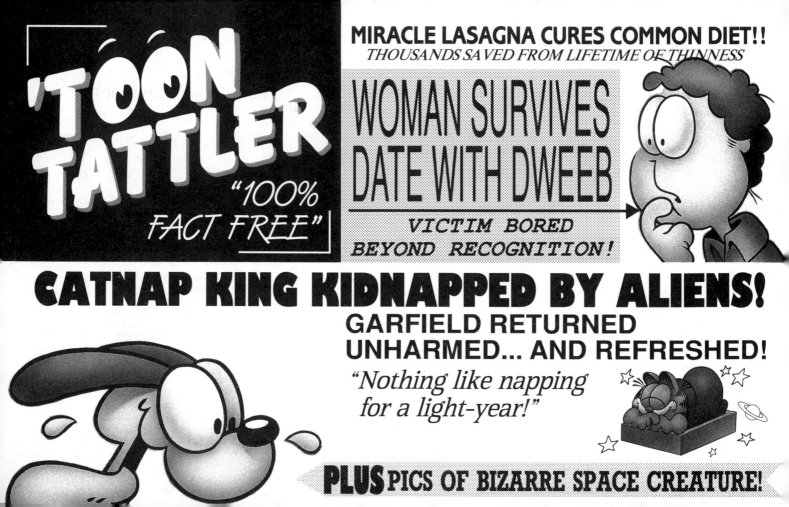

STRIPS, SPECIALS OR BESTSELLING BOOKS...
GARFIELD'S ON EVERYONE'S MENU

Don't miss even one episode in the Tubby Tabby's hilarious series!

___GARFIELD AT LARGE (#1)   32013/$6.95
___GARFIELD GAINS WEIGHT (#2)   32008/$6.95
___GARFIELD BIGGER THAN LIFE (#3)   32007/$6.95
___GARFIELD WEIGHS IN (#4)   32010/$6.95
___GARFIELD TAKES THE CAKE (#5)   32009/$6.95
___GARFIELD EATS HIS HEART OUT (#6)   32018/$6.95
___GARFIELD SITS AROUND THE HOUSE (#7)   32011/$6.95
___GARFIELD TIPS THE SCALE (#8)   33580/$6.95
___GARFIELD LOSES HIS FEET (#9)   31805/$6.95
___GARFIELD MAKES IT BIG (#10)   31928/$6.95
___GARFIELD ROLLS ON (#11)   32634/$6.95
___GARFIELD OUT TO LUNCH (#12)   33118/$6.95
___GARFIELD FOOD FOR THOUGHT (#13)   34129/$6.95

___GARFIELD SWALLOWS HIS PRIDE (#14)   34725/$6.95
___GARFIELD WORLDWIDE (#15)   35158/$6.95
___GARFIELD ROUNDS OUT (#16)   35388/$6.95
___GARFIELD CHEWS THE FAT (#17)   35956/$6.95
___GARFIELD GOES TO WAIST (#18)   36430/$6.95
___GARFIELD HANGS OUT (#19)   36835/$6.95
___GARFIELD TAKES UP SPACE (#20)   37029/$6.95
___GARFIELD SAYS A MOUTHFUL (#21)   37368/$6.95
___GARFIELD BY THE POUND (#22)   37579/$6.95
___GARFIELD KEEPS HIS CHINS UP (#23)   37959/$6.95

GARFIELD AT HIS SUNDAY BEST!
___GARFIELD TREASURY   33106/$9.95
___THE SECOND GARFIELD TREASURY   33276/$10.95
___THE THIRD GARFIELD TREASURY   32635/$9.95
___THE FOURTH GARFIELD TREASURY   34726/$10.95
___THE FIFTH GARFIELD TREASURY   36268/$9.95
___THE SIXTH GARFIELD TREASURY   37367/$10.95

BALLANTINE SALES
Dept. TA, 201 E. 50th St., New York, N.Y. 10022

Please send me the BALLANTINE BOOKS I have checked above. I am enclosing $ .... (add $2.00 for the first book and 50¢ for each additional book to cover postage and handling). Send check or money order—no cash or C.O.D.'s please. Prices are subject to change without notice.

Name _____

Address _____

City _____ State _____ Zip Code _____
30   Allow at least 4 weeks for delivery   3/90 TA-135

BIRTHDAYS, HOLIDAYS, OR ANY DAY...
Keep GARFIELD on your calendar all year 'round!

GARFIELD TV SPECIALS
___BABES & BULLETS   36339/$6.95
___A GARFIELD CHRISTMAS   34368/$6.95
___GARFIELD GOES HOLLYWOOD   34580/$6.95
___GARFIELD'S HALLOWEEN ADVENTURE   33045/$6.95
(formerly GARFIELD in Disguise)
___GARFIELD'S FELINE FANTASIES   36903/$6.95
___GARFIELD IN PARADISE   33796/$6.95
___GARFIELD IN THE ROUGH   32242/$6.95
___GARFIELD ON THE TOWN   31542/$6.95
___A GARFIELD THANKSGIVING   35650/$6.95
___HERE COMES GARFIELD   32012/$6.95
___GARFIELD GETS A LIFE   37375/$6.95

BALLANTINE SALES
Dept. TA, 201 E. 50th St., New York, N.Y. 10022

Please send me the BALLANTINE BOOKS I have checked above. I am enclosing $ .... (add $2.00 for the first book and 50¢ for each additional book to cover postage and handling). Send check or money order—no cash or C.O.D.'s please. Prices are subject to change without notice.

GREETINGS FROM GARFIELD!
GARFIELD POSTCARD BOOKS FOR ALL OCCASIONS.
___THINKING OF YOU   36516/$6.95
___WORDS TO LIVE BY   36679/$6.95
___GARFIELD BIRTHDAY GREETINGS   36770/$7.95
___BE MY VALENTINE   37121/$7.95
___SEASON'S GREETINGS   37435/$8.95
___VACATION GREETINGS   37774/$10.00

Also from GARFIELD:
___GARFIELD: HIS NINE LIVES   32061/$9.95
___THE GARFIELD BOOK OF CAT NAMES   35082/$5.95
___THE GARFIELD TRIVIA BOOK   33771/$5.95
___THE UNABRIDGED UNCENSORED
UNBELIEVABLE GARFIELD   33772/$5.95
___GARFIELD: THE ME BOOK   36545/$7.95
___GARFIELD'S JUDGMENT DAY   36755/$6.95
___THE TRUTH ABOUT CATS   37226/$6.95

Name _____

Address _____

City _____ State _____ Zip Code _____
30   Allow at least 4 weeks for delivery   3/90 TA-267